AF522294

Electronic Communication in Digital Library

Electronic Communication in Digital Library

M. Ram

Electronic Communication in Digital Library

ISBN 978-93-5111-489-5

Published in 2015 in India by

RANDOM PUBLICATIONS

4376-A/4B, Gali Murari Lal, Ansari Road
New Delhi-110 002
Phone : +9111-43580356, 011-23289044, 011-43142548
e-mail: sales@randompublications.com,
info@randompublications.com, randomexports@gmail.com

Reprint 2021

Type Setting by : Friends Media, Delhi-110089
Digitally Printed at : Replika Press Pvt. Ltd.

Preface

The advancement of information technology, digital telecommunication technology, CD-ROMs, multimedia, computer networks, internet etc. have paved the way towards electronic publishing and changed the traditional libraries to digital library. ICT have transformed the way of information generated, disseminated, preserved and made accessible with technology providing such incomparable access to digital resources and information services, digital libraries and information repositories are now worldwide accessible. The idea of converting traditional library into digital formats by using computer and web applications are emerging out as an important era in the library services. Thus, the process is leading to the concept of a virtual or a library without walls. It allows flexible learning and distant education accessing online available to the users readily.

With the availability of computers capable of computing at very high speed and having large disc storage space it will be possible to digitize and store information in the form of high quality, graphics, colour images and video clips. WWW tech based on HTML and advance web browsers have provided a very easy to use interface to the users. Digital library have tremendous capacity to store huge data, which promote universal accessibility, protects rare books that are rapidly deteriorating due to over use and poor storage conditions, a tool for preservation of heritage. The importance of digital library is to provide instant access to digitized information from remote database throughout the world.

Designed to present a holistic view of the digital library scene, this text is based on evidence from examples of major digital library research projects around the globe. It is intended for students of digital librarianship and related courses at departments of information science and computer science, and also for practitioners and researchers who need to get a good grasp of issues and developments in the field.

Author

Contents

1

Electronic Communication and Information Services

The Internet and electronic communications doesn't just mean new tools for communication; it means new ways to communicate. Today your organization interacts with its various constituents differently - employees, board members, customers, partners and others - depending upon the nature of the message, the goals you are trying to achieve and the strengths (and weaknesses) of the available media - telephones, voice mail, fax machines, print, etc.

Electronic communications adds a powerful new channel that not only will change how you use this mix of options, but it will create entirely new ways to interact. For example:

— Electronic communications lets you combine numerous media - text, graphics sound, video, etc. - into a single message. That can result in far more meaningful communications tailored to the nature of your particular audience. In contrast to broadcasting, *narrowcasting*reflects the ability to develop numerous communications for subsets of your market or constituencies.

— Electronic communications is interactive. It engages audiences in active, two-way communications. That requires a new way of thinking about advertising copy and the handling of public relations. The pay-off, however, is a self-selected audience, engaged and actively participating in the communications process.

— Two-way communication is nothing new. But electronic communications creates a new form of many-to-many communications that lets geographically distributed groups communicate interactively and simultaneously through text, sound and video. You can hold inexpensive video conferences or press conferences from your desk, or conference with people at several desks located across the world. One of the burgeoning phenomena of the Internet is businesses and organizations sponsoring, supporting and moderating discussion groups about issues, products, strategies - anything of interest to the organization and its constituents. Sponsorships are also solicited for popular resources, such as indexes and other Internet search tools, and these provide a further communications and marketing opportunity.

— Many organizations are using electronic communications facilities, such as the World Wide Web, as internal communications tools to enhance team work. Many individuals at different locations can work on the same documents, hold meetings and integrate research findings.

— Electronic communications removes the power of communications *gatekeepers* to both positive and negative effects. Most organizations are used to controlling the messages that go out to its constituents through managers, spokespeople and others. But with the Internet, constituents begin to talk among themselves, requiring new approaches and a new emphasis on listening and reacting, not just talking.

— With the Internet you have the ability to transmit and receive large amounts of information quickly to and from individuals and workgroups around the world. This changes the way activists, for example, can galvanize communities, inform legislators and change public opinion. It changes the sources and depth of your constituents' knowledge levels. It also lets those constituents reach you with new kinds of communications they may never have attempted before.

Electronic Library

There are many definitions of an "electronic library", terms such as "digital library", "electronic library" and "virtual library" are often used synonymously. In order to define these terms we have to consider these elements:

— The digital library is not a single entity.

— The digital library requires technology to link the resources.

— Universal access to digital libraries and information services is a goal.

Digital library collections are not limited to be a document replacement: they extend to be digital view that cannot be represented or distributed in printed formats.

The first use of the term digital library in print may have been in a 1988 report to the Corporation for National Research InitiativesThe term digital libraries was first popularized by the NSF/DARPA/NASA Digital Libraries Initiative in 1994. These draw heavily on As We May Think by Vannevar Bush in 1945, which set out a vision not in terms of technology, but user experience. The term virtual library was initially used interchangeably with digital library, but is now primarily used for libraries that are virtual in other senses.

A distinction is often made between content that was created in a digital format, known as born-digital, and information that has been converted from a physical medium, e.g. paper, by digitizing. The term hybrid library is sometimes used for libraries that have both physical collections and digital collections. For example, American Memory is a digital library within the Library of Congress.

Some important digital libraries also serve as long term archives, such as arXiv and the Internet Archive. Others, such as the Digital Public Library of America, seek to make digital information widely accessible through public libraries.

Large scale digitization projects are underway at Google, the Million Book Project, and Internet Archive. With continued improvements in book handling and presentation technologies such as optical character recognition and ebooks, and development of alternative depositories and business models, digital libraries are rapidly growing in popularity. Just as libraries have ventured into audio and video collections, so have digital libraries such as the Internet Archive.

According to Larry Lannom, Director of Information Management Technology at the nonprofit Corporation should be for National Research Initiatives, “all the problems associated with digital libraries are wrapped up in archiving.” He goes on to state, “If in 100 years people can still read your article, we’ll have solved the problem.” Daniel Akst, author of The Webster Chronicle, proposes that “the future of libraries — and of information — is digital." Peter Lyman and Hal Varian, information scientists at the University of California, Berkeley, estimate that "the world's total yearly production of print, film, optical, and magnetic content would require roughly 1.5 billion gigabytes of storage." Therefore, they believe that "soon it will be technologically possible for an average person to access virtually all recorded information.

The advantages of digital libraries as a means of easily and rapidly accessing books, archives and images of various types are now widely recognized by commercial interests and public bodies alike.

Traditional libraries are limited by storage space; digital libraries have the potential to store much more information, simply because digital information requires very little physical space to contain it. As such, the cost of maintaining a digital library can be much lower than that of a traditional library. A physical library must spend large sums of money paying for staff, book maintenance, rent, and additional books. Digital libraries may reduce or, in some instances, do away with these fees. Both types of library require cataloguing input to allow users to locate and retrieve material. Digital libraries may be more willing to adopt innovations in technology providing users with improvements in electronic and audio book technology as well as presenting new forms of communication such as wikis and blogs; conventional libraries may consider that providing online access to their OPAC catalogue is sufficient. An important advantage to digital conversion is increased accessibility to users. They also increase availability to individuals who may not be traditional patrons of a library, due to geographic location or organizational affiliation.

Information Society

An information society is a society where the creation, distribution,use, integration and manipulation of information is a significant economic, political, and cultural activity. The aim of the information society is to gain competitive advantage internationally, through using information technology (IT) in a creative and productive way. The knowledge economy is its economic counterpart, whereby wealth is created through the economic exploitation of understanding. People who have the means to partake in this form of society are sometimes called digital citizens. This is one of many dozen labels that have been identified to suggest that humans are entering a new phase of society.

The markers of this rapid change may be technological, economic, occupational, spatial, cultural, or some combination of all of these. Information society is seen as the successor to industrial society. Closely related concepts are the post-industrial society (Daniel Bell), post-fordism, post-modern society, knowledge society, Telematic Society, Information Revolution, Liquid modernity, and network society (Manuel Castells).

There is currently no universally accepted concept of what exactly can be termed information society and what shall rather not so be termed. Most theoreticians agree that a transformation can be seen that started somewhere between the 1970s and today and is changing the way societies work fundamentally. Information technology is not only internet, and there are discussions about how big the influence of specific media or specific modes of production really is.

Some people, such as Antonio Negri, characterize the information society as one in which people do immaterial labour. By this, they appear to refer to the production of knowledge or cultural artifacts. One problem with this model is that it ignores the material and essentially industrial basis of the society. However it does point to a problem for workers, namely how many creative people does this society need to function? For example, it may be that you only need a few star performers, rather than a plethora of non-celebrities, as the work of those performers can be easily distributed, forcing all secondary players to the bottom of the market. It is now common for publishers to promote only their best selling authors and to try to avoid the rest—even if they still sell steadily. Films are becoming more and more judged, in terms of distribution, by their first weekend's performance, in many cases cutting out opportunity for word-of-mouth development.

Considering that metaphors and technologies of information move forward in a reciprocal relationship, we can describe some societies (especially the Japanese society) as an information society because we think of it as such as letters.

The growth of technologically mediated information has been quantified in different ways, including society's technological capacity to store information, to communicate information, and to compute information. It is estimated that the world's technological capacity to store information grew from 2.6 (optimally compressed) exabytes in 1986, which is the informational equivalent to less than one 730-MB CD-ROM per person in

1986 (539 MB per person), to 295 (optimally compressed) exabytes in 2007. This is the informational equivalent of 60 CD-ROM per person in 2007 and represents a sustained annual growth rate of some 25%. The world's combined technological capacity to receive information through one-way broadcast networks was the informational equivalent of 174 newspapers per person per day in 2007. The world's combined effective capacity to exchange information through two-way telecommunication networks was 281 petabytes of (optimally compressed) information in 1986, 471 petabytes in 1993, 2.2 (optimally compressed) exabytes in 2000, and 65 (optimally compressed) exabytes in 2007, which is the informational equivalent of 6 newspapers per person per day in 2007. The world's technological capacity to compute information with humanly guided general-purpose computers grew from 3.0 × 10^8 MIPS in 1986, to 6.4 x 10^12 MIPS in 2007, experiencing the fastest growth rate of over 60% per year during the last two decades.

Digital Library Infrastructure

The digital library is an electronic or virtual library where information is selected, acquired, processed, organised , stored and retrieved in digital form. The developed countries have already digitized their libraries. The developing countries are in the process of digitization of their libraries. The users of digital libraries are the universal users who should have facility to access to all created and acquired digital sources of information in the form of electronic text, image, map, sound, video and multimedia. Thus the digital libraries are attributed to electronic databases and capable of handling large data and servicing users effectively in resource sharing environment.

A digital library has certain technological requirements such as:

i. Locally developed database
ii. Local library system with adequate personal computers having LAN and CD-ROM Drives.
iii. Electronic mail service
iv. Network connection to have access to other data bases
v. Various functions to coordinate, manage the entry and retrieve data.
vi. Multimedia Kit
vii. Well trained manpower

viii. Computer Hardware with Audio-Visuals, Video Conferencing Kit, Pentium Web Server, Laser Printer, Scanner, Barcode Scanner, Barcode Printer, Digital graphic printer and UPS.

ix. Software and its accessories.

The supeŕ structure of digital library rests on some important factors like: (i)the human need for information especially that is timely and relevant and (ii) accumulation of information, and all the supporting infrastructure that includes research community, professional associations, libraries and publishers, advances in methods and technology leading to developments in net working, information science, information storage and retireval, hyper-media, human-computer interaction, artificial intelligence and other areas of computer science that make digital libraries a possible proposition.

Digital Library Services

Always library services are followed by library works. But now the advancement in information technology has brought changes in the concept of traditional library work as well as service. The recent trend and change in the information related field especially in collection, storing, processing and dissemination of information have resulted in to the evolution of digital libraries . Now most of the reference books like encyclopaedias , dictionaries, directories, hand books, etc. are published in electronic form. Similarly about 50% of the existing secondary resources like abstracting and indexing services are available in electronic form for example, Chemical Abstracts Service, Index Medicus, Engineering Index. At present most of the digital libraries have been highlighted mainly on providing access to diverse digital information resources. The provision of personalized reference and information services is considered as one of the important characteristics of the library and information profession. However reference services include (I) Either finding the required information on behalf of users, or assisting users in finding information themselves; (ii) Instruction in the use of library resources and services, and (iii) user guidance in which users are guided in selecting the most appropriate information sources and services.

In this changing scenario, reference works of modern libraries are influenced by a set of related technical and economic factors, especially the increasing use of technology and techniques. To cite some examples, the recent developments in the INTERNET and in Web Technologies have brought significant changes in the concept of traditional reference services and a number of web-based "expert services" , that are now offered by many non-library organisation. Information services are provided to the users on demand as well as anticipating the user needs including various forms of current awareness and selective dissemination of information services. Such services are provided to the users to keep them abreast of the latest developments in their field of interest through on-line search services in digital information environment, even by the non-library organisations like Dialog.

Personalized Services

Most of the researches on digital library development have focused on access to and retrieval of digital information but they have overlooked the personalized service aspects, as primary goal of library information services. However the technology and information resources, on their own, can not make up an effective digital library. On priority basis the personalized services in a digital library environment would help the users to find information resources available in a digitally chaotic world. In a Delphy study it was revealed that (I) the primary roles library professionals play in digital libraries include organization of macro and micro-documents (Cataloguing and indexing), selection and acquisition and acting as gateways to the provision of information services, and (ii) the best reasons of developing a digital library include: increasing access to information serving and users needs and bringing organization to the unstructured universe of electronically available information. However there is a demand for end-user instruction on the use of digital libraries and the digital library professionals who are subject specialists should help users to formulate disciplinary search strategies and provide assistance in developing new digital information resources.

Web-based Reference and Information Services

Several reference and information services are now available on the web and many of these services are provided by non-library organization. Also a web site that provides a categorized listing of libraries that offer real-time reference services using specific software, live interactive communication tools, call centre management software, bulletin board services and other INTERNET technologies. Of course, most of these services are designed for registered users of some specific libraries in-digital information environment. HodgKin has made an aggregation approach to reference and information services. According to which more than one reference sources is made accessible digitally and also it is more practicable in terms of visibility and profitability than a single reference source. Further (I) it's reference service becomes much better known to professional users and thus easier to find, by providing access to several reference works, (ii) by tackling a number of reference works at a time, the publishers can achieve economics of scale in production and development (iii) the user's search session is likely to be much more powerful and fruitful.

According to Chowudhury and Chowudhury online reference and information services can be broadly categorized into three groups : (I) those from publishers , database search services and specialized institutions (ii) those provided by libraries and /or experts through the INTERNET and (iii) where the users need to conduct a search and find information through the web. Also they have listed several online information services that belong to the first category comprising various current awareness, and SDI services, for example :

a) Contents pages services from commercial publishers, such as Elsevier's Contents Direct Service and IDEAL Alert from Academic Press.

b) Information on new books available for free from publishers and vendors, such as Wiley Book, Notification Service from Wiley, and Amazon.com.

c) SDI services from online search services providers, such as Dialog (Dialog Alerts)

d) Current contents and ISI Alerting Services from ISI and so on.

However some of these services, particularly the contents page services from publishers of journals, are free, while for others, such as Dialog Alerts, or Current Contents from ISI, users need to register and pay for the services. There are also some web-based reference services where users need to conduct a search in order to answer their reference query. For example, the Internet Public Library (www.pl.org.), Britannica(www.britanica.com), the Electric Library (http/ask.library.com/refdesk.asp) and the Internet Library for librarians (www.company.com/inforetriever/). Most of these web-based reference services are available free of charge but some charge a small amount as fee. For example, the Electric Library charges an annual subscription fee.

Search Engine Services

Sherman made a comparision among three web-based reference services like (a) Ask Jeeves, (b) the Electric Library, and (c) Information please and observed that:

(a) Ask Jeeves (www.askjeeves.co.uk) basically a search engine, is useful for complex questions and is a good choice for searchers who lack Boolean or other searching skills, because of its strong natural language parser and question- and- answer template structure. The users can ask a question on a given topic and it comes up with a list of questions on the same or similar topics; the users can select any of those predefined questions and then it provides further answers. It processes each query syntactically (to analyse the grammer) and semantically (to determine meaning) and then its answer processing engine provides the question template response (listof questions the users see after they ask a question). When the users clicks on a response, the answer-processing engine retrieves the answer template that contains links to the answer locations. Thus Ask Jeeves can help users to select a query from a pre-defined set of queries on a given topic. So it is considered as a useful model for reference and information services in digital libraries.

(b) The Electric Library is an excellent choice for a serious researcher in need of timely content from a wide array of otherwise unavailable sources. It provides access to various on line reference sources and allows users to either select a specific source or conduct a search on a range, or all, of the sources.

(c) Information please is a suitable tool for students and other researchers, as an authoritative source of facts and pointers for further investigation.

Moreover Chowdhury and Chowdhury have suggested some other useful search engine services like (I) Web help.com (www.about.com) that claims to offer real time search assistance with a real live expert-any time, day or night, (ii) About.com (www.about.com) is a service that shows a number of pre-defined categories related to a search topic given by the user. For example, a simple search on 'e-commerce' not only produces a list of sites, but also provides a set of topics related to e-commerce, such as e-commerce-definition, e-commerce security, the advantages and disadvantages of e-commerce, e-commerce statistics and so on.

Digital Reference Services for General Public

Today web-based digital reference services are being provided by a network of public libraries. The users make their query on an enquiry page and it is automatically routed to one of the participating libraries which records it as an e-mail message to the user containing necessary and available information. For example, the British Library, London provides special reference services for business, scientific, technical, medical, patent and environmental information which range from answering simple queries up to complex questions involving on line data base searches. Of course some of these services are free if users put simple queries, but for complex queries users need to pay at the prescribed rate which covers the costs of staff time, on-line searching and value added tax (VAT).The British Library provides STM (Science, Technology and Medicine) Search Service for which users need to pay (www.bl.uk/services/ current/stm-search.html). Similarly New York Public Library (Digital Library), American Library of Congress, Alexandria Digital Library, Berkeley Digital Library, Bibliotheque Nationale de France, Victoria State Library, Vatican Library, etc. are some other libraries which provide digital reference services for users.

Digital Reference Services of Academic Libraries

Web based reference services are also now being provided by academic libraries, Recently a study report on web-based reference services reflects the current practices of digital library services in seventy academic libraries of USA. The study shows that university libraries allow their patrons to put reference questions in a variety ways: 99% offer e-mail reference, 96% offer reference services by appointment while 29% of the libraries offer real-time virtual reference. These libraries use customer relationship management (CRM) software packages for providing web-based reference services in the virtual reference environment.

Co-operative Digital Library Services

The rising cost of digital reference sources and its proper processing by the trained manpower and also the initial infrastructural investment for introducing new services in libraries have influenced different organisations to choose a co-operative model of digital reference services. As a result some co-operative projects have been launched for providing web-based reference services to the users who can ask for such services from a remote location at any time. The Library of Congress, USA has launched the collaborative digital reference service with a mission to provide the users, anywhere anytime through an international digital network of libraries. This network has three main components consisting of (I) Member Profiles (ii) Request Manager-Software for entering, routing and answering reference queries; and (iii) knowledge Base- a searchable database of questions and answer sets. In this network a participating library sends a question to the system on behalf of a user and the system looks in to the knowledge base for a match. Then a reply is sent to the relevant library through e-mail. Incase the question and its corresponding answer is not found in the knowledge base, then it is passed on to the Request Manager where using the profiles of participating libraries and their information resources collection, expertise etc, relevant query is passed on to an appropriate library. This library receives the query, finds an answer and sends back reply to the results store and answer to the knowledge base. Thus the Knowledge Base and Request Manager become able to provide reference service in digital environment. However, the Library of Congress and OCLC have developed a co-operative "Question Point" the advanced generation of collaborative Digital Reference Service (CDTS) in June 2002 which integrates local as well as global electronic reference networks.

Library Networking

The world has been witnessing a knowledge and information explosion during the past few decades. Over 10 million journal articles are published every year besides news items, editorials and articles that are appearing in popular print media. Information professionals who would be the leaders in the twenty-first century depend on information for their work. Access to information holds the key to development. Libraries, which are storehouses of knowledge and information, and information centers, which disseminate knowledge and information, form two important components of present day society. While there is a deluge of information on one hand, the cost of collecting, processing, storing and disseminating information has been spiraling up on the other hand this his calls for heavy budgets for libraries even to maintain a reasonable level of acquisition of journals, books and reports. Estimates show that a three to fourfold rise in library budgets will be needed by AD 2000 to maintain the same acquisition level as in 1990. Information buying power of libraries has been declining year after year.

Because of this, resource sharing and cooperative functioning through networking have become inescapable for libraries and information centres worldwide. India is no exception; for that matter, it is even more necessary to network libraries in newly developing countries like India than in the developed nations. Efficient resource sharing can be achieved by using the recent advances in information technology for realizing a network of libraries.

During the last six to seven years, library and information activities in the country have entered a new era. Individual libraries are coming out of the proverbial "Berlin Wall" around them. They are trying to form a larger community in an effort to tackle the ever increasing demands for better services, quantitatively and qualitatively, in an environment already over strained by financial pressures. Forced, motivated, or logic driven, the librarians are coming out of their shell in large numbers.

This has resulted in discernible change in the information scenario. Now a large number of library resource sharing networks like the Metropolitan Area Networks, such as CALIBNET (Calcutta), DELNET (Delhi), BONET (Bombay), PUNENET (Pune), MALIBNET (Madras), MYLIBNET (Mysore), HYLIBNET (Hyderabad), ADNET (Ahmedabad), and countrywide ones like ERNET (Educational and Research Institutions), SIRNET (CSIR Laboratories), INFLIBNET (Universities and Research Institutions) and DESINET (Defence Laboratories), and sectoral ones like BTISNET (Biotechnology) and TIFACLINE (Technology per se) are under various stages of conceptualization, design and development. A host of agencies, like the National Information System for Science and Technology (NISSAT), Dept. of Electronics, NISCAIR/ CSIR, DESIDOC/DRDO, DBT, NIC, and TIFAC/DST, are involved. Looking from the participant's side, it is common to find an institution participating in more than one network. The ultimate goal of information/library networks is to interlink information resources in a metropolitan area, so that users could access information irrespective of its location, format, medium, language, script etc. Further, the development of such networks requires actions in several areas such as training, rationalization of information resource acquisition, diffusion of standards, preparation of union lists and generation of database services apart from setting up hardware, software and communication facilities.

The concept of library networking to aid information resource sharing and support activities in libraries has become a real necessity. The shortcomings observed are mainly related to two aspects:

a) Non-availability of materials and services, and

b) Efficient administrative control.

In India, the need for resource sharing has been well recognized but the technology options available until now were limited. NISSAT has taken up networking of libraries in Calcutta (CALIBNET), Delhi (DELNET), Madras (MALIBNET), Mysore (MYLIBNET), Hyderabad (HYLIBNET), Ahmedabad (ADNET), Pune (PUNENET), and Bombay (BONET). The present study highlights only some of the major library networks in India.

Towards library networking activities in India NISSAT has taken the initiative for promoting resource-sharing activities. These initiatives are aimed at ensuring better utilization of science and technology information resources, minimization of functional load of information centres and encouragement of motivational factors to a large extent by better means of communication. NISSAT only goes to the extent of setting up general infrastructural facilities like network service centres including hardware, software, manpower and other organizational requirements, communication facilities etc. With a change in the development and implementation strategy, the participating institutions in a network are to arrange their own terminal hardware, software, manpower and data conversion.

Objectives:

- To promote and support adoption of standards in library operations.
- To create databases for projects, specialists and institutions to provide online information services
- To improve the efficiency of housekeeping operations
- To coordinate with other regional, national & international network for exchange of information and documents
- To generate new services and to improve the efficiency of existing ones

Library Consortia

Library consortia means to co-operation, co-ordination and collaboration between, and among, libraries for the purpose of sharing information resources. Libraries in developing countries have been working on consortia at national, regional and international level. However, some barriers such as poor technological and communication infrastructure, inadequate finances, culture and context, attitudes toward consortia and multiple efforts are reported to be limitations of consortia activities in developing in India.

The Council of Scientific and Industrial Research (CSIR) in India has 40 scientific laboratories involved in basic and applied research in various disciplines. Many of the laboratories have well equipped libraries, and some of them act as the main information centres for different subjects, functioning as consultant libraries at the national level. Access to e-journals through the use of state-of-the art technology is possible in many of the libraries belonging to these laboratories. Each of the laboratories has a well-established library or documentation center. National Institute of Science Communication and Information Resource (NISCAIR), a constituent establishment of CSIR. To augment CSIR research and development activities, NISCAIR implemented an agency for providing access to globally available e-journals to the entire scientific and technical staff of CSIR and its constituent units through a consortia approach. As a first step, NISCAIR, on behalf of CSIR, has entered into an agreement with Elsevier Science to access its 1,500 e-journals and further intends to strengthen its information resource base by subscribing e-access of more and more journals published globally. The CSIR consortium extended its access by creating appropriate agreements on a consortium basis with the other providers of e-journals. The major focus is on emerging sectors such as, biotechnology, pharmaceuticals, information/ communications/ entertainment (ICE) and financial services.

INDEST is an open-ended proposition, and welcomes other institutions with the similar area of interest and who can join for sharing benefits. The INDEST Consortium is the most ambitious initiative taken up so far in India in the area of engineering and technology disciplines. The Ministry of Human Resource Development (MHRD) has set up the Indian National Digital Library in Science and Technology (INDEST) Consortium. Institutions including the Indian Institutes of Science (IIScs), the Indian Institutes of Technology (IITs), the National Institutes of Technology (NITs), Regional Engineering, Indian Institutes of Management (IIMs) and a few other centrally funded government institutions through the consortium. Besides that, 60 government or government-aided engineering colleges and technical departments in universities have also joined the consortium with the financial support from the All India Council for Technical Education. In addition, a total of 26 other engineering colleges and institutions have also joined the consortium on a payment basis.

The Indian Astrophysics Consortium called Forum for Resource Sharing in Astronomy (FORSA) is a typical example of a homogeneous group of members wherein the libraries have a common area of interest and establishing the consortium is slightly easier than in a heterogeneous type of members. The FORSA consortium consists of five members who joined together for negotiating licensing for astronomy journals and identified a subscription agent as a supplier of journals. Subscriptions for both print and electronic format are paid through their supplier. The agreement was originally meant for only astronomy journals, published by a particular publisher.

Type of Networks

Local Area Network (LAN)

A LAN is a number of related computers and electronic devices that share information over a transmission media. A typical use of LAN is to tie together personal computers in an office so that they can all use a single printer and a file server. The LAN can be within a building or a campus wide network.

Metropolitan Area Network (MAN)

Attempts are being made to develop this type of network in metropolitan areas such Delhi, Calcutta, Bangalore, Madras, etc.

Wide Area Network (WAN)

A large-scale network, involving offices in different cities and countries is referred to as WAN, which is specially designed to interconnect data transmission devices over wide geographical areas.

Major Library Networks

DELNET

DELNET is a major resource-sharing library network in South Asia, which covers a wide spectrum of member-libraries and their resources connecting more than 1630 libraries in thirty-two states in India and seven overseas countries. It was registered as a society in 1992. DELNET is committed to pool the information about resources. Scattered in the libraries in the country and consolidate information through union. Catalogues, union lists and other databases. This is being done to satisfy the major information requirements of students, researchers, scholars and the public in the country.

DELNET is extensively providing Interlibrary Loan facilities to its member libraries in and outside the country and is one of the most widely used and popular services of DELNET databases have crossed over 90 Lac records. DELNET has shifted to its newly constructed building in JNU Campus in October 2005.

The limitation of financial resources and space for housing library collections in the libraries in Delhi led to the promotion of sharing of resources by automation and networking and establishment of the DELNET in 1988. NISSAT took the initiative in setting up DELNET. It has emerged as an important resource centre for the libraries in Delhi. In Delhi the libraries have been growing very fast in number and site during the last four decades. They cater to specialized and general clientele and are of various types which include institutional libraries, research libraries, government libraries, public libraries, departmental libraries and libraries of the universities, colleges and schools. During the recent years, cumulative information has been increasing at a very fast pace and with it the increase in demands of the users. It has been noticed that in the era of information explosion the libraries in India are generally ill equipped to handle and retrieve information effectively. As already mentioned, the financial resources and the space for housing library collections are limited in almost all of the libraries. The option left with the forward looking librarians has been to promote the sharing of resources by automation and networking.

Initially, 40 libraries were directly linked to the DELNET host system through e-mail to promote library mailing, interlibrary requests, transfer of files, exchange of messages, interlibrary services, etc. Side by side with the automation of participating libraries, the functions and services have also started. Presently about 90 libraries are members of DELNET. Almost all participating libraries are now computerized by means of acquisition and fund accounting, cataloguing, circulation, serials control and local users services. Users are able to locate books and serials through Online Public Access Catalogue (OPAC). A union catalogue of current periodicals available in Delhi libraries, and a union list of current serials available in Indian libraries are available on online for DELNET participant libraries. A central database of DELNET has been created and made operational. This central database includes the library holdings of DELNET member libraries used as union catalogues of books/monographs.

DELNET provides access to the central union catalogue for books and monographs, efficient electronic mailing facilities to access databases of member libraries. It also proposes to develop a network for accessing CD–ROM databases available at member libraries in the near future. DELNET also provides CAS and SDI services, consultancy in library computerization, training and H.R.D. and assistance to libraries on standardization, local automation, retrospective conversion etc. DELNET is likely to emerge as a co–operative network incorporating all disciplines of science, technology, social sciences and humanities.

CALIBNET

The Calcutta Library Network (CALIBNET) was inaugurated on 21 December 1993. NISSAT, Department of Scientific and Industrial Research (DSIR), Govt. of India, took the initiative in setting up CALIBNET, which has adopted a two-way system for networking:

1. The networking route with a library automation and networking through its own application software "Maitrayee"
2. The e-mail route connecting member libraries with on-line access to various databases within network and Internet access.

CALIBNET established a high-tech resource base and provides the following services:

- Online/CDROM based global information search and retrieval services
- Full-text document delivery
- Database services

MALIBNET

The need for interconnecting libraries and information centres in Madras was visualized in the Indian National Scientific Documentation Centre (INSDOC) in 1991. Initially six major academic institutions were directly linked to the MALIBNET host system. Two important databases have been created utilizing the resources available in Madras libraries. One is a Directory Database of Current Serials in Madras covering 30 libraries, and the other is a Contents Database covering articles published in 300 journals available in Madras libraries. Both these databases are continuously updated and also expanded. They are available for online- access to any user and the information is also supplied in diskettes and hard copy. Photocopies of articles from member libraries can be supplied within two days.

Madras has about 60 important libraries besides information centres like INSDOC. About 15 of these libraries have a holding of well over 100,000 items. These libraries act as good resource centres on the network. As of December 1993, all the 60 libraries together invest about Rupees 8,000,000 on acquiring journals and books every year. It is estimated that 40% of the information acquired is redundant. With the libraries networked and resource sharing implemented, each user on the network can get access to a vast amount of literature, and redundancy can be brought down significantly. A novel and unique feature of MALIBNET is that the members will be permitted to offer their own innovative information services on the network. A membership in MALIBNET is open to universities, colleges, R&D institutions, industries and individuals.

MALIBNET presently offers the following information services:

- Current serials acquired in about 60 libraries
- Full journal holdings of about 60 libraries
- Contents information of about 500 important journals
- Electronic mail including internet connectivity
- Door delivery system for document photocopies
- It also offers access to about 1000 international databases

MYLIBNET

It is the first library network established in a small city. The launching of MYLIBNET in association with Mysore city library consortium (MCLC) took place on 12th June 1995. There are 16 institutional members. The holding list of Mysore city libraries has been computerised and software has been developed to enable users to access the catalogue and information on-line. MYLIBNET provides e-mail facilities to its members.

BONET

The Bombay Library Network (BONET) was setup at the National Centre for Software Technology (NCST), Bombay, on 6 November 1992. The Network is sponsored by NISSAT. The aim of BONET is to build a low cost library information system which can possibly be used as a model for future expansion of this service even outside Bombay. BONET also benefits significantly from the experience gained, and facilities created, by the Education and Research Networking (ERNET) project of the Department of Electronics, Govt. of India, assisted by the United Nations Development Programme (UNDP). BONET is aimed at promoting cooperation between libraries in Bombay. The focus is on inter-library activities, rather than on computerizing individual libraries, which will no doubt computerize their own operations and are likely to share their experiences with each other. BONET offers training related to library computerization and networking, and speed up computerization of Bombay libraries. BONET membership provides for access to its centralized catalogues and for E-mail among BONET members. However, access to library related services outside Bombay in India and abroad would require use of ERNET.

PUNENET

Presently, 30 libraries and 15 professionals from Pune city are accessing the PUNENET through modem. The users not only access PUNENET data, but also use the e-mail and internet facilities. Following databases are available on PUNENET for its members:

- Catalogues of holding of all member libraries
- Union catalogue of current periodicals in Pune libraries and information centres
- Publishers and book sellers database
- Database on international grants and fellowships in the health sciences
- Hard databanks in biotechnology
- Access to NICNET and databases available on NICNET e.g., MEDLANS, AIDS database, US patent database
- Access to internet and various databases available on internet
- Patent information
- Union catalogue of books available in British libraries in India

ADINET

Ahmedabad Library Network (ADINET) was formally inaugurated in February 1995 when a memorandum of understanding was signed between NISSAT and ADINET at Ahmedabad. ADINET has ten institutional members, five associate institutional members and two professional members. A centralized database has been created at ADINET, which contains institute master, journal master and book databases. It also organized six work and training programmes. ADINET provided e-mail connectivity to 30 libraries of Ahmedabad.

INFLIBNET

Information and Library Network (INFLIBNET), a programme of the University Grants Commission, was launched in May 1991. The main aim of INFLIBNET is to establish a national computer-communication network to link libraries and information centres in universities, colleges, universities, UGC information centres, institutions of national importance, R&D institutions, etc., and thereby improve capability in information handling and services. It is a programme for academic excellence to be achieved through establishment of a mechanism for information transfer and access to support scholarship and academic work. It facilitates pooling, sharing and optimization of scarce library resources in the country. As a major programme it helps modernize libraries and information centres in the country through application of information technology.

The National Centre of INFLIBNET is located in Gujarat University campus at Ahmedabad. At present, INFLIBNET aims at computerizing and networking of university/college libraries. Every year, INFLIBNET programme is identifying a number of university libraries for automation depending on the budget allocation. The selected institutions are given funds for procuring computer systems, retro conversion and networking. Application software for data entry and other library functions, library standards and formats, etc., are provided by INFLIBNET to the participating libraries. Manpower development is an important part of the programme. Training courses for core library staff engaged in computerised library operations, have been conducted since 1992-93. Development of suitable software, standards for various library operations and communication based services (e.g., e-mail, bulletin boards) designing suitable network architecture and preparation of union catalogues of serials, books, non-book materials, and cooperation with other networking organizations like NISSAT, NICNET, etc., are other important activities

Library Services and Information Highways

Libraries help us adapt to our changing world. They are a source of information on different cultures and religions, different times and places. For example, many people have recently sought information on Islam to help them understand the tensions and historical context of our world today.

Libraries are also a source of economic development information for our knowledge-based society and for small businesses or others seeking success. In Arizona, people looking for information to write a resume, start a new business, or to nurture their small business, turn to the Economic Development Information Centres (EDIC) in libraries.

EDIC libraries have helped people obtain patents, test the potential of markets through demographic information, and helped small businesses find suppliers. Many libraries have legal collections and most state or university libraries have extensive law libraries that serve members of the public as well as all of you. People who need access to the Internet, or basic computer instruction, come to their community library.

And, children begin reading with their parents, go on to story hours, through Internet exploration, college or employment searches and through career skill set changes and elder care information-all at their local library. We are the only public institution that provides life-long service that changes as individuals change. The role of libraries in the digital age, rather than being usurped as many predicted, has been expanded.

Libraries provide content through digital collections and perform editorial functions-insuring the information gathered is authoritative, accurate, and authentic. We work with all aspects of the digital divide-the haves and the have nots, the can and the can nots, and the will and the will nots-providing not just access and assistance, but training and mediation. It is not enough to have a computer or connectivity-you have to know how to use it, and want to use it, to be successful in online research.

Public policy, including legislation attempting to protect our economic and security interests in the digital world, has evoked profound disagreement between publishers, some technology corporations and the education community. The resulting discussions have left some fearing that libraries may be unable to provide services necessary to economic growth and life-long learning.

Some proposed "downstream" database legislation would replace footnotes with royalty checks-creating even more of a have not population. Information has a life cycle that must be nurtured and respected. Libraries are the heart of a community. They are the only public meeting space open to all without institutional barriers of authority, cost, age, or other restrictions.

They provide a safe physical place for the community to exchange ideas; serving as the information commons of the 21 century. Libraries have always been places where everyone in a community can find common ground. Libraries provide no-cost access for the public to all types of information in a variety of formats and media. They are the institution most concerned with providing a level playing field for all to participate.

Libraries invest their resources for you to have access to information. That includes not only making the material physically or electronically available, but also providing services that make the available material meaningful. These services include basic computer instruction, literacy classes, and reference services, or mediation, to help people identify the most useful material in an avalanche of information.

The need to provide internet access and these related services is a growing portion of the traditional library role of providing access to the information that people need to live fulfilling and productive lives-or to participate as informed voters in the governance of our nation. "The library is central to our free society. It is a critical element in the free exchange of information at the heart of our democracy."

Libraries provide opportunities and tools for life-long learning. Public libraries serve as the research library for the University of Life. In today's economic culture, continuously learning new skill sets is a prerequisite for economic viability and is frequently not possible within the traditional educational system.

Twenty-first century learners are self-directed and actively pursue new knowledge on an individual basis. Their community libraries serve as both a source of materials and as a resource to help them identify the materials and services that best meet their needs. Such a society must become a learning society in which all people share in the opportunities to increase skills, knowledge, understanding, and the capacity to reflect on and adapt to change.

Learning across a lifetime, supported throughout our communities, is increasingly essential to a healthy and productive society. Much of the education and research and development activities which fuel our economy and define our culture are possible because of the legal doctrines of fair use and first sale, and the research assumption of permanence of information through the public domain.

Fair use means being able to refer to earlier research, to build on it, and in turn to provide new information for others to build on and use. First sale allows libraries to share materials between institutions (inter-library loan) and to allow you to borrow material to use and return for others to use. Libraries believe that fair use is essential for the learning enterprise.

Fair use is a lawful use of copyrighted material without prior permission from the copyright holder. It means that, for example, a student can photocopy a journal article for research without checking with the publisher first and could refer to that article in a subsequent paper with a footnote. At the same time, licensors of digital works worry about the vulnerability of these technology-based products to unlawful multiple use, and therefore loss of distribution control resulting in a reduced profit.

The US Constitution Clause 8 states that Congress shall have power "To promote the progress of science and useful arts, by securing for limited times to authors and inventors the exclusive right to their respective writings and discoveries." Our patent and copyright laws are based on that clause. Congressional authority was intended to be constrained by the concept of originality; the purpose of promoting science and the useful arts; and to operate within limited periods of time.

Historically, copyrighted works have been sold and the purchaser received a right of use over a particular physical copy of that work, while the creator retained the copyright, or the rights to the intellectual property. The owner of a physical copy is free to sell, loan, or discard that copy.

In the digital environment, the created work is licensed not purchased. The licensee of a copy might not be free to transfer, or share that copy if the license prohibits such actions. Librarians are concerned that current legislative activity seeking to foster the market place for digital information may result in limiting activities legally a part of the promotion of research.

Activities such as fair use, and first sale under gird our educational and research and development efforts. Section 107 of the Copyright Act provides that "the fair use of a copyrighted work, including such use by reproduction in copies....for purposes such as criticism, comment, news reporting, teaching (including multiple copies for classroom use), scholarship, or research, is not an infringement of copyright."

The "first sale" doctrine, embodied in Section 109 of the Copyright Act, limits the copyright holder's "distribution right" by providing that once the owner authorizes the release of lawfully made copies of a work, those copies may in turn be passed along to others by sale, rental, loan, gift, or other transfer. It is this provision that allows libraries to lend books without infringing the copyright.

Information highways

The term 'information highway' gained prominence as a political vision. The information highway is not simply a matter of political will, however. In many ways the political will has been a bandwagon effort to tip national scales in favour of competing most successfully for the increasingly obvious and potent economic benefits of a whole range of groundbreaking, technological R&D which has taken place over several decades.

Basically, the information highway may be defined as the convergence of computer and communication technologies. Not surprisingly, given its complex array of components and transformative power, perceptions of what constitutes the information highway differ, often according to vested interests. Academics, for example, tend to think of the information highway and the Internet as synonymous.

Some use the term 'information highway' as a catch-all to describe the technological revolution, the transformative process that is sweeping most of the globe. For others, the words 'information highway' identify the individual technological innovations that affect our everyday life: most prominently, the Internet, interactive television and electronic banking.

Yet others view it as a massive infrastructure, constituting a 'seamless and transparent network of networks' capable of transmitting a full range of interactive, audio, video, and data services. No matter which component is emphasized, the phenomenon of the information highway is massive, transformative and inevitable, given the enabling power of the technologies involved. As Al Gore (1995) has stated:

> New technologies that enhance the ability to create and understand information have always led to dramatic changes in civilization.... There is no longer any doubt that [these new] machines will reshape human civilization even more quickly and more thoroughly than did the printing press.

Although the 'information highway' initiative was given its name in the United States, the phenomenon was recognized simultaneously in many places in the world. Developmental stages differ, however. Singapore was one of the first countries worldwide to perceive and capitalize upon the economic benefits to be gained from the development of an IT-based infrastructure.

The incentives were strong: upon achieving self-rule in 1959, Singapore was saddled with severe poverty and chronic unemployment of its poorly educated population. From 1965 Singapore switched to a development strategy of export production, first in the industrial and manufacturing sector and then in technological diversification, a strategy which met with exceptional success.

This remarkable result of high-tech leading to information highway development can be attributed to the activist policies of the government in creating macro-economic stability (low inflation, positive real interest rates, sound fiscal management) and above all a liberal foreign trade environment.

Europe, in the early stages of forming itself as a world trading block, had reasons similar to Singapore's to seize upon the economic opportunities provided by the emerging information technologies. Seeking to bolster private sector growth, it did this particularly in terms of research and development. From the mid-1980s, the European Strategic Programme for Research in Information Technology (ESPRIT) has been a remarkable source of R&D funding.

Convinced that information technology would be a large factor not only in the successful formation of the European Union itself but also in its effectiveness in global trade, the European Commission established the first ESPRIT programme with the aim of strengthening an already growing information technology industry.

The overall objective is to contribute to the healthy growth of the information infrastructure so as to improve the competitiveness of all industry in Europe, not just the IT industry, and to help enhance the quality of life. Outlining plans for the Common European Information Area, it provided the impetus for the establishment at the 1993 Brussels Summit of a group of prominent persons to prepare a report on the information society with concrete recommendations for action.

Although this High-Level Group on the Information Society, chaired by Martin Bangemann, was not charged to advise on the information highway *per se*, nearly all of the recommendations of the subsequent report relate to its development. Overriding the specific recommendations of the Bangemann Report concerning competition rules, protection of intellectual property, interconnection, interoperability and other information highway issues is the urge for the European Union 'to put its faith in market mechanisms as the motive power to carry us into the Information Age'.

The report continues: 'This means that actions must be taken at the European level and by Member States to strike down entrenched positions which put Europe at a competitive disadvantage.' This should be done by fostering an entrepreneurial mentality and developing a common regulatory approach rather than using more public money, financial assistance, subsidies, dirigisme, or protectionism.

The Group also proposed an action plan of concrete initiatives based on a partnership between the private and public sectors to carry Europe forward into the information society. The Bangeman Report, presented at the Corfu Summit, gave way in July 1994 to a European Commission Action Plan (1994) which urged activity in the following four areas: the required regulatory and legal framework for trans-European networks; basic services and content applications; social, societal and cultural aspects; and the promotion of the Information Society.

Within the European Union itself, several member countries have undertaken their own initiatives regarding national information highway development and related policies. France, in fact, can rightly be called the pre-information highway 'pioneer' with the development of Minitel by France Telecom in the early 1980s.

Minitel, now an integral part of daily life for French people, both at home and at work, currently offers a wide range of electronic directories including the International Minitel Directory covering over 200 million telephone subscribers in Europe (Belgium, Germany, Portugal, Spain, Switzerland) and the United States. In addition to its directories, popular Minitel electronic services have expanded to include banking, transport information, mail-order selling, tourist information, weather reports, classified advertisements, radio and television information, and various business services.

With over fourteen years of online service experience, France Telecom made its approximately 25,000 Minitel services available on the Internet in May 1996 and is moving into multimedia applications. In February 1994 Gérard Théry, father of Minitel and former Directeur Général des Telecommunications, was appointed to analyse and report on measures for the development of information highways in France.

The Théry report, completed in October 1994, recommended four major actions: the deployment of fibre-optic networks; the launching of platforms for experimentation similar to those in the United States; the promotion of applications software and content; and the acceleration of high-speed transmissions on the network. Other countries in Europe which have proceeded with government policies for information highway development at the national level include Denmark, Finland, Norway and Spain.

The United States, meanwhile, was the first government to call for action and advice focused specifically on the information highway. An Information Infrastructure Task Force (IITF) was established by the White House Office of Science and Technology Policy and by the National Economic Council as part of the NII Agenda for Action initiative. The Council was established by Executive Order 12864 in September 1993 to advise the IITF.

Major issues for the Council were: the appropriate roles of the private and public sectors in NII development; a vision for the evolution of the NII and its public and commercial applications; the impact of current and proposed regulatory regimes on the evolution of the NII; privacy, security and copyright issues; national strategies for maximizing interconnection and interpretability of communications networks; and universal access.

In April 1994 the Council organized itself into three MegaProject Working Groups to explore: the vision and goals for the information superhighway; access to the superhighway; and intellectual property, privacy and security issues. The purpose of the MegaProjects was to frame discussion and draft recommendations to facilitate the full Council's ability to reach consensus in these areas.

The Council met across the United States from February 1994 to the end of 1995, receiving voluminous public comment. In March 1995 it published its emerging framework, an articulation of basic principles, the first of which addressed five areas: universal access and service, privacy and security, intellectual property, education and lifelong learning, and electronic commerce.

The Council concluded that the most efficient way to develop the information highway ('super-highway') in the United States was through community effort. Its KickStart Initiatives document offered guidelines for achieving universal access by connecting the nation's schools, libraries and community centres.

In Canada, the Final Report of the Information Highway Advisory Council (IHAC), produced in September 1995, addresses many of the issues mandated to the United States Council. It also echoes to a large extent the policy stance recommended by the Bangemann Report. Established by the Minister of Industry Canada in May 1994, with McGill University Professor David Johnston as Chair, IHAC was a high-level group of twenty-nine Canadians from the private sector (telecommunication, cable television, computer and networking technologies), government, education, and other interested groups such as consumers, labour and libraries.

IHAC was charged to advise the Canadian Government specifically on fifteen issues, including competitiveness, culture, access to learning, and research and development. The Council's deliberations were guided by three objectives: to create jobs through innovation and investment in Canada; to reinforce Canadian sovereignty and cultural identity; and to ensure universal access at reasonable cost.

The Council also established five principles: an interconnected and interoperable network of networks; collaborative public-and private-sector development; competition in facilities, products and services; privacy protection and network security; and lifelong learning as a key design element of the information highway.

In Asia, despite recent progress in China, the Republic of Korea, Malaysia and Thailand, no country compares with frontrunner Singapore in information highway development. However, it is also important to note the progress of Japan. Despite its history as one of the most 'informatized' societies of the world, Japan was in fact slower than the United States to progress toward formalizing its information highway development.

This was due partly to the proliferation of government departments and other agencies which claimed responsibility, including the Ministry of International Trade and Industry (MITI), the Ministry of Posts and

Telecommunications (MPT), Nippon Telephone and Telegraph (NTT), numerous cable television companies, telecommunication equipment suppliers and media owners.

In June 1993 the Information Industry Subcommittee of MITI's Industrial Structure Council published a report on improving the social infrastructure for the information society. Later in 1993 NTT announced its grand plan, at a cost of US$400 billion, to install optical fibre throughout Japan by the year 2015. Also in 1993 the MPT was framing new regulatory policies for infrastructure development.

A new vision for an advanced information society, with Japan taking the lead in Asia in the multimedia industry, was announced in September 1994 by Prime Minister Murayama's Advanced Information and Telecommunications Society Promotion Headquarters. In recent years the ministerial meetings and conferences of the G-7 member countries have provided a focal point for global information highway development by the industrialized nations.

Following the Bangemann Report, the central theme of the G-7 Ministerial Conference in Brussels on 24-26 February 1995 was the information society transforming the quality of life for a growing number of peoples around the world. Global interconnection was discussed, with recommendations for worldwide co-operation, especially for the less developed countries.

The outcome of this conference was the designation of eleven specific projects in selected theme areas. The themes, which offer a glimpse of the already incredible sweep and breadth of the information highway phenomenon, are: creation of a global inventory of information relevant to the development of the global information society; global interoperability for broadband networks; cross-cultural training and education; electronic libraries; electronic museums and galleries; environment and natural resources management; global emergency management; global health-care application; governments online; a global marketplace for small and medium enterprises (SMEs); and maritime information systems. The projects were assigned to the various G-7 countries.

The Organization's programmes in this area are designed to assist all Member States to respond to the new challenges of the information society. More particularly, they aim to ensure that all sectors of society benefit from the potential of information and communication technologies to support development processes. At the centre of the challenges posed by the emerging information society is the concept of universal access and how a 'right to communicate' will evolve in an increasingly digital world.

Access in this context involves not only physical availability and cost, but also ensuring that the user can benefit from the services concerned, with a minimum level of 'digital literacy'. In the increasingly competitive and commercial world of information and communication, the risks of excluding disadvantaged populations are substantial, both within and among societies as well as among developed and developing countries.

An important facet of the 'right to communicate' concerns access to telematics facilities at affordable cost by the 'intellectual' sectors - education, science, culture, media, libraries and archives - which have a crucial role to play in the development of national information infrastructures. Another important issue is the maintenance of linguistic and cultural diversity in the information society.

Technology-induced globalization is seen by many as a threat to local customs, values and beliefs, as exemplified by the fact that, today, a large majority of the data on the Internet is in English. Increased access to interconnected networks and databases raises major ethical and legal issues. These include:

— privacy of information and the right of individuals to check data pertaining to themselves;

— regulation for the content of information circulating through information highways; computer piracy and other informatics crimes; and

— copyright, where efforts are required to extend legitimate intellectual property protection while maintaining access to information.

At the twenty-eighth session of the UNESCO General Conference (1995), a joint meeting of the Programme Commissions discussed the 'educational, scientific and cultural challenges of the new communication and information technologies'. The General Conference also adopted 28C/ Resolution VII.15, which stressed the societal problems of information technologies and potential dangers of information highways to developing nations.

UNESCO has undertaken a wide range of activities which may be described under three headings: Overall societal impact, at the global level, of new information and communication technologies. Co-operative links have been established with the International Telecommunications Union (ITU) and other IGOs and NGOs; and various meetings have been or are being organized: Copyright in the Information Society; Education and Informatics; and Ethical, Legal and Societal Aspects of Digital Information.

In 1994, in the framework of their Joint Programme on Promotion of Telematics for Development, ITU and UNESCO completed a study entitled The Right to Communicate - At What Price: Economic Constraints to the Effective Use of Telecommunications in Education, Science, Culture and in the Circulation of Information. This defined a new strategy for ensuring access to modern telematics facilities at affordable cost for users in UNESCO's fields of competence in the developing countries.

More recently, a United Nations system-wide, Special Initiative on Africa was launched 'Harnessing Information Technology for Development' - for which ECA, the World Bank, UNESCO, the ITU and UNCTAD are identified as the lead agencies. A large number of projects are under way, in many areas related to new information technologies and information highways.

Examples are the linking of African countries to the Internet, improved access to telematics services in the Caribbean, the application of electronic information technologies to distance education, safeguarding Internet use by journalists and the media, and the Memory of the World Programme.

Telecommunication Infrastructure

The essence of the information highway revolution lies in the convergence of information processing and telecommunication technologies. This has eroded the traditional distinction in communication between carrier and content, resulting in several profoundly new challenges, not least of which is regulatory turmoil. Clearly, the technological issues related to the development of the information highway infrastructure are complex, the costs are immense, and with convergence the stakes for the major carriers are extremely high.

Whereas the governments of Singapore and others in East Asia have intervened strongly to ensure the benefits of a strong infrastructure for their countries, Western governments have attempted to stimulate private sector development. In the countries of the West, where the private sector is expected to drive information highway development, deregulation currently holds centre stage. There is widespread agreement that the United States has taken the lead, beginning with the break-up of the AT&T monopoly in 1984 and culminating to date in the signing by President Clinton of the Telecommunications Act of 1996.

In one sweep, the new Act ends United States Government regulations that have maintained barriers between local and long-distance telephone services, cable television, broadcasting and wireless services. In the age of digital communications, those regulations have become anachronistic. The microchip is placing all forms of communication - from satellite-television images and long-distance telephone calls to e-mail and World Wide Web pages.

Finland, Sweden and the United Kingdom have already at least partially opened their markets to carrier competition. Fifteen European Union countries together with Switzerland and Norway, face a deadline to do this formally on 1 January 1998. In anticipation, new players are already investing many millions of dollars in networking and building alliances; for example, Olivetti of Italy has a joint venture with Bell Atlantic Corporation, with plans to team up with France Telecom and Deutsche Telekom to challenge the monopoly of Telecom Italia.

Meanwhile, amid fears that the 1998 liberalization agreement will be a case of 'too little too late', new competitors in Europe will be permitted as of July 1996 to lease telephone lines from cable companies, railways and utilities, bypassing the monopoly of national operators and paving the way for a billion-dollar trans-European backbone network.

Meanwhile, liberalization of trade in basic telecommunication services is currently being negotiated at the international level through the General Agreement on Trade in Services (GATS). In the midst of all this activity, encouragement of standards becomes a crucial governmental role. The key to an effective and efficient global information highway, for competition as well as for society as a whole, is interoperability.

Most obviously, open (as opposed to proprietary) technical standards are required for the infrastructure, but because of digitization this infrastructure increasingly includes content as well as the carriers. Accordingly, international content/carrier standards are necessary for digital compression, data transmission protocols, software, consumer equipment, etc.

The development of international standards in such a fast-moving area of activity is not without risks; at best, flexibility is required to avoid the costly mistakes of going down wrong developmental paths, technical myopia and monopolistic pressures.

Multimedia Revolution

Because development of content and applications on the information highway depends upon the infrastructure, this latter aspect initially captured attention. In North America and Europe, too, content and applications have come more sharply into focus - both through reoriented, newly-allied carriers and through the new multimedia players.

Within Europe, the INFO2000 initiative illustrates the push for multimedia production growth. In a Communication to the European Parliament and Council in 1995 the European Commission defines the content industry as involving the creation, development, packaging and distribution of content-based products and services, and describes the different segments of the industry as follows:

— Print publishing (newspapers, books, magazines, corporate publishing).

— Electronic publishing (online databases; video-tex, audiotex, fax- and CD-based services; video games).

— The audiovisual industry (television, video, radio, audio and cinema).

The INFO2000 initiative has three action lines to facilitate the transition by the private sector to electronic publishing and interactive multimedia: stimulating demand and raising awareness; exploiting Europe's public sector information; and triggering European multimedia potential.

In general, the [information highway] will be driven by the content carried over the network - services, applications and information. According to consumer surveys, likely areas for success are: entertainment, including a broad variety of interactive, user-driven arts, music, video and games; information sharing, such as news groups and bulletin boards; medical databases and consultation; interpersonal communication, such as voice, video, fax and electronic mail; news gathering and research; educational applications; banking, insurance and securities trading; and monitoring services, including home security, fire protection and home environment regulation.

Although many of these products are not new, to succeed, the new mode of delivery over the [information highway] must provide additional value to the consumer. While many carriers have targeted entertainment, video-on-demand in particular, as the top choice of consumers, recent surveys reveal different priorities. Four key areas of consumer demand for content and new services have been identified in order of priority as: education and training; health care; leisure and entertainment; and government information.

Education is clearly an area where traditional structures are crumbling. To begin with, 'facilitated by the power of information technology, classroom learning now extends beyond a single campus to distant sites across the country'. Beyond that, dramatic changes in student demographics, the current knowledge explosion, new tools for accessing, creating, displaying and assessing information, and many other factors, are transforming the nature of the learning process itself.

Educational software and CD-based products abound, as do videoconferencing, audiotex and other technologies for distance delivery. The drive for multimedia products extends to all ages and levels of education, from preschoolers to pensioners. Huge markets exist for courseware and other curriculum delivery products for students from primary schools to universities.

In addition, there is growing demand for training packages in the workplace to increase skills, and for upgrading and retraining programmes for workers displaced by redundancies, early retirements, etc.

Indeed, as in all areas of life affected by the information highway, the ability to access these products from home has exacerbated the loss of boundaries between home and work and school (and allied institutions such as libraries), transforming the consumer's living room into a 'virtual' school, office or library as required.

This blurring of distinctions profoundly increases the overlaps between education and entertainment, between work and play. Much of the current market for home-based learning and training involves cable vendors and/or the Internet, causing direct competition in the United States, for example, between current online service providers,

Telecommunications Inc., another United States cable giant, has announced plans for a trial next year of its home online service, and Netcom, the largest American Internet access provider, has plans to meet Bell Canada's new Sympatico Internet service head-on. Meanwhile, Le Groupe Videotron, a Canadian-based cable company, already has an operational home service available by subscription in Montreal and in the United Kingdom, offering an array of services on cable television including banking, video-on-demand, and fast food ordering; the only additional equipment required is an IBM-designed modem and a card swiping device for payment.

The growth of electronic payment systems is a concomitant feature of the new content services -indeed, all forms of commerce - on the information highway. The shift to electronic 'cash' is a further instance of the general transition from paper to electronic documentation. Sophisticated financial transaction systems based on direct payment, payroll, electronic data exchange and credit card transactions are being developed.

The development of payment/credit systems for electronic commerce on the information highway, secure against counterfeiting and fraud, is big business in itself. Currently Visa and MasterCard are at a standoff, Visa working with Microsoft to develop a Secure Transaction Technology Protocol and MasterCard working with Netscape and other vendors on a Secure Electronic Payment Protocol.

Beyond matters of payment, however, is the development of smartcards that include a wealth of personnel data that can be used in transactions ranging from user verification to insurance purchase to health care. For example, Motorola, the world's leading supplier for smartcards, has recently announced major contracts with two new European government health and social security projects.

Spain will take delivery of 7 million card chips as part of an eventual countrywide social-security-linked smart-card programme; and the Czech Republic will take 10,000 chips for a pilot scheme as part of a countrywide health project to reach 10 million people and provide vital health-care information. Health care on the information highway is an explosive development area, with services from distance diagnostics to consumer health information.

Telemedicine is appearing in areas of the world where distance is a factor; in Canada, for example, a system links rural doctors in Alberta with specialists in the city of Calgary. Still in early stages of delivery, this system is estimated to have significantly decreased health-care costs, including the wear-and-tear, travel and accommodation costs of patients. Soaring health-care expenditures, driving the trend to hospital closures and increased emphasis on community care, have made the potential benefits of telemedicine particularly attractive.

Coupled with the smartcard phenomenon that enables patients to access their entire medical records, the possibilities (and pitfalls) for electronic health-care delivery are still in their infancy. It is evident that, along with convergence and restructuring on a massive scale in the information technology industries, the new content industries (multimedia, imaging, etc.) are bringing about the global de-institutionalization of schools and hospitals.

Sweeping changes are being brought about by the information highway revolution in other institutions, too. 'One of the first pieces of evidence that this is a "big one", as far as revolutions go, is that three of the oldest institutions of human civilization schools, hospitals and libraries - are undergoing this sort of fundamental, structural change'.

Indeed, the concept 'library', difficult enough to define in the traditional sense, has become almost impossible to define today. It has been a long time since a library was merely a collection of books. For centuries libraries were essentially archives for the storage and preservation of recorded thought. Not until the early twentieth century, in fact, did libraries emerge as distinct from archives, with an emphasis upon information retrieval and use.

In other words, although the revolution brought about by the invention of the printing press had a direct and profound impact upon libraries, its ramifications were slow to develop fully. In contrast, the impact of the current information revolution is happening with breathtaking speed. It has been said that, increasingly, new nurses are getting jobs not in hospitals, but as partners in health-care delivery. The same can be said for librarians who, as libraries close, are beginning to be placed more strategically as knowledge workers within organizations.

There is a vast array of opportunities for librarians, who adopt new names like data analysts, information managers, information consultants and the like, in today's knowledge-intensive organizations (for example, consulting firms, software companies and other SMEs). In the public sector, the Freenet phenomenon in North America has opened possibilities for the 'wired' public library.

Some librarians, not yet grasping the speed of the transformation, still mount their catalogues on the Internet so that people will come to the library.

With remote access to library catalogues, electronic publication and document delivery, that walk to the library is becoming irrelevant. The virtual library is in the consumers' offices, classrooms and homes.

As electronic communication grows, the need for the traditional intermediary skills of librarians lessens. Long the facilitators between people and information, today's librarians face not just the crumbling of their institutions but the more positive cognitive task of seeing themselves as information highway 'content people'. In other words, their professional future lies within the multimedia and content provision industry as a whole.

Preserving and providing access to 'the cultural memory' in today's global village is at least as important as it has been in centuries past; the stakes for all content providers -librarians and archivists included - are as high as the opportunities. The race toward global interconnectivity and content delivery brings with it the important issue of cultural sovereignty.

Cultural and linguistic aspects of the information society are of particular relevance. The nature and operation of the global information infrastructure must respect cultural and linguistic diversities. The content of new networked applications, especially in the sphere of education and entertainment, is likely to become as essential as the traditional media as a vehicle for shaping cultural values.

Audiovisual programmes are a key component of content. Encouraging the circulation of diversified content is highly desirable in order to promote mutual understanding and cultural enrichment. However, it is also very important to preserve and promote cultural and linguistic specificity, whose importance as an objective is justified by the contribution diversity makes to human progress and mutual enrichment.

Cultural diversity and the appropriate presence of indigenous cultural products and services will be facilitated by the impressive potential of low cost delivery of multimedia content over the information infrastructure. Linguistic minorities find themselves especially vulnerable in a world increasingly connected by information in the English language.

Strong public cultural policies have become extremely important in non-English-speaking or bilingual countries. Equally important are the legal and ethical aspects of electronic content control, the most vexing (and unresolved) of which have to do with intellectual property, privacy and security.

'Browsing' is a particular thorny copyright issue: authors, on the one hand, fear loss of control over their works in an electronic environment, and on the other hand consumers, readers especially, fear loss of their traditional right to browse through a document (book, newspaper, etc.) before photocopying, borrowing or buying it.

The latter has become especially critical in the light of at least one recent court decision, in the United States, that the act of browsing a work in a digital environment (that is, viewing it on a computer screen) constitutes an act of reproduction. The twin issues of privacy (confidentiality) and security (protection, authentication and verification) of data are significant enough to have spurred the growth of entire new industries.

Privacy is of deep personal concern to consumers, particularly with the advancement of smartcards. Data security is crucial for today's individuals and organizations wholly dependent upon electronic databases for accurate (often sensitive) information free from the threat of 'computer crime' such as tampering or 'hacking', fraud and unauthorized deletion.

Interconnection of networks is dramatically increasing the number of electronic transactions, credit ratings, financial accounts, education records, medical and driving records, etc., that can be amassed in individual or company profiles. These masses of data cross national boundaries (an aspect of the disturbing issue of transborder data flow), and are often resold, re-used or integrated with other databases - often without knowledge, consent or remuneration.

References

Bertot, John C., "Libraries and Networked Information Services: Issues and Considerations in Measurement." *Performance Measurement and Metrics*, 2004.

Schatz, Bruce R. "Information Retrieval in Digital Libraries: Bringing Search to the Net." *Science*, 17 January 1997.

Schwartz, Candy. "Digital Libraries: An Overview." *The Journal of Academic Librarianship* 26, November 2000.

Shiri, Ali. "Digital Library Research: Current Developments and Trends." *Library Review* 52, no. 5, 2003.

Smith, Abby. *Strategies for Building Digitized Collection*s. Washington, DC: Digital Library Federation, Council on Library and Information Resources, 2001.

Suleman, Hussein,et.al., "Networked Digital Library of Theses and Dissertations: Bridging the Gaps for Global Access—Part 1: Mission and Progress." *D-Lib Magazine* 7, September 2001.

2

Information Access

Digital technologies open a world that paradoxically is simultaneously more complex and, in some ways, simpler. It is more complex because now the same document or document format may intrinsically be represented in different media for different purposes, forcefully motivating the need to distinguish carefully between the format and the medium. Furthermore, different media may be used interchangeably for different stages of document handling, that is, for capture, storage, access, distribution, and use. To complicate the situation even more, the documents may be encoded in a myriad of ways at each of these stages. And yet, separation of the format and the medium—and treating each stage of document handling separately—may open up a more logical structure free from traditional constraints. In this sense, digital technologies may simplify certain aspects of librarianship. Digital technologies present many new challenges, however, that must be considered. For example, although these varying formats may be decoded and translated back and forth among each other, many fear that the means of decoding may become lost as a result of technological obsolescence, conceivably making digitally stored documents inaccessible.

There are also many who question the longevity of the physical media used in digital technologies. Others suggest that the appropriate way to address both of these problems—as well as to take advantage of the declining costs of computer storage and of increasing storage densities—may well be to copy stored documents periodically onto new media. Indeed the main advantage of the world of digital technologies, namely that they represent a kind of "esperanto" of mutually comprehensible and interchangeable formats, may, if not properly managed, also represent their biggest weakness, because of the rapidity of change and obsolescence, and because of the wide range of choices available at any given time.

Periodic recopying onto new media represents a whole new approach for libraries to the operation and financing of "inventory management". The implications could be quite extensive. Librarians tend to think in terms of periods of centuries rather than having to recopy every few years. Such considerations may either hinder the adoption of digital technologies for preservation or other purposes or eventually cause some rethinking of the underlying economics of librarianship. The incentive for such potential reevaluation, however, is not limited to the preservation of older materials, nor is the influence of technology the only driving factor. The underlying stimulus is a gradual transition over the centuries—perhaps spurred by the exponential growth of recorded knowledge and information—from documents with associated physical or conceptually useful lifetimes, times between new editions, or, more generically, times between "instances", that can be measured in decades or centuries; to documents with associated times between instances measured in much shorter units of time—even, in the case of "active documents", measured in minutes or seconds. The financial and other implications of this could undoubtedly be far-reaching for libraries, introducing into the library milieu unfamiliar concepts associated with continuous processes or processes with relatively short lifetimes, such as "depreciation" and "lifecycle costing."

These are concepts that are familiar to the world of digital electronic processing and quite normal outside of universities, but that have been avoided in worlds—such as research libraries—that depend to a greater or lesser extent upon irregular gifts or grants of varying or unpredictable size, donations directed to the purchase and immediate storage of documents, but not to their maintenance. Indeed, one of the most serious questions facing librarians in the future may be how to effect a match between the changing economic demands of "continuous processes" and the traditional nature of many funding sources. Yet the potential of digital technologies and of the flexibility they offer is boundless.

Over the coming decades, these technologies may open up vistas of ever-increasing storage densities to where entire libraries can be electronically stored in the space of a single room; of blinding access and distribution speeds allowing whole documents to be moved almost instantly across the nation's (and indeed the world's) data networks, leading to the concept of the "distributed library;" of ease of replication at very modest cost (another cause for alarm, particularly to those concerned with protection of intellectual property); of "print-on-demand" where paper copies of documents are only printed "just in time" and not inventoried in advance of need; of accessibility at a distance away from where the "digital document" or preservation copy was created or is stored; and of intelligent automated document analysis. Indeed, the means of creation and production of documents have already been revolutionised by these technologies. These technologies also open up horizons for totally new document formats, such as active documents whose contents may combine different media such as text, sound, video or voice; or whose contents may change dynamically with time, what Harvey Wheeler called "the fungible book."

The preservation of these new "active" formats is not of direct interest to the subject of preservation of more traditional formats, but is of indirect interest because digitally preserved traditional documents can be incorporated into such active documents. Some view the introduction of digital technologies into the world of libraries as likely to cause a revolution as far-reaching as that caused by the printing-press: a massive paradigm shift. Others view the introduction with concern, an intimidating perturbation that disturbs an equilibrium and modalities of scholarship that have served well for many decades or even for centuries. Either way, digital technologies cannot be ignored.

The next twenty years are likely to be times of extraordinary change. Our libraries—indeed our universities, colleges, and our scholarly communities—may well be remade by the consequences of this technological revolution. And yet—in spite of technology's impact and of the revolutionary consequences of that impact—it must be recognised that technology itself is not the ultimate driving force. It is the inexorable pressure caused by the exponential growth of recorded knowledge, and the ever-increasing complexity, costs, and other problems associated with the storage and distribution of, and access to, such information. Technology can provide some solutions: it is not an end in itself. Furthermore—for many reasons too numerous to detail here—the "digital library" is not about to replace the "paper library." Both will need to coexist in a shifting environment, at least for the foreseeable future. This in itself will present librarians with many economic, organisational, social, technical, and other challenges. Between the eager apostles of technology and those who approach change with extreme caution lies the mass of professionals who are trying to understand and grapple with the potential of this shifting environment, many of them implementing prototype activities designed to elucidate greater insight, many working to close the gap between promise and reality.

The rash of new information technology has raised major problems for librarians and archivists, faced with a flood of new kinds of media such as audio and video tape or computer disks. Most of these technologies were designed and manufactured without permanence as a prime consideration. A worse problem is the short life of the reading devices; even the less than permanent tapes or disks often do not deteriorate until long after the machines to read them become unavailable.

Digital preservation thus depends upon copying, not on the survival of the physical media. Librarians and archivists must prepare for reformatting as a regular step in information management. In this, they must join with computer center managers, individual computer owners, and all others who need to keep machine-readable data for more than a few years.

Computer-based Archives

There is great economy of scale in maintaining new media—not so much the devices, but in sharing the expertise. Cooperation is essential for libraries to manage. Not only will standard formats help a great deal, but copying digital information is much easier than generating it. Particularly where lots of intellectual effort is required it makes no sense for different groups to work on the same file. It will be much easier for libraries to obtain updated versions from central sources than for each library to manage all its own reformatting. A cooperative program for converting digital information would be appropriate. It should involve both maintaining records of who has what, seeing that conversions are done only once, and seeing to it that important materials are kept in more than one place. There are a great many existing computer-based archives. Efforts should be made to find funding to put archives of this sort on a firm footing. In the long run, it will be cheaper to have sites of responsibility for particular materials than to attempt to duplicate expertise in specialised records conversion.

Furthermore, sites of this form will function in the traditional way to link scholars working in the same area, even if these links are now via electronic mail rather than by physical travel to the site. Most of the computer-based archives above are textually oriented. Support is needed to extend computer-based archives in the multimedia areas, and also in the areas of numerical data and programs. Some attention is also needed to ways of indexing the material in these archives, as there is no straightforward way to locate information, particularly non-textual information, in machine-readable form. Bibliographic guides will have to be developed, and even the format these should take is not clear. Industrial and government computing groups have often had the problem of maintaining old tape files, and have stimulated much of the work in records management for machine-readable files. Unfortunately the history here is often poor: it is said that we know more about the 1860 census than the 1960 census, which was written on a very early form of computer tape and which no one realised in time should be copied to newer media.

Copyright rules may pose a severe problem. The copyright life of much material greatly exceeds the technological life of the media it is recorded on. A library may well be able to preserve something only by copying it, but may have difficulty obtaining permission to do that. With luck the original issuer will publish the material in a new format, but as the devotees of old records and movies can testify, this does not always happen. Leaving aside the question of how it is accomplished, through either amendment or court interpretation, the concept of "fair use" should be extended to include the copying to new media of a publication which is no longer available for sale, and the distribution of the copy to other libraries. At the moment, there is an exemption for copying of a publication that a library already owns, but not for distribution to libraries that do not own the original being copied.

The law may also pose problems even for information where the copyright law does not bar conversion. A library or archives might wish to store information derived from old, copyright-expired publications; or from public domain sources; or from publications of the university to which it belongs. However, it is doubtful that a copyright can be asserted in a straightforward transcription to machine-readable form of a non-copyrighted document or audiotape. The rule that a copyright can only be claimed for the result of creative activity is somewhat unclear. It has recently been interpreted to say that (a) collecting and alphabetising names into a telephone book is not copyrightable but at the very least (b) numbering the pages in a Government-provided text is copyrightable. Although measuring the creativity in these publications is like arguing whether a concrete block is more or less intelligent than a 2x4, the legal uncertainty causes all vendors of electronic information to require specific contracts limiting the use of the purchased data, imposing administrative burdens on everyone.

Libraries and archives, depending on the circumstances, might be on either side of this issue. Presumably, the ability to enforce a copyright in a converted text will encourage someone to do a conversion. On the other hand, if the issuer then disappears, it becomes difficult to get permission to do the next conversion when that becomes necessary. Again, it would be useful to have a rule that the copyright lasts only as long as someone is willing to sell the protected item. The copyright law also affects the question of multiple copies. The United States is developing a very high speed digital network which will soon provide 45 Mbits/second between major sites and should be at 1 Gbit/second before the end of the decade. Thus, libraries and archives may well feel that there is no need to have their own copy of something, since the delay in getting it remotely may be negligible.

But, depending on copyright rules and the developing business practices in the electronic information industry, it may be difficult to arrange access permission. On the other side, it would be unfortunate if the existence of the network meant that important documents were kept in only one copy which was at risk of disappearing. Finally, the insertion of copy-protection into sound recordings acts against the interests of libraries and long-term permanence of the original material. Deposit of an unprotected copy in some trustworthy institution is probably the best solution, but not something the industry is pursuing.

OI Usability

We have identified the commercially available online information resources (OI) which are relevant to digital libraries as online databases, CD-ROMs and bulletin boards. This definition is dictated in part by the association of these resources within the literature, and in part by the interdependent nature of the technologies that comprise them. New and existing OI resource providers are variously constrained and enabled in their efforts to take advantage of advances in data transfer (like fiber-optics), processing (like massively parallel architectures) and information storage (like terabyte hard drives and CD-ROM.) These technological components define an accessibility baseline of OI resource usability. Digital libraries which contain

OI products and services must at least facilitate physical connection to these resources. Beyond this point, there are many aspects to usability that make using OI resources more enjoyable, less expedient, more expensive, less effective, and so on.

The aspects of OI usability can be classified into four major categories:

1. HCI Usability,
2. Content Usability,
3. Organisational Usability and
4. Interorganisational Usability.

HCI Usability involves issues of individual access and individual resource usage on a personal level or within working groups. It highlights human-computer interaction with the OI resource interface, but also takes into consideration how individuals might need to coordinate resource usage in a work group setting.

Content Usability involves characteristics of the information itself. It addresses issues of information relevance, information awareness, information retrieval methods, and expertise.

Organisational Usability involves the situated use of OI and OI resources. A library or organisation may provide training and support staff to help people use the available resources, or it may not. The information itself may be used collaboratively among working groups or symbolically as post-decision support.

Interorganisational Usability involves use of OI and OI resources within interorganisational networks. This may entail uses of OI to achieve competitive advantage, or to coordinate professionals of the virtual organisation.

OI Users

Non-scholarly users of OI resources in the digital library may be today's consumers of commercial OI services. Martha E. Williams has been accumulating and analysing the statistics of the online database industry for a number of years. Her classifications of "users" are at the institutional level: academics, information brokers, government, industry, legal institutions, medical institutions, not-for-profits and libraries. Levy and Marshall also confirm that digital libraries are "users" of OI resources. The people searching these databases are also called "users", and they are often segmented on the basis of their information usage into two groups: end-users and intermediaries. Intermediaries are usually associated with libraries or corporate information centers. They search the OI resources at their disposal on behalf of others who will use the information retrieved in decision-making or other tasks. Aumente quotes 1987 DIALOG usage statistics as 80% by search intermediaries. End-users are commonly considered to be individuals who use the information they retrieve directly in their own work tasks.

There has been a significant amount of research attention paid to the end-user. However, some researchers have found it difficult to segregate the intermediary from the end-user in situated use. They have concluded that in their studies all individual OI resource users were essentially intermediaries because "the work practices of their settings led them to share their search results with others, either by request or on their own initiative". Who the user is and what the user does has been the quintessentially interesting research question of the OI resource provider and the digital library architect. However, as was demonstrated by the videotext fiasco, the providers and architects are not always willing or able to perform the research and evaluate the results before constructing or marketing the resources. When empirical usability research does not exist or cannot be done because the technologies under construction have no current equivalent, OI resource providers in industry and academia rely on theoretical perspectives that are widely espoused by respected members of their communities to guide them.

One perspective on OI usability is widely and tenaciously held. It can be characterised as optimistically rational, and it is espoused as a complex array of social, political and organisational strategies which emphasize the importance of information, information resources and information technology for economic survival and social progress. These strategies call be called as "informational imperatives." They guide organisations and individuals to adopt more information-intensive practices, and they set expectations for particular socio-technical results.

OI Reserach

Currently, most empirical studies indicate that the use of online databases in particular, and the use of libraries and information resources in general, has not been integrated into decision-making and strategic planning activities to the degree that informational imperatives might project. Explanations of why this may be so are guided by identifiable themes. The dominant perspective is rationalist, but strong currents of institutionalism, human relations theory, critical theory and postmodernism run through the discourse on many OI usability aspects.

Rational Utility

HCI Usability: It involves issues of access and resource usage on an individual level or within working groups. It highlights human-computer interaction with the OI resource interface, but also takes into consideration how individuals might need to coordinate resource usage in a work group setting. Rationalist discussions of online database usage begin with the assumption that an individual will naturally want to conduct his or her own search. So, providing quick and easy access to OI resources is their primary concern. Their solutions to problems of usability focus on the human-computer interface—usually the computer screen or application presentation layer. They may suggest adding "richer", multimedia formats or the development of natural language interfaces. Michael Eisenberg discusses some studies which tried to measure the effectiveness of bibliographic database searching by untrained users. For the most part, these studies were conducted as experiments on undergraduate and graduate students. They all seem to conclude that anyone can search effectively, given the right interface, although the only researcher to report situated results was somewhat baffled: "Results were surprising in that the online searches resulted in few references in the students' bibliographies" Rationalists expect the aggregate use of OI resources by working groups to yield productivity benefits and stimulate additional use.

Content Usability. Content Usability involves characteristics of the information itself. It addresses issues of information relevance, information awareness, information retrieval methods, and expertise. Rationalists believe that when individuals learn about OI resources, they will recognise the potential value of OI contents and use them accordingly. If OI resources are not being used, then it must be because people just don't know enough about them. They believe, as Jon Kaye does, that "to take full advantage of on-line database services, the threshold of awareness of the value of information must be raised. Users are still not understanding the value of information as a strategic tool".

However, rationalists working with content usability understand that establishing awareness is only one facet of the problem. Once access and awareness have been established, there are still issues of information retrieval and information overload. Some researchers, like Ray R. Larson, try to resolve both of these problems simultaneously by developing online systems which use techniques derived from information retrieval research. Recognising that users sometimes just "give up" when their queries don't return relevant results immediately, Larson attempts to cluster the data into meaningful classifications that, when coupled with statistical ranking mechanisms, can "reduce the cognitive load on the user in selecting relevant documents".

Organisational Usability. It involves the situated use of OI and OI resources. An organisation may provide training and support staff to help people use the available resources, or it may not. The information itself may be used collaboratively among working groups or symbolically as post-decision support. One of the reasons why rationalist managers of an organisation may choose not to provide technical support or training on OI resources is because it costs too much. Researchers like Michael Koenig seek to convince them otherwise by extrapolating from economic theory to affirm that organisations systematically underinvest in OI support services and libraries. He then goes on to assert that the existence of these organisational infrastructures enhances the free-flow of information throughout the organisation, and leads directly to productivity gains and improved decision-making, but his studies do not identify the mechanism by which they do so.

Along with providing OI resource usage support, rational organisations in the Information Age are expected to develop formal organisational strategies to guide the optimised use of both internal and external information available through these resources. But a survey of IS managers by King and Grover found that "[n]early 55% reported either 'irregular' or 'no formal process', suggesting that analyses dealing with information technology and information as a strategic resource have not yet become a routine and regular part of the planning process". King and Grover suggest that, in order to successfully 'mine' online databases for potentially powerful information, organisations should adopt a model of competitive advantage like those developed by rationalists concerned with interorganisational OI usability.

Interorganisational Usability. Marchand and Horton adopt the view that efficiently functioning markets are the highest good. And, for rationalists, healthy competition is the hallmark of efficiently functioning markets. Interorganisational Usability involves use of OI and OI resources within interorganisational networks. This may entail uses of OI to achieve competitive advantage, or to coordinate professionals of the virtual organisation. According to Marchand and Horton, managers must learn to use information strategically, in order to correctly assess environmental changes in their own industries and to spot potential opportunities in heretofore "other" industries. To do this, managers will have to realign the organisational structure with TQM-like methodologies.

The profitability and efficiency concerns of corporate information consumers may not be motivating concepts for digital library planners, but an interorganisational usability awareness may allow them to consider that "outsourcing" organisations may take advantage of publicly available digital libraries. Rational perspectives which encourage efficiency and the attainment of competitive advantage rarely consider the consequences of shifting the productivity burden to public institutions.

Human Resourcefulness

A preponderant proportion of the OI usability literature reflects a rational point of view. But, within the HCI community, there is a large contingent of researchers who are interested not only in enhancing productivity but also in designing OI resources which enhance the work experience.

HCI Usability. While rationalists assume that OI resource access naturally leads to use, human relations (HR) theorists seek to broaden the definition of accessibility. Mary Culnan has personalised the access question by breaking it down into three behaviorally oriented components: physical access (i.e. finding a terminal), interface access (i.e. using a query command language) and informational access (i.e. displaying data.) We have classified the last two components as aspects of Content Usability, largely on Culnan's findings that "physical access to the terminal used to access the system and access to the actual information system are independent dimensions". Furthermore, on the physical access dimension, she suggests that physical accessibility does not necessarily lead to use. Contrary to rationalist expectations, she finds that experience with a resource improves perceptions of accessibility and potential usefulness of the information attainable through that resource.

HR theorists researching at the group level are also very different from rationalists in one important respect—their expectations incorporate a notion of equity. Unlike Flores et al., who suggest that efficient control is the answer to group work coordination problems, Grudin suggests that a balance in terms of who does the work and who benefits from that work would go further to alleviate coordination issues. Although Grudin's work focuses on internal OI resources, like scheduling systems; his concepts can be seen to apply to external OI resources and digital libraries as well—especially when research functions are organisationally segmented.

Content Usability. HR theorists do not approach OI resource content usability from a perspective which assumes that mere awareness of the potential usefulness of a resource is enough to ensure use. In fact, Nicholas and Erbach conclude their examination of end-user searching in four commercially available OI resources with an important observation. They find that the services are dissimilar, the pricing structures are divergent, downloading speeds are highly variable independent of baud rates, and in-depth knowledge about even a small set of OI services is difficult for any one person to obtain and maintain. Their findings are based on end-user observations and are motivated by a concern for lowering the frustration level of the end-user by identifying user behaviors which are not well-accommodated by the OI resources in the study. Nicholas and Erbach make numerous suggestions for improving these existing resources, which if followed, would lead to a standard approach to OI resource design. However, they do not explicitly make this recommendation. Pfaffenberger agrees that there are a great many obstacles to end-user searching in OI resources. He points out that equal opportunity of information access was rhetoricised as the inevitable by-product of technologically enhanced information networks. But he identifies inequity of expertise as the most serious threat to equity of access. Pfaffenberger suggests that online databases will only attract end-users who are highly educated and are able to judge the significance of the material they encounter online. Much of his discussion takes on a critical theory perspective, especially when he refers to the decline in public education quality and the proletarianisation of the white collar work force, but we have included it here because his suggestion to restructure the online information formats so they are more accessible to end-users is a human-factors solution to the problem of expertise.

Organisational Usability. HR guided researchers are nearly unanimous in their advocacy of training and support infrastructures for OI resource usage. They may suggest that an organisation provide basic skills training and technical support for its OI workforce, or they may suggest a kind of self-help system which blends humans and technology into a single package. Mark S. Ackerman describes how one such system has been developed to combine information sharing with expertise sharing. His system is not merely a factual repository, it is a device for growing organisational memory, and so it encourages managers to reorganise work—especially how expertise is captured and how it is made available to all levels of the workforce.

Mintzberg takes a different tack. Rather than suggesting a technological solution to information access, he concentrates his attention on intermediaries and collaboration. While trying to answer the question: "Why do managers not use information as they apparently should?", he focuses on identifying how managers work. He suggests that organisational impediments to OI resource usage arise from dysfunctional goal setting and the nature of managerial work and advancement. Mintzberg also encourages the reorganisation of work to alleviate the problem, but he states that "[m]anagers need broad-based formal information systems, in large part independent of the computer...There is reason to believe that the best filters and pattern recognisers are intelligent human beings—bright specialists (and alter egos) who can stand between the manager and mass of data out there".

Interorganisational Usability. The Human Relations perspective usually focuses on issues of job satisfaction and worker productivity, so there is not much HR literature which addresses OI resource usability at an interorganisational level. One notable exception is a report issued in 1982 by the United Nations Centre on Transnational Corporations. The UN was worried that the "information gap" between developed and developing countries had been widening and lessening the potential for real competition by developing countries in world markets. They commissioned this study which suggested two organisational solutions to level the playing field: build human resource infrastructures in the developing countries, like the Mexican information center, or establish search centers in the information-rich countries. Whereas the rationalist is interested in allowing markets to function and information to flow, researchers with an HR view are more interested in removing barriers to entry and leveling the playing field.

The digital library community has taken many of the guiding principles of the public service library community to heart, and it strongly embraces the concepts of HR theorists. But concerns for equity of access, fairness in the distribution of work and advocacy for adequate training in distributed, multi-organisational environments should be guided by an awareness of these non-academic contexts of use in addition to traditional academic contexts.

Institutionalised Use

A small but significant body of the OI usability literature reflects an institutional perspective. These researchers are interested in how organisational and institutional environments constrain or enable use of OI resources and their contents. Although, institutionalists may recommend technological fixes to OI resources, they are more likely to recommend policy or procedural modifications that are within an organisation's power to change.

HCI Usability. Institutional discussions of OI resource usage do not assign an active, rational decision-making role to the individual. They are more likely to present OI resource user choices as a complex set of constraints set up by the various organisations and institutions which provide and administer OI services. Aumente presents a historical overview of the videotext and online database industry, with an accent on HCI usability aspects. He finds fault with the usability of videotext formats and the communication exchange capabilities of the medium, but notes that similarly constrained services, like online databases, have been successful. He looks to see where the technological constraints have been overcome within the videotext arena, for example France's Minitel, and identifies the external political factors as key enablers. Aumente's set of recommendations for the establishment of usable and viable OI resources involves technological enhancements which are tightly coupled with political support for developing a national OI infrastructure. Wanda Orlikowski has examined the introduction of groupware databases which served as digital libraries throughout a large, geographically dispersed organisation. Her study found that the groupware had been developed expressly for collaborative use. For those groups within her organisation who shared information in a cooperative mode, the system was usable. But for the consultants, who worked in a competitive, non-information sharing mode, the system was largely unusable. They did not have any established norms for sharing information through digital libraries.

Furthermore, they had real economic incentives not to share, but to retain and obtain as much expertise for themselves as possible. Orlikowski does not assume that everyone will want to use the resource, and she does not assume that equal access brings with it any incentives to use. She locates the implementation problem of her study outside the technological infrastructure, within the competitively-focused organisational incentive structures for the consultants, and suggests that modifications will have to be made here before the OI resource usage practices of the consultants can be expected to change.

Content Usability. Institutionalist information retrieval approaches try to acknowledge the taken-for-granted ways of doing things that can be discerned in particular organisations or environments. Oddy et al. have tried to incorporate situational information into OI retrieval systems. They attempt to generate generic research scripts and to match search processes with markers in the script so that the system will "know" where the searcher is in his or her research project. Oddy et al. believe that "[p]eople engaged in empirical work can be viewed as members of a community: they complete similar tasks, espouse shared social and technical norms, and operate within a unique reward structure". So knowing where a researcher is in a research project can help a search intermediary determine what is the most relevant information. Oddy et al. were able to identify some important patterns along these lines, but their study results suggest that "both users and intermediaries are constrained by their expectations about current systems and by their views of their own roles in the search process".

Organisational Usability. Kling and Elliott have investigated how the organisational environment can influence the use of OI resources and have made some suggestions for organisational support of the use of OI resources in digital libraries. They focus attention on how these systems can be effectively integrated into the work practices of specific organisations. They suggest that the systems could be more organisationally usable if they were designed to include the infrastructure necessary to support and accommodate people as they learn to maintain and use these resources. However, Kling and Elliott recognise that their advice may be ignored by OI systems designers and digital library architects who make assumptions about how their systems will be used which are based on the taken-for-granted concepts of their own cultural and organisational ways of doing things.

Organisational use of OI resources is often associated with a library or an information center. Research services may be provided to an entire organisation by a small group of information specialists who make use of OI resources, and print information resources, on behalf of others. This confounds the issue of who is actually the "user"— someone who performs the OI search, or someone who uses the information retrieved by the searcher. In cooperative work settings, identifying the end-user of the information as someone separate from the information intermediary becomes even more difficult. O'Day and Jeffries have concluded that, in the organisations they studied, virtually everyone functioned as an intermediary in some fashion; either by updating team members, consulting, broadcasting or putting the information into a shared archive.

Although rationalists might suggest that the intermediary represents an inefficiency in the system of getting relevant information directly and quickly to the end-user, O'Day and Jeffries show that modes of work which involve information sharing, as opposed to intensive, individualised use, are prevalent. While informational imperatives may encourage intensive information gathering practices, not all the information gathered is actually used in decision making. In fact, Feldman and March suggest that information gathering is largely a symbolic act of the decision making process. They cite studies which show that little systematic relation can be established between the time of receiving the results of an information search and the time of making a decision. However, these studies do find that when the intrinsic quality of a decision is difficult to assess, the signals generated by information gathering during the decision making process may impart a legitimacy that affects the perceived quality of that decision. So, when managers cannot show that their decision is "correct", they can at least build confidence by showing that they have followed accepted practice in formulating it. With respect to OI resources, the conclusions of Feldman and March would suggest that organisational decision makers might be more likely to use them in a "scanning" mode when decision criteria are ambiguous, performance measures are vague or when decision quality requires a long period to become established.

Interorganisational Usability. There are a number of environmental constraints on OI resource use at individual, group and organisational levels. When a resource is constructed expressly for use at the interorganisational level, the reasons for its underutilisation may be attributed to these constraints and to additional environmental influences. Francois Libmann's study of European online technology transfer databases shows that reasons for OI resource implementation failure can be linked to cultural concepts. He finds that "[n]o one has sought to create synergies between databases and other elements in the world of technology transfer (interpersonal networks for example)...databases are on the whole little or inefficiently used to optimise innovatory process. This is a cultural problem and should be dealt with as such, and is one which is not exclusive to technology transfer databases". Libmann suggests that national policy must be modified to address this need. US policy makers have encouraged the construction of digital libraries, and have stressed the importance of their educational support functions. But organisations on the periphery of academia, such as Libmann's who are promoting university/industry technology transfer efforts, are also interested in constructing or using digital library services. Digital libraries may serve these organisations, or may be embedded within them, depending on how central or supplemental the research function is to their core organisational processes.

Using Postmodernity

A recent and growing body of OI literature assumes a postmodern perspective. The philosophical discourse of postmodernists is suffused with an awareness of the power of language and the malleability of 'the text.' They see network technologies, digital libraries and OI resources as important components of the postmodern condition, and variously discuss online databases as new structures of domination and electronic writing as another level of reality—"textuality" or "hyperreality"

HCI Usability. Postmodern views of OI usability do not fall neatly into the admittedly rationalist framework. According to Amiran, Unsworth and Chaski, "There is no psycholinguistic evidence that the process of reading suddenly changes when it is conducted in a different medium". But they do find significant differences in the malleability of electronic texts, and suggest that a shift toward electronic scholarly publications may encourage a reinterpretation of the concepts of authorship, ownership and scholarship at individual and institutional levels.

Content Usability. Usability of 'the text', according to Timothy W. Luke, lies in its ability to serve as a site of shared cultural consciousness. Luke examines Baudrillard's concept of 'hyperreality' and presents it, not as a future capability, but as an extension of existing social and political simulations which use current implementations of electronic media. He suggests that simulation and the shared cultural consciousness it can achieve are important contributions to the social infrastructure. Luke and postmodernists see fiction and simulation as preceding and defining reality for those residents involved—that's hyperreality. Although this perspective takes environmental and institutional factors into account, the postmodern view of content usability differs greatly from the institutional view, which is focused on how OI resources are manipulated by users. Postmodernists examine how users' perceptions are modified by the contents of OI resources.

Organisational Usability. With respect to organisational use, the postmodern emphasis is less concerned with training organisational members to use OI resources effectively, and is more focused on understanding how OI resources, as critical components of the technical infrastructure, sustain organisational bureaucracy. Mark Poster presents an insightful overview of the impacts of Bell's forecasts for the Information Society. He identifies information as the sustaining materiel of bureaucracy, and he acknowledges Foucault's interpretation of online databases as the major structural component of domination in postindustrial society. But he suggests that databases also have a democratic side. In personal communication, he has associated democratic empowerment with database exchanges on the Internet to exemplify the dual potential of OI resources. In either case, the postmodern view of organisational OI resource usability can be seen to resemble the institutional view in some important ways. The end-user of the information is often difficult to identify. She may be the intermediary, the bureaucrat, or some collective identity that is amorpously referred to as 'the organisation.'

Interorganisational Usability. In postmodern discussions, the terms 'organisational' and 'interorganisational' may be used interchangeably. Clegg's analysis of modern organisations defines one of the more recent examples, the Benneton firm, "less as an organisation per se and rather more as an organised network of market relations premised on complex forms of contracting made possible by advances in microelectronics technology". Clegg does not refer exclusively to OI resources, but to IT generally speaking, when he suggests that the classic Weberian bureaucracy may be replaced by technologically enabled organisational forms such as Benneton's.

Unlike Marchand and Horton's rational analysis of interorganisational use of OI resources, Clegg's analysis does not stop at the managerial methodology level. And unlike institutional analyses which call for governmental intervention to enact cultural change so that existing organisational forms can make more effective use of OI resources and traditional library bureaucracies, Clegg identifies environmental and cultural changes which are redefining the boundaries of the organisations themselves. The postmodern perspective encourages us to recognise that the boundaries which separate digital libraries, academic enclaves and commercial organisations are permeable and changeable. The roles of librarians and information intermediaries may be equally transmutable.

Temporary Archiving

The archive is in flux. Much of this has to do with the pace of technological change, and the perceived locus of control. The concept of "temporary" measures rests on an assumption that one day we will all catch up with technology. This assumption underlies much of the technology purchasing, that if we buy the "right" computer or software at the "right" time, we will finally be state-of-the-art. The reality is that Microsoft and others will continue to change operating platforms, hardware, and software every year. Manufacturers operate within a structure of premeditated obsolescence, of staggered improvement and alteration, ensuring that there will be no "end-state" program upon which we can all settle.

Because electronic media, software applications, and computer hardware will all continue to change at a rapid rate, and because policies must be developed to address that reality, the archive must change. The very notion of a permanent or fixed archive may have to give way to an ecological preservation system that is in a state of constant change.

Data grows, lives, and dies, as do delivery systems. As never before, the task of keeping data alive requires frequent adaptations to and perpetual evolution of the archival system. To keep pace with technological flux, an ongoing process of selection — of media platforms, of preservation structures, of migratory patterns — is necessary to avoid data extinction. In these various ways, there is an ecological force at work.

In fact, there are several ecological themes already in play in electronic archives. These include the encouragement of symbiotic relationships, the use of anti-extinction preservation and migratory schemes, and the deliberate adoption of cloning/breeding campaigns.

Symbiotic Archiving

Successful archiving involves assessing appropriate storage and delivery methods for documents based on cost, usage, appropriateness, and longevity. In this case the best solution was symbiosis of electronic and paper media. By combining paper and electronic means, twin goals are achieved: an original record is maintained, and worldwide access to the material is provided.

The symbiotic, ecological relationship exists in the fact that the paper version needs the electronic version for the sake of its own preservation against constant usage, and the electronic version needs the paper version as a backup in case of technical problems or obsolescence. Symbiotic double conservation contrasts with some previous "preservation" practices such as the effective destruction of books through the removal of bindings to facilitate the microfilming process.

A careful consideration of the archival ecosystem allows for effective migration while maximising conservation in the long term. By identifying how a book or journal is most easily accessed with current technology, and best preserved, the text stands a better chance of lasting through time.

Of course, HTML, SGML, Java, JPEG, MPEG, and WAV files, etc. might go the way of the Commodore 64, and Canadian Architect and Builder and other journals archived on the Web may suffer a similar fate: technologically unreachable and/or unreadable by the Web advancements in the next five to one hundred years, they will be lost to the interested reader. They will be extinct.

Further, a Web site with a forgotten URL may, in the long term, be even harder to find than a mis-shelved book. While some search engines can be tremendously efficient at locating relevant sites by keyword now, we do not know if the search engines of fifty years hence will be able to locate the historic, first-generation sites coded late in the twentieth century and in the early years of the twenty-first century.

Preservation and Migratory Schemes

Migration is a set of organised tasks designed to achieve the periodic transfer of digital materials from one hardware/software configuration to another, or from one generation of computer technology to a subsequent generation. The purpose of migration is to preserve the integrity of digital objects and to retain the ability for clients to retrieve, display, and otherwise use them in the face of constantly changing technology.

Crucial to that overall process is the independent certification of digital archives and a critical fail-safe mechanism. The primary function of the critical fail-safe mechanism is to enact "an aggressive rescue function to save culturally significant digital information" that may be at risk. The independent certification is a mechanism through which digital archive standards are reviewed, and whose indicators include the accessibility of stored data and the long-term protection of culturally valuable information. In 2001, Harvard University Library was awarded a major planning grant to look into repository techniques for electronic journals. Funded by the Andrew W. Mellon Foundation, the project explored the mechanism through which electronic journals are selected for preservation, commercial intellectual property negotiations with publishers, delivery format for users, costs, and the overall storage strategies to be employed.

Stanford University's LOCKSS project (LOCKSS stands for Lots of Copies Keep Stuff Safe) seek to assure the integrity of electronic publications through the maintenance of copies on multiple sites, and with periodic checks between these copies to verify informational congruency. Through cloning and distributed storage, LOCKSS hopes to minimise in advance the impact a catastrophe at any individual site may have upon (data) populations as a whole.

This list of archiving and migration methodologies is by no means exhaustive. Of particular concern are the long-term prospects for the electronic resources and research undertaken in developing countries. While research libraries in the United States and other industrialised nations may have the financial resources and the available workforce to facilitate "perpetual care" activities, in other parts of the world the resources are simply not available. "Digital aid" to the universities and publishers of the developing world may prove imperative in the coming years. The ecology of the archiving process requires that the whole biosphere of electronic data must be considered in the push for preservation, not just the material of discrete territories. Even where the necessary will and resources are in place, for some electronic data the issue of long-term preservation and/or migration is somewhat more difficult. Central examples are the presentations and publications produced only in multimedia format. As one report put it, there is no "safety net" for purely digital data, "no analogous tangible version you can recapture if you lose the digital version."

While projects such as LOCKSS may provide some degree of safety, a further complication remains. If all computer platforms and software packages steadily lose their cutting-edge status via the computer industry's (apparent) maxim of premeditated obsolescence, multimedia format documents combining complex interactions of moving images, sound, and text stand the greatest risk of being lost or degraded over time. If there is a high degree of dependence between a given multimedia presentation and specific hardware or software, the process of "refreshing" — copying digital information from one medium to another — may be insufficiently compatible to maintain the exact interplay of image, sound, and text captured in the original. A two-dimensional replica may still be preserved, but the subtleties of the original may be lost, degraded in the transfer.

As has always been the case, decisions will have to be made regarding what will be preserved, either in the symbiotic sense, or in the broader ecological migration to next-generation systems. This process, as always, takes time and resources. Priorities will be set and value judgments will be made regarding what should be preserved, and how well. Despite the massive technological advances in recent decades, it is a surety that information and data will still be lost in the passage of time.

Archiving as Metaphor

The fate of data will largely depend on the strategies adopted by libraries, publishers, archivists, and individual researchers. The future of the archive depends on how information storage is conceptualised. Rather than making temporary plans in the hopes of a future permanent solution, it is advantageous to visualise all information preservation as an evolving, ever-changing ecosystem.

As technology continues to develop apace, those seeking to preserve and to update are faced with ever-expanding options of how best to do this. It is an exercise in futility to try to pick the technological winner, for "the latest" will be hopelessly outdated in ten years' time. What is necessary is a permanent strategy for handling perpetual change. This will involve periodic reassessment, the migration of material from one platform to the next, and the allocation of resources.

Bibliographic Access

Bibliography used in making of lists of books, articles, and other documents — by subject, by author, and by other attributes--and the making of indexes to those lists. The term bibliography is used in several ways to denote the study of books and the making of descriptions of books. Bibliographic access is perhaps the best available term for the whole apparatus of access to records of all kinds (textual, numerical, visual, musical, etc.), in all kinds of storage media. Bibliographic access includes three central concerns:

— *Identifying documents:* Which documents exist that might be of interest? The essence of bibliography is the identification and enumeration of documents that would be of interest. Which writings by some specified author? Which articles about some subject? Which books published in some time, place, or language? It is a matter, on the one hand, of creating useful descriptions of documents, and, on the other, of identifying documents that fit any given description.

— *Locating documents:* Bibliographies describe documents, but they do not usually tell you where a copy can be found, least of all where the nearest copy can be found. It is catalogs that indicate where copies may be found. During the nineteenth century catalogs became more elaborate in their descriptions and came to look like and, indeed, to be bibliographies of local holdings. The differentiating characteristic of a catalog is that it indicates a location.

— *Physical access to material:* Identifying and establishing the supposed location of a document is not the same as having a copy of the document in ones hands, close enough to read.

Bibliogrphies

The components of this bibliographical universe are numerous as well as varied. An important feature of bibliography in this sense is that it is primarily concerned with works and editions of works rather than with individual copies of documents. Bibliographies are not ordinarily concerned with specific copies of an edition. Information about individual copies is usually included only in exceptional circumstances: one copy is somehow different, or may be the only extant copy known.

For rare materials and early printing it is customary to note where individual copies can be found or which individual copy was inspected by the bibliographer. Nevertheless, as a general rule, bibliography deals with published editions rather than with individual copies of an edition.

Because bibliographies describe works rather than individual copies, they are of general interest to anyone who might benefit from knowing of the works that are listed. For this reason publication of, or at least widespread public access to, bibliographies is highly desirable. Bibliographies, especially continuing ones, lend themselves well to computer-based production which reduces the tedium of the mechanical tasks of sorting, cumulating, updating, rearranging, and indexing a large number of individually brief records. It has become difficult to imagine creation of a bibliography without using a computer and the logical next step to make the bibliography available on-line.

It is reasonable to expect the number of bibliographies that are available in machine-readable form to increase and for them to account for a growing proportion of all use of bibliographies. It is also reasonable to expect that these bibliographies will become available in more different ways: accessible through commercial database services; available as tapes that can be mounted at computer centers; or available on optical digital disks, such as CD-ROMs, attachable to microcomputers.

The next logical development would be to provide links from the references in the bibliographies to libraries' holdings records. If one were to find an interesting reference to an article while searching Chemical Abstracts on-line, for example, it would be an obvious amenity if one could move automatically from the bibliographic reference to a statement of local libraries' holdings of the periodical concerned. This kind of service is beginning to be provided. Even better, one would like to know whether that particular volume is currently available and to be able to send a request for a copy of it.

Bibliography deals with published works in a general fashion and is not ordinarily concerned with individual copies of works. In contrast, library records are, of necessity, very much concerned with individual libraries, individual copies, and, for that matter, with individual library users.

Library catalogs, as currently know them, are composed of a combination of bibliographic records and of library holdings records, containing both general statements about editions of works and also specific statements about individual copies and their individual locations in particular libraries. One might even argue that, given the limitations of the technology of paper and of cardboard, the only practical way of achieving this linking of bibliographies and library records in the nineteenth century was to create an additional third set of records containing elements derived from each: the modern library catalog.

Library catalogs vary considerably in format according to the technology in use: in book form; on cards; in microform; on-line. Further, if library catalogs are seen as a bridge between bibliographies and library records, it has to be recognised that this is a bridge between two moving and changing objects as bibliographies and internal library procedures both evolve. Early library catalogs were inventories of what was on the shelves. The printed catalog of 1620 of the Bodleian Library of Oxford University is regarded as significant because it listed books in author order regardless of where they were shelved. This, then, was the library catalog as an author-ordered finding list of books.

The transformation of library cataloging to its present form came in the nineteenth century when it was argued that simple author access was not enough and that a different, more sophisticated, and more elaborate approach was needed. In effect, the new library techniques of the mid and late nineteenth century can be viewed as a building up on top of simple finding lists a superstructure of bibliographical access: complex subject headings, added entries, cross references, systematic shelf-arrangements, and so on. The form of display moved from catalogs in book form to catalogs in card form, which are easier to update, but the principal change was the local development of more elaborate access to the contents of the collection. Modern library catalogs are essentially as defined in the nineteenth century.

A catalog includes an essential element that is normally absent from bibliographies, the call number, although this is in practice an incomplete and imperfect reflection of the precise status of the library's holdings. To determine the actual status it may also be necessary to refer to library holdings records: to the circulation file for the best information on what is where, to serials records to know which pieces have arrived, to the "in process" file to know what has arrived but has not yet been cataloged; and to acquisitions files to know what is believed to be on its way. Although the catalog may show that the library has the book, the book may have been lost.

The present set of relationships can be expressed as follows: Records found in bibliographies may help one find corresponding records in catalogs, if present, and vice-versa. The catalog usually indicates the official location of a copy of a document. But one may choose to (or need to) consult other library holdings records (acquisitions, circulation, serials) for more precise information concerning actual copies of documents and their location. The present relationship between bibliography, library records, and the catalog is shown in Fig 1.

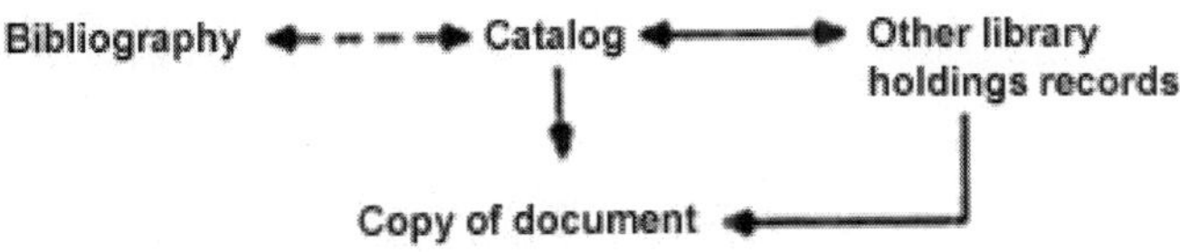

Figure 1. Conventional relationship between bibliographies, catalogs, library holdingsrecords, and documents

The purpose of a library catalog, almost all of the data needed are bibliographical and would be common to any other library catalog or bibliography that listed the same edition. The exception is the locational information: the particular call number and details of each copy, as needed. The locational data would not be the same as those found in other libraries' catalogs listing the same work.

In the broader perspective of bibliographic control, library cataloging can be seen as a special case of bibliography defined by the intersection of two subsets:

— Library catalogs use one particular level of description: the edition of the monograph and the title of the periodical.

— The set of records in a library catalog is further defined geographically: the records that pertain to the holdings of a collection, a library, or, for a "union catalog", to two or more libraries.

It is important to stress that the limitation by level of description, which excludes the more detailed levels of access commonly needed, is a matter of standard practice, not of principle. Excellent examples can be found of library catalogs that also provide entries for articles in periodicals and individual contributions within books. One example is the Index-Catalogue of the Library of the Surgeon-General's Office, United States Army, published in 1880, which evolved into the Index Medicus and now MEDLINE.

However, technical and cost considerations resulted in the general practice of omitting access, especially to articles in periodicals, leaving that important role to publishers of bibliographies and indexes mainly operating outside of librarianship. Library catalogs should be seen as a form of bibliography. That they are not normally thought of as bibliography is largely an accident of semantic custom and of a tradition of library organisation that associates the catalog with catalogers in technical services departments and bibliography with reference librarians in public services departments.

From an operational perspective the library catalog can be seen as a useful amplification of records that are unavoidably needed anyway. The information in a catalog can be useful in a variety of ways to library staff and library users. The difference between modern library catalogs and those before the late nineteenth century is essentially that the modern catalogs have a much larger bibliographical superstructure added to the locational information than had previously been the case. However, a library catalog has some significant shortcomings as a tool of access. In contrast, published bibliographies are, or can be:

— more complete,

— more selective,

— more capable of special arrangements,

— more flexible,

— more detailed,

— more descriptive,

— more easily deployed to cover new topics of interest as needed,

— more expertly compiled

— more coherent,

— more cost-effective.

Catalogers have denied these assertions and made counterarguments that, for example, local cataloging permits access to be adapted to local circumstances and can include items not included in published bibliographies. In the late nineteenth-century debate between bibliographers and catalogers, bibliographers unsuccessfully argued that the investment made in local library cataloging would be better spent in the improvement of bibliographies that could be published and would be, therefore, of widespread usefulness.

Subject bibliography has developed during the twentieth century largely outside the mainstream of librarianship, with major roles in the creation of and provision of access to bibliography played by individual scholars, professional and scholarly societies, government agencies, and private firms.

The difference between a bibliographer's perspective and that of a cataloger can be illustrated by considering how each might approach the provision of bibliographical access to, say, a chemistry library. Both fantasies are exaggerated for the sake of emphasis. A bibliographer responsible for a chemistry library might take the point of view that there is a published bibliography of the literature of chemistry that should be the users' principal tool of access to the entire relevant literature including the subset that happens to be held in a particular library.

The strategy might then be to arrange for plentiful use of Chemical Abstracts, perhaps by mounting a copy on-line locally, then seeking to link the citations in Chemical Abstracts to the library's holdings records. Perhaps the link could be made by using the International Standard Serials Number (ISSN) for each periodical title and the Library of Congress catalog card number (LCCN) or International Standard Book Number (ISBN) for each monograph. In the meanwhile the library's records would also have ISSN, LCCN, ISBN, or similar numbers attached. The library user would search Chemical Abstracts and be able to ascertain the library's holdings when interested. Possibly, as an option, searches could be automatically limited, at least initially, to entries with links to library holdings records.

Alternatively, that subset with library holdings links could be separated out as an unusually detailed "catalog" of locally held material. Locally-held material not or not yet in Chemical Abstracts would pose a problem. Possibly such material could be contributed to Chemical Abstracts if on chemistry; perhaps other bibliographies would need to be used for other subjects. Some local supplementation of the files would probably be unavoidable.

A cataloger setting out to provide access to locally held materials might also note that a traditional library catalog provides almost no direct access to the literature of greatest interest: the individual papers on chemistry, usually published as articles in periodicals. From a cataloger's perspective it would seem logical and traditional to expand the catalog by cataloging each of the articles in the periodicals received by the library and only in those periodicals.

The cataloging would be based on national standards but would be adapted to local needs. A significant concern in each library would be the maintenance of local authority control. Possibly with modern technology and the traditions of interlibrary cooperation, costs would be reduced by using a consortial approach to catalog construction. A shared database of catalog descriptions of articles, technical reports, and books could be developed for chemistry library catalogs, an "on-line chemistry library center," perhaps.

Catalog records contributed by one chemistry library would be available as a convenient basis for the derivation of records for the local catalog. This cooperative database, with much broader coverage than any one library, would be available to the librarians, but not, in practice, to library users. Chemical Abstracts would be of greatly reduced value because it would duplicate catalog records for everything in the library. This small vignette identifies the extravagance of a catalog-based approach compared with a bibliography-based approach and invites more extensive examination of the potential role of bibliographies in the future of the catalog.

How should the identification and location functions be approached in the future? To the extent that the card catalog was a product of the limitations of what is no longer the preferred technology, the development of even the most sophisticated electronic version of the card catalog could represent misguided creativity, reminiscent of the continued refinement of sailing ships after steam had become the preferred source of power. To get a better perspective on future library service we should stand back from the conventional catalog and try to view it from first principles.

Three elements — bibliography, library records, and documents — provide the needed ingredients. Bibliographies will continue to be published; documents continue to be collected; and libraries have to have their copy-specific inventory and status records. Computer-based procedures enable records to be linked in ways not previously feasible. The following approach is suggested:

— Since bibliographies constitute the principal means of identification, there should be extensive, convenient access to bibliographies regardless of technology.

— Because it is necessary not only to identify but also to locate material, it should be made possible when searching bibliographies to ascertain the location, call-number, and availability of copies of documents in local library holdings.

— It would be convenient to have an option whereby searches in bibliographies could be limited to the holdings of one or more particular libraries.

— It should also be possible for a library user to forward a copy of a bibliographic record to library staff as a request that a copy of the document represented be sent in the original, in photocopy, or by telefacsimile.

These relationships are represented in figure 2.

Figure 2: Simplified relationship between bibliographies, holdings records, and documents

There are practical problems to be solved in linking bibliographies with libraries' holdings records. However, there appears to be no obvious technical reason why on-line bibliographies should not routinely be linked to libraries' holdings records, call-numbers, and circulation status for documents.

Once that is appreciated who would want to settle for less? Another way of describing this change in the relationship between bibliographies, catalogs, library holdings records can also be shown in terms of the contents of the records involved. The use of computer-based techniques to achieve the goal of extensive bibliographical access combined with call-number and availability information for documents invites a major reconsideration of the roles and relationships between library collections, bibliographies, and internal library processes:

— Bibliographies should be viewed, not so merely as library resources, but rather as a dramatic enrichment of bibliographic access far greater than can be provided by the catalog. Not only does the access provided by bibliographies greatly exceed that of catalogs in fineness of indexing but also the sheer quantity of records and their variety are both far greater. Non-trivial intellectual access to the published record depends on access to bibliographies. Conventional catalog records, limited as they are to editions of monographs and titles of serials and to locally owned material only, are simply not in the same league in terms of providing bibliographical access.

— Operating records of libraries should be automated whenever feasible. In the case of acquisitions, circulation, and other useful information, these records should be made accessible to users, and to other libraries, to the extent security and privacy considerations permit.

— The records in bibliographies will need to be linked to libraries' holdings records. This implies some changes. Neither the traditional marketing through centralised retailers (e.g. DIALOG) nor the newer, isolated, "stand-alone" systems on CD-ROMS deliver what is needed. Either could do so if standardised interfaces to local libraries' records were provided. Another likely option is for libraries to mount on-line bibliographies locally in conjunction with their library automation systems.

A bibliographical search would continue to be a two stage process, as it is with manual searching: The first stage is to identify what exists; the second is to locate a copy. The difference would be that computer-based procedures should be designed not only to handle each stage but also the transition between them. It would be a natural and logical extension of the "Search and Retrieve" protocol to have a standard interface whereby a set of bibliographical records retrieved from a bibliography could be searched against a set of library records. This would include three separable tasks: transferring back the retrieved set of references from a bibliography, searching that set against a file of library holdings records, and coping with data deficiencies in either file that would impede matching.

There are two views of the future of the library catalog emerge. From one point of view, the library catalog. Given an ability to link records in bibliographies to holdings records, there is no longer any role for the catalog to play.

This is entirely to be expected if one accepts that it was the limitations of the technology of paper that prevented the effective combining of bibliographies with library records; the solution adopted in the nineteenth century was to create in the catalog what is, in effect, an alternative local bibliographical structure, a duplicative set of bibliographical records which are also present in bibliographies; and the limitations of the technology of paper and of cardboard are ceasing to be relevant as the newer, more flexible technology of computers replaces it. Expect the massive bibliographical apparatus of the catalog to abandoned.

In this view the "new" catalog blossoms as means of providing access to the works in a library with a richness of detail to match the nineteenth-century catalogers' most ambitious dreams. This approach is not really inconsistent with traditional catalog practice. A century ago catalogers sought to add entries for parts of books and periodicals. This and the practice of providing annotations stopped only because it was too expensive.

In recent years almost all of each library's catalog records have been copied, through cooperative arrangements, from the Library of Congress card service, from large shared databases of catalog records, or elsewhere. Even "original" cataloging is usually derived from extant bibliographic records as far as is practical.

The many different forms of subject indexing found in bibliographies is a complication. Users with specialised interests should benefit more from specialised indexing than from the standardised approach to subject cataloging used in general libraries. Attempting to harmonise a Babel of different kinds of subject headings, indexes, and classification schemes would pose serious difficulties. This variety is already present in existing bibliographies, but without the benefit of links to holdings records. The prospect of providing library users not only with extensive, convenient on-line access to a wide range of bibliographies, but also with interconnected access to bibliographies, catalogs, and to libraries holdings is an exciting prospect.

New developments in telecommunications enable on-line catalogs to be consulted from a distance. One consequence is that it becomes possible for several libraries to share the same catalog, should they wish. A union catalog brings together the records of two or more libraries, whether a union catalog for all branches of a single system, or a shared on-line catalog for two or more different library systems, or a resource of catalog records for catalogers and interlibrary loan staff.

Another consequence is that it becomes possible for the user of one library to use the on-line catalog of another, remote library, though formalities of telecommunications, passwords, and unfamiliar commands may make it more or less inconvenient to do so. Since computers can be programmed to handle tedious routines, it would make much more sense to tell one's local, familiar on-line catalog to extend any given search to remote, unfamiliar catalogs on one's behalf.

The new "Search and Retrieve" are designed to facilitate just that. By making any remote catalog a temporary extension of the local catalog, one is, in effect, creating not so much a union catalog but temporary ad hoc unions of catalogs as and when needed. This will achieve in the automated library what was done in the paper library when copies of the printed book-form catalogs of remote libraries were exchanged and collected in reference collections.

Research on information retrieval effectiveness has shown that different retrieval systems all work imperfectly, generally work comparably imperfectly, and tend to retrieve different items from the same file. It is wise to use a multiplicity of approaches and to combine the results. But in the Paper Library maintaining even one subject approach is very onerous. Investing in the creation of multiple approaches in catalogs is very expensive. Yet any experienced bibliographer, any experienced researcher, knows that for the best results it is prudent to look in a variety of different sources and the more different they are in their approach the better.

Libraries in the United States have felt able to afford subject headings as well as subject classification, but additional approaches, although clearly desirable, would be unthinkable in the Paper Library. In the shift from the Paper Library to the Automated Library the technological constraints have changed. Indexing that is merely mechanical can now be provided without investing local labor in their creation. Using the words in titles for "title keyword" searching in an on-line catalog is a good example: Only computer programming and computer hardware need be added, not more cataloging staff. Citation indexes constitute another good example of a useful, mechanical, supplementary approach. Indexing that is not simply mechanical can in principle be obtained, by acquiring bibliographies, for example, and used to "enrich" the catalog.

Future Bibliographic Strategy

Since it no longer matters much where a catalog or bibliography is located, a change of perspective becomes possible: Instead of concentrating on the local catalog and locally held bibliographies, one can think more sensibly in terms of all bibliographies and catalogs, or, at least, of all "networked" bibliographic resources. In practice this means all bibliographic files that are available through networks and held by institutions willing to collaborate. The basic functional requirements for a more general, "networked," collaborative, or universal approach to library collections include the following:

— The overall bibliographic coverage should be as complete as possible in providing access to the whole of human knowledge.

— Multiple access points should be provided, minimally by subject as well as author.

— It should be a distributed system in that everyone should be able to have access to it and that it should be possible for files to be partitioned and copied for efficiency.

— Bibliographic records should be correct, concise, correctable, and expandable.

— The bibliographic universe should be built up peicemeal from existing sources.

— Bibliographic records should state where copies of the documents are located.

— The bibliographic records should provide a basis for quantitative studies of publication patterns.

— The bibliographic system should help to protect intellectual property.

Automating a catalog or placing a bibliography on-line each represents a substantial technological development. But to think only of an individual on-line catalog or of an individual on-line bibliography--even being aware that there are several different on-line catalogs and numerous individual bibliographies available on-line--is to think in terms of the card catalogs and published paper bibliographies of the Paper Library.

A major constraint of the technology of paper is that files cannot easily be reformatted, linked, interfiled, or otherwise combined in dynamic ways. This constraint is not characteristic of on-line systems. What if, instead of thinking of individual bibliographies,swere to base our thinking on the knowledge that there are large and growing populations of bibliographies and catalogs on-line, increasingly connected by telecommunications networks, and containing records that can, in principle, be linked, combined, and rearranged? What could happen if instead of thinking of "on-line bibliography" as using a bibliography on-line,The logic of electronic technology step further and think instead of a collectivity of bibliographies on-line, in effect of using a reference library--a sizeable universe of bibliographies--on-line?

When considering multiple bibliographies it can be helpful to think of the various differences between systems:

— Different bibliographies represent different, more or less overlapping populations of documents;

— Different bibliographies will have more or less different descriptions, even for the same document;

— The access points which can be searched vary between systems;

— Different systems can have more or fewer reference between different related terms; and

— Different retrieval systems support different types of searching even in the same bibliographic files. Some allow complex search requests or searches for keywords, others do not.

So, correspondingly, one can immediately identify five different classes of reasons for extending searches to two or more on-line bibliographies and/ or on-line catalogs. Depending on the circumstances, one might want to:

— Extend a search to another bibliography or catalog because what was desired was not found in the first source, and a new population of documents may contain the information.

— Extend a search to another bibliography or catalog for a document that has been found because differing bibliographic descriptions can be used to accumulate additional information. For example, consider a medical book present in a library catalog, in a medical bibliography, and in a citation index. All three will have more or less differing bibliographic records for the same document:

— Extend a search to other access points. Citations have to be searched in a citation index. The ability to search on other features such as searching by words within a title or abstract, or by the language or date of the document, varies significantly between systems.

— Try another system that has a better or different network of cross references.

— Extend a search to another system because it has special searching abilities, such as identifying pairs of words that occur close to each other, or extend the search by downloading results into a personal computer for more detailed analysis.

Bibliographic access comprises three elements: identifying documents, the realm of bibliographies; locating copies of documents, the underlying purpose of catalogs; and obtaining a copy of a document, the role of document delivery and collection development. In the late nineteenth century catalogs were made available on cards and an elaborate bibliographic superstructure was added. After two decades of automating existing bibliographies and catalogs, it has become possible to rethink what should be done in terms of the capabilities and constraints of computers rather than those of paper.

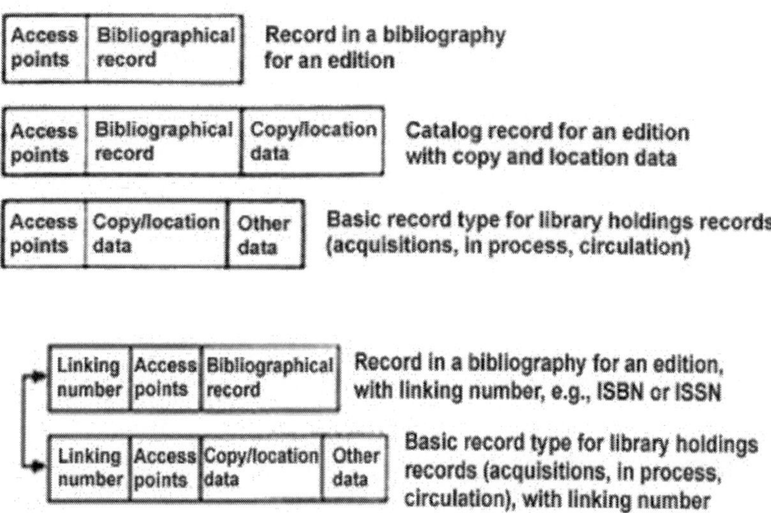

Figure 3. Conventional and linked record structures

Part a of figure 3 shows the conventional records structure of figure 1.

The prospect of a new-found ability to link bibliographies and library holdings records suggests a reconsideration of the bibliographic elements of catalogs and a new perspective on the use of bibliographies as a dramatic enhancement and, in a sense, a partial replacement for conventional catalogs. The rise of telecommunications and the flexibility of computers mean that it becomes practical to use bibliographies and catalogs that are at a distance as well as those that are local. It also becomes more feasible to use more different indexes than previously. The general effect of these changes is to change the perspective from local to general and to extend our view of on-line searching from searching on individual bibliographies to extended searches on multiple bibliographies using multiple retrieval systems. The linking of bibliographic systems through a "Search and Retrieve" standard (Z39:50) provides a basis both for adding access to more different files and for using more different retrieval techniques on any given file.

Number of Retrieval Systems	Number of Files	
	One	Multiple
One	Typical search of bibliography or catalog	One search on multiple files, e.g., DIALOG "Onesearch"
Multiple	Linked systems searching (Z39:50); Postprocessing of retrieved records	Multiple systems accessing multiple files

Figure 4. The four combinations that emerge as retrieval is extended from one file to multiple files and from one retrieval system to combinations of retrieval systems.

These possibilities suggest that, in future library services, bibliographic access could be developed to support, from any workstation anywhere, the kind of searching that could be done, tediously and imperfectly, in a well-equipped reference collection of a very large, research-oriented Paper Library. However, "could be" and "will be" are not the same. Here concentrated on questions of design and technology.

REFERENCES

Schatz, Bruce R. "Information Retrieval in Digital Libraries: Bringing Search to the Net." *Science*, 17 January 1997.

Smith, Abby. *Strategies for Building Digitized Collection*s. Washington, DC: Digital Library Federation, Council on Library and Information Resources, 2001.

Suleman, Hussein,et.al., "Networked Digital Library of Theses and Dissertations: Bridging the Gaps for Global Access—Part 1: Mission and Progress." *D-Lib Magazine* 7, September 2001.

3

Management of Digital Library Collections

A digital library is much more than just the collection of material in its repositories. It provides a variety of services to all of its users (both humans and machines, and producers, managers, and consumers of information). Thus we start our definition with the notion of the collection of services that the digital library represents. There are a large and varied set of such services, including services to support management of collections, services to provide replicated and reliable storage, services to aid in query formulation and execution, services to assist in name resolution and location, etc.

The basis for a digital library, however, must be the information objects that provide the content. A basic characteristic of the digital library is that the information objects are found in collections with associated management and support functions. The types of information objects vary from traditional "documents" through to live objects (e.g. sensor readings) or dynamic query results.

The goal of the digital library is to assist users by satisfying their needs and requirements for management, access, storage, and manipulation of the variety of information stored in the collection of material that represents the "holdings" of the library. Users may be humans or they may be automated processes acting on behalf of or in support of human needs. Users also vary and include those who are "end" users (those not involved in the management and operation of the library but rather are the customers), library operators, and information "producers" who want their material available through the library.

The key to effective collections management is to implement simple structural organizations and be able to present those organizations in a way that library users find useful and can understand easily. In traditional libraries, books are primarily stored by subject, title, author, and date, and accessed by following signs to the appropriate floor, room, bookcase, shelf, and spine-labeled book. The size and relative celebration of each portion of the collection gives patrons information about the collection and can reveal the library's collection management objectives as well.

A library is created to serve a community of users. Users who participate in the digital library should be aware of its design and be able collectively to refine that design to better serve their own information needs. Therefore, the ongoing human usability of a digital library depends on the clear and unobtrusive exposure of the library's design, its near-term goals, and its overall objectives.

Furthermore, digital libraries should continue the ongoing tradition of coupling utility with aesthetics in the organization and presentation of materials.

These information objects may be digital objects or they may be in other media (e.g. paper) but represented in the library via digital means (e.g. metadata). They may be available directly over the network (e.g., using a query service of the library to find and then retrieve electronically the information object) or indirectly (e.g., the result of the query may give instructions on how to obtain the object, but that is done outside the scope of the library itself.)

Although the objects may not even be electronic, and although the objects themselves may not be available directly over the network, the objects must be represented electronically in some manner through, e.g., metadata or catalogs. Otherwise, we would not consider the objects to be part of the *digital* library.

Development and Management of Collections

There is likely to be a growing recognition of the need to co-operate in the development and management of collections. This will raise questions about the feasibility and means of co-ordinating acquisition, retention and disposal. A pre-requisite for such co-operation will be a better understanding of the present pattern of collections, which will generate more regional and national collection mapping initiatives.

Organisations are likely to come under increased pressure to publish and share information about their collections. This will be stimulated by the public agenda for increased knowledge of, and access to, collections via public networks. Political and funding authorities in turn will put pressure on organisations to avoid unnecessary duplication by sharing information. The concept of the distributed national collection is therefore likely to become more widely accepted.

There will be a growing need to address the issues raised by digital material and the recorded cultural heritage will encompass an increased range, diversity and volume of digital collections. 'Born-digital' local and national records will form an increasingly important part of archivists' responsibilities, stimulating a changing focus in education and training programmes.

In many higher education libraries, electronic scholarly publications will make up the majority of research and special collection acquisitions. There is already some concern over the reluctance expressed by publishers of preserving and maintaining long-term access to their electronic publications and pressure is being put on libraries to take on this responsibility. Cross-sectoral digitisation programmes are likely to underpin local and regional strategies to meet learning needs.

There is an increasing recognition of the need for a national approach to solving certain collections management problems. English Heritage is considering the option of establishing large regional stores-cum-study centres to house the archives of archaeological excavations. A legacy of severe financial constraint means that there is a significant shortfall in the resources available to museums, archives and libraries, and this is inhibiting the effective management of our cultural heritage. The care of our collections is being neglected because managers are having to operate with insufficient financial resources, inadequate numbers of appropriately skilled staff and, in many cases, unsuitable buildings.

To an extent, the impact of this shortfall can be ameliorated by a reallocation of resources, but this will not solve the problem completely. Resource believes that all institutions should receive, or should have a clear prospect of receiving, a level of funding that enables them to act as effective stewards of the collections for which they are responsible. This would enable them to reach and maintain defined standards of collections management.

Resource is actively advocating that stewardship of collections is at the heart of the access, education and social inclusion agendas, and that good management, acquisition, cataloguing and preservation are crucial to the maintenance of sustainable access to collections.

Information and communications technology (ICT) offers considerable potential for raising the level of collections management. It has particular applications in cataloguing and documentation and in reaching wider audiences through digital networks. Yet many institutions feel that they are lagging behind other public sector bodies in the application of technology.

In some cases the problem is the lack of hardware, in others, institutions are using inappropriate software. Many also feel that they have inadequate access to the skills needed to make the most of the technology. Resource is contributing to the development of a co-ordinated approach to digital preservation across the sector through the Digital Preservation Coalition and other collaborations.

The starting point for strategic management of the cultural heritage is a better understanding of the nature and location of the various collections that make up the distributed national collection. Such understanding is also a pre-requisite for co-operation between institutions with common interests. People need to know what exists and where it is located.

The process of describing and documenting collections of material is, however, far from straightforward. Much work needs to be done to facilitate the development of regional and national maps. The Scottish National Audit is already addressing this in Scotland. Resource will support and co-ordinate, where appropriate, the mapping of collections. Significant cataloguing and documentation backlogs are associated with too many important collections.

At present, insufficient importance is attached to conservation and collections management. As a consequence, there is a risk that unconsidered neglect of collections will result in a loss to future generations of users.

There is a particular need to raise awareness and shape attitudes among governing bodies and funding agencies More generally, Resource will work to promote a more informed public understanding of stewardship issues and how they impact upon both users and non-users of cultural heritage services.

Managing Personnel Collections

The first wave of library computerisation took place in the seventies. During that period manual back-room activities, such as acquisition, distribution and cataloguing, were turned into computer-controlled activities. As a result, the library's traditional customers had to fundamentally reorient themselves to the new way in which bibliographic information was now becoming available, that is through an on-line public access catalogue (OPAC).

This period also saw the introduction of the first local bibliographic and indexing databases, as well as various other databases. During the second wave of library computerisation, which started in the 90s, the focus was on the deployment of computer networks providing access to remote electronic information by means of library information systems.

Access to electronic information is no longer limited to so-called secondary information (catalogues, bibliographic databases). Primary information has now become electronically available as well. For instance, users will have access to the electronic full-text versions of scientific journals. Electronic textbooks and readers enable users to consult information outside the library, i.e. at the professional and private workplaces of the library's traditional customer.

One very important trend is the decreasing prominence of the library's physical collection, and the corresponding increase in the importance of information reference. The library is developing into a gateway, referring users to information irrespective of the location where that information is physically stored. A second trend is taking place in the traditional appreciation of library tasks as some kind of overhead.

In the future, library tasks will be regarded as directly productive forces. It is becoming ever more difficult to distinguish between the actual provision of information and the various processes in which that information is used. A university library, for example, is connected to a university, whose primary tasks are education and research. At its most fundamental level, education is characterised by the transfer of knowledge from teacher to student.

The traditional borderline between knowledge transfer through teaching on the one hand and the provision of information by the library on the other is fading fast, due to the use of information technology in education. To a growing extent, library services are blending with the teaching process.

Similar trends can be observed in the process of research and in other primary processes supported by library tasks, for example in policy-making and legal consultancy. A third trend is eroding the self-evident position of the library in the process from information production to information consumption. However, while some of the traditional library tasks are under threat, new activities also present opportunities for strengthening the library's position.

In order to understand the way in which the library's activities are influenced by the implementation of new technology, we should take a look at the so-called information chain. The role of the library is often described as one link in that chain. In the traditional information chain the main functions, i.e. the production, distribution, acquisition, and consumption of information, were always accommodated in strictly separated stages.

However, the configuration of functions within the information chain has begun to change, and within this changing constellation all the parties involved are struggling to determine their positions. These developments show how important it is for those parties to innovate themselves and to experiment creatively with new roles instead of adhering to traditional patterns.

Any forceful attempt to preserve the old structure will not only impede any development as such, but will also expose that structure to the increasing threat of arbitrary disintegration. One of the conclusions to be drawn from this analysis is that libraries should try to become publishers of electronic documents instead of merely relying on agreements with commercial publishers.

At this moment the full and long-term implications of these developments are far from clear. One effect might very well be that the role of the library as an institution becomes less obvious. It is quite conceivable that the functions performed by the library in society and within institutions will merge with other functions that are performed by other parties than traditional libraries.

Features of Digital Library Collections

One of the distinguishing features of the digital library is that it provides access to digital information irrespective of the location where that information is stored. A modern library's policy should aim to make as much relevant information as possible accessible by electronic means, while allowing the library to retain paper subscriptions where necessary.

A library can of course store information on its own server, but in general this is not very efficient unless the data involved is information in respect of which the library itself fulfils the publisher's role. Most of the information to which the library provides access is stored on servers of publishers or intermediary organisations. How can the access to that information be guaranteed? In practice, a number of possibilities can be distinguished.

1. Free access. This holds especially for Internet sites.
2. Full licenses for well-defined user groups. University staff and students are examples of such user groups. The costs tend to be high; quite a few scientific journals combine such licenses with compulsory subscriptions to paper journals, and sometimes include long-term non-cancellation clauses.
3. Licenses for well-defined user groups with a maximum number of concurrent users, an extreme variant of which would be to restrict access to one user at one specified workstation.
4. Pay per view licenses
5. No access.

Ideally, users have access to all sources of information. The financial conditions may of course vary among the different information sources and user groups. This ideal situation cannot be achieved unless flexible arrangements are in place between libraries and publishers. For that purpose, the automatic paper subscriptions in licenses for access to electronic information should be cancelled.

There are three main workable variants for licenses.

1. Free access.
2. Full licenses for well-defined user groups.
3. Pay per view.

Combinations between variants 2 and 3 will increase flexibility. Suppose a publisher has 500 journals, all of which are electronically available. Suppose also that 300 of these can be considered to be part of Library A's core collection. In this case, an effective model would grant the library full licenses for those 300 journals and pay per view licenses for the other 200. If any of the 200 non-core journals is viewed so often that the pay per view price exceeds the full license fee for that particular title, the pay per view license is automatically turned into a full license.

Conversely, the journal in the core collection that is consulted least often would be transferred to the pay per view collection. Such an arrangement would obviously call for adequate administrative tools to obviate the risk of users being continually confronted with administrative processes, such as repeated requests for a password or a credit card number.

Publishers often present their electronic databases with the help of a user-interface developed specifically for their own products, and tend to regard that interface as an added value item. However, this approach presents a number of problems.

— Firstly, given that they are geared towards the "broadcasting" of information, such interfaces generally fail to take into account the users' wishes in a sufficient manner. This is not surprising, since most publishers only maintain limited contacts with end users.

— Secondly, these interfaces are developed mainly for the publisher's own products. Some publishers, e.g. Elsevier, have successfully opened their interfaces for use by some other publishers, but those interfaces only provide access to a limited amount of information. Intermediary parties, such as subscription agents, also offer access to databases through their own interfaces. Again, however, the amount of information accessible through these interfaces is quite limited.

The consequence of this from the user's point of view is that he/she will have to perform the complicated task of scanning the information sources from different publishers by means of different interfaces. In other words, if you look for information you will have to know by which publisher it is offered in order to find it. From a user's point of view this is highly inefficient, to say the least.

Technically it is possible to offer a software solution to the multiple interface problem. There are different types of software available that perform information retrieval tasks independently of the interfaces developed by the publishers. In order to do so, they need direct access to the structured data of the publisher's information sources (coded mostly in very effective XML or SGML).

Utrecht University Library has implemented software that enables this type of information retrieval (Muscat). In practice, however, there are obstacles that prevent this solution from realising its full potential. Several publishers are rather reluctant to provide access to their structured data, or ask a high additional fee in return.

Information retrieval is not a service to be delivered exclusively by publishers. The libraries in particular have an important role as facilitators of the navigation possibilities available to the users. There are several reasons for this. Traditionally, libraries operate in close contact with their users and communicate with them in order to establish specific user needs.

If libraries know who their users are, have developed good and close relationships with them and are also well informed about user demands, what possibilities do they have to further improve their services in a changing technological environment? The first thing they must do is prevent themselves from becoming an obstacle in that new environment as a redundant logistic or functional intermediary stage in the process. In other words, the libraries themselves should become invisible. The invisible library could offer the following services to its users.

Search facilities are subject to a number of basic user requirements, the most important of which can be summarised as follows. Users will want to be able to start the search process immediately, without first having to study complex interfaces and codes. They are looking for information and cannot be expected to be interested in the technical structure or format of the data involved.

Neither are users likely to be interested in the origin of the source (the identity of the publisher or intermediary), or in the location where the information they need is physically stored. They just want to find an answer to a particular question. During the search process, moreover, users will only want to be presented answers that are fully relevant to their question, without being swamped by thousands of articles only marginally related to the subject.

These general user requirements must be translated into functional requirements that the Information Retrieval (IR) system should be able to fulfil. Most importantly, the IR system is required to:

— allow search questions to be asked in natural language;

— allow all data sources to be searched simultaneously on the basis of a single search question;

— make use of high-quality and professional software (including high recall and precision scores; most software developed under time pressure by unqualified staff fails to meet these strict criteria)

— enable users to search through sub-collections of the sources, which implies that it must be possible for the sources themselves to be divided into sub-disciplines so as to reduce the search domain.

These functional requirements are clearly derived from user needs and should serve as guiding principles in the purchase or development of IR systems.

Personal alerting system is vital to provide an easily accessible information universe which the user can enter independently provided he is equipped with the proper IR tools. In addition, the user should be served by his own personal assistant, who offers packages of information tailored to the user's individual reader profile.

Such assistants have already been created in self-learning software known as intelligent agents technology. These assistants, or agents, are used in the construction of a personal alerting system. The set-up and testing of such personal alerting systems is the responsibility of support organisations, for example university libraries; their use requires no additional intermediaries.

Researchers, teachers and students will all make use of this tool independently and will only require assistance from the library when they need specific instructions or are confronted with specific problems.

The traditional library organisation was characterised by a decentralised structure in which individual libraries were found in the locations where teaching and research activities actually took place (mostly in the university professors' rooms). In order to improve efficiency, to solve logistic problems and, above all, to cut costs books and magazines were relocated to central or faculty libraries.

Double subscriptions were cancelled. While obviously provoking some protest from among faculty members, this operation was in many cases inevitable. Due to the advent of the Internet and electronic sources of information, the physical location of those sources has become irrelevant. From behind a PC in his or her own office, today's scientist has access to a range of sources that is incomparable to the access provided by the traditional library in the professor's lecture room.

While the range of sources offers clear and major advantages, its very extensiveness also causes a number of problems. Some of these can be obviated by IR systems and personal agents, but more tools are required; tools that help the user to create and manage his/her own limited but tailor-made collection. These tools allow the scientist to become a librarian himself, but a librarian who has no other clients.

Scientists need tools to perform this role, tools that help them organise their own articles, research data, teaching material, etc.; tools which respect the preferences of their users and can deal with even the most idiosyncratic approach to building up personal collections. It is one of the library's tasks to make such tools available. They can be described as the creation of facilities, the supply of user instructions for those facilities and the provision of assistance when problems occur, and are all consistent with user demands.

Information cannot be separated from the purpose it is used for. At universities, that purpose can be found in the primary processes of education and research. This is why the university library's tasks are focused on the integration of information services in the user's primary processes. Such integration is not achieved automatically, however. A teacher who is preparing a new online reader will need access not only to all relevant sources and search and selection tools, but also to online publishing facilities.

These may be templates provided with conversion programmes which adapt the content (text, image, video) for presentation on the world wide web, or old readers already converted from the old, illegible formats to formats that enable the teacher to cut and paste selected items for use in his new reader. They may be interfaces for database publishing, or administrative procedures that affect the available space on the server, security measures or technical privileges granted to the teacher in question. Another example is the virtual 'primer'.

In addition to preparing new material for their lectures, it is not unusual for teachers to draw up primers for their students, including books, journals and other sources of information which the students are supposed to read within the context of the course.

In these examples, the tools that help teachers compile virtual primers and the online publishing facilities are perfectly geared towards the primary process. The library consists of information and software and has been fully integrated into the teaching process. The tasks of the library may reach beyond the efficient and effective supply of information.

Researchers do not merely consume information, but also communicate intensively with their colleagues. When they read a scientific article, many researchers will want to respond, ask the author questions or give critical comments. In effect, the first academic journals, which appeared in the seventeenth century, supported this type of academic dialogue.

The exchange of research results and attempts to refute and validate them through debate and comments are no less important than the access to the relevant sources of information. Given that library tasks focus on improvement and facilitation of the entire primary process, it seems obvious to extend them so as to include the facilitation of academic communication.

The user not only creates his/her own library; via the library access, he/she can actually participate in the academic dialogue with colleagues. This is why the provision (and maintenance) of linkage between interaction facilities and sources of information should be included in the library's task package. The integration of the library in primary processes can advance to such a degree that the library becomes altogether invisible as a separate institute.

The user takes on the role of the librarian. He gains access to a vast amount of information and is provided with a set of tools and aids that will help him extract the data he needs and arrange and process it in the manner that suits him best. Library services in which libraries provide access to as much electronic information as possible and offer additional services that enable users to organise the sources of information they need for personal professional purposes.

The future of the library, the 'collection' tends to be seen as a concept that will continue to play a prominent role. The question is whether that prominence will be borne out by future developments. A key feature of collections is their status as sources of information gathered for the benefit of the library's users. This implies that the information they contain has been deliberately selected. However, this kind of explicit and deliberate selection is absent from most of the library services described above.

The library provides 'anything, anytime, anywhere' from the collection of high-quality academic sources. The financial conditions may differ (campus-wide license or pay-per-view), but these are not so much influenced by a library's selection than by the actual behaviour of its users. In other words, it is not realistic to regard the provision of access to electronic journals as an activity that forms part of a library's 'collection'. These sources together constitute something like a universal collection, which will continue to grow.

We are witnessing the advent of a truly global certified scientific collection. In this view, it is no longer the library that decides which data to select, but the individual user himself. The user can arrange the information sources relevant to his own professional needs into a tailor-made collection with the help of the tools presented by the library, organise those sources according to the use he expects to make of them, and integrate them into his own publications or educational programmes.

These considerations do not apply to certified sources, such as freely accessible sources on the Internet. In that area, libraries will continue to be responsible for the selection of high-quality scientific material; a selection in the form of pointers, sets of references. However, the selection of material is not the prerogative of the library.

On the contrary; the library should restrict itself primarily to the collection of references (bookmarks) which in turn are collected by scientists for their own use. As a secondary task, the library should (automatically) cancel double references, arrange references into disciplines and present them via homepages. These activities are necessary in order to allow the various IR tools and agents to function optimally and to visualise the designated sources.

In this field, cooperation with scientists will be extremely efficient. Far-reaching forms of cooperation among the libraries themselves are also quite conceivable. What is known in the physical world as the alignment of collection formation profiles, or priority area formation, is, understandably, only rarely successful.

This concept may yield countless advantages for the virtual selection of Internet sources. The task of designating quality sources can be distributed due to the very fact that the physical location of the information is irrelevant and, hence, allows universal access. This is because this task does not involve the development of a central collection, but rather the certification of a sub-collection of information.

In part, collection management is limited to measuring the frequency with which the sources are consulted and the type of use that is made of them. Related to, and indeed derived from this is the management not of the collection itself, but of various types of licenses. In addition, collection management refers to a distributed process of assessment of the quality of freely accessible sources on the Internet.

Changing Nature of Collection Management

Information overload may be the greatest challenge that scholars and librarians have faced in the twentieth century. Librarians whose careers spanned the pre- and post-1950s worlds noted a marked expansion in the scope of scholarship in America. Before World War II, academic research in America concentrated on Western culture and classical areas of science. After the war, American research horizons expanded to cover all areas of the world as well as applied and specialized fields of science.

Library collections grew rapidly to house the products of this expanded research effort. In the 1950s and 60s many university librarians found themselves in the midst of a "golden age" of collection development when acquisitions funds seemed plentiful, U.S. currency was strong, and there was still room in academic library book stacks.

Cooperative collection development, which in some sense is the ultimate activity of this new functional field of librarianship, has proved difficult to implement and to sustain. It is clear, both in theory and practice, that no single library can collect the entire - and exploding - record of knowledge; and, as use studies show, no library really needs to do so to satisfy most of its users' needs.

A reasonable approach would be to coordinate collection development locally, regionally, nationally, and internationally to maximize local use of library collections and broad coverage of all fields of knowledge. The Center for Research Libraries, however, emerged as a viable model for depositing and sharing highly specialized research material, and some carefully focused regional efforts, such as the one involving the academic libraries in North Carolina's Research Triangle, did provide some long-standing cooperative collection development opportunities for the libraries involved.

By and large, however, most cooperative collection development experiments from the 1950s through the mid-1980s were not successful. The strong political pull of local library autonomy, combined with the technical difficulty of moving print material quickly and economically over geographic distances, tended to make cooperative collection development difficult and impractical.

In the mid-1980s many universities and research libraries found themselves in a period of fiscal constraint and even decline. Economic constraints affected all aspects of research library operations. In fact, personnel reductions seem to have been steeper than acquisitions declines. Between 1982 and 1991 the typical portion of a total research library budget spent on acquisitions remained constant at 35 percent, while the portion of a total library budget spent on salaries declined from 56 to 52 percent.

Anecdotal evidence points to fewer full-time heads of collection development, bibliographers and subject specialists in research libraries as the 20th century closes. In 1989, John Howe, a history professor and interim director of libraries at the University of Minnesota, described the emerging situation as the "decentering of the library" within institutions of higher education. According to Howe, the library might still be the symbolic heart of the university, but for several reasons it was losing its central place as a funding priority on many campuses.

First, new information technology was creating "alternative paths" for access to scholarly information, and investments in technical infrastructure and computing centers were diverting funding from the traditional library. Second, the decline in arts and sciences and the rise of science and technology programs in universities were eroding the power of disciplines that most directly supported the traditional library. Third, the profession of librarianship itself seemed to be in disarray, fraught with uncertainty and anxiety over its future in the computer age. Fourth, libraries were not competitive enough in the new, aggressive environment of higher education.

Howe emphasized that new leadership was required to assert that libraries still played a central role in supporting teaching and research. The library could no longer take for granted a special status in the university. While confronting adverse economic conditions in the 1980s and 90s, collection management librarians were faced with an even more powerful force for change: the emergence of the digital information system.

The online catalog was followed by electronic reference databases, and by the mid-1990s full-text digital articles and journals and digital collections were vying for collection management librarians' attention. Librarians now had to balance the demands of print and digital materials, even as they sought to understand the nature and consequences of digital, networked information and the impact a new information system would have on library operations, including the budget.

At the same time, scholarly publishing was also experiencing dramatic change. With fewer orders from libraries, university presses had to cut back the number of monograph titles they published, while commercial journal publishers, at least some of the largest science and technology publishers, were expanding and flourishing. All concerned struggled with the impact of the Internet.

A constricted library economy, the emergence of information in digital format, and the commercialization and consolidation of the publishing sector have combined to produce profound and surprising changes in collection management in research libraries at the beginning of the 21st century.

Collection management librarians - and library directors - are faced with a new and uncharted environment. Libraries have much less buying power than they had a decade ago. With fewer staff in collection management full time, many selectors and bibliographers work at collection management part time while handling a much broader range of disciplines and formats.

The technical advances in digitization are truly revolutionizing the way scholarly information is published, organized, and maintained, and both the scope and extent of this change are difficult to comprehend and manage. As difficult as it was to manage a print collection, librarians now have two equally formidable formats to consider: print and digital.

When digital resources were first introduced in research libraries, there was a good deal of conflict between the old and new format. What might be called the cultural wars between print and electronic proponents began with the demise of the card catalog and moved to the fear of digital content taking over from print.

In fact, current practices and traditions in scholarly communication are at the base of the conflicts within collection management. The divergence among disciplines is noteworthy. Scholars in the sciences publish their research results in journals, rather than in monographs, in part to be able to report as rapidly as possible.

They are, for the most part, comfortable with digital access to journal articles and, in many cases, communicate widely electronically and share initial results of their research, e.g., electronic preprints. In some disciplines, such as mathematics, scholars regularly use back issues of journals in their fields; others, such as computer science, do not. In some areas of the humanities, however, such as history, monographs, not journal articles, are required for tenure and promotion.

Rapid dissemination of results is less important in the humanities (and hence different editing practices exist) than in the sciences, and older publications are consulted more frequently than in many scientific disciplines. There are some areas of the humanities, such as philosophy, however, where monographs play a much smaller role than do journal articles.

Blaise Cronin, Dean of the School of Library and Information Science at Indiana University, commented recently on the differences among academic disciplines within the changing world of electronic publishing: "Interestingly, cross-field variations are largely independent of the highly visible tools and technologies associated with electronic publishing. Common platforms don't breed common approaches.

Rather, publishing practices and expectations within a given research community are shaped by prevailing norms and conventions. Nothing new in that. Traditionally, a refereed conference paper has counted for something in computer science, but is likely to be given short shrift by a promotion and tenure committee in a business school. A monograph will be expected of a junior scholar in English, but not of an aspiring mathematician. This being so, our ex cathedra pronouncements about publishing really should be grounded in the multiple realities of tribal life in academe."

Within this complicated picture of needs and traditions, the rapidly increasing prices of science journals has literally eaten up limited collection budgets. In fact, despite cancellation of hundreds of thousands of dollars worth of journals since 1986, the 110 largest research libraries in the United States and Canada have spent 124% more on serials to purchase 7% fewer titles, according to the Association for Research Libraries. Although monographs are increasing in price at a slower rate than are journals, fewer monographs are purchased by libraries because of the need to fund expensive journals (both electronic and print) in the sciences.

With fewer orders from libraries, scholarly presses have reduced the number of titles and the quantity of print runs; therefore, it becomes more and more difficult for a scholar to find a publisher for a monograph. To complicate the picture further, universities and libraries have had to scramble to develop the technical infrastructure and staff expertise necessary to fully participate in the new digital information system. Some departments in the academy still lack up-to-date computer equipment and support, while others have long had a strong information technology infrastructure and continue to improve it.

Library organization and the education of many library staff were designed for work in a print information system. It is not easy to change operational procedures, organizational structures, and established work habits and outlooks—such social changes generally lag behind technological change. The amount of digital information is growing faster than most librarians would have predicted.

Despite this phenomenal growth, research libraries, for reasons stated above, are still largely dominated by print resources, both in acquisitions and collection management. It is unlikely that more than 10 to 15 percent of a research library's collection budget is used today to purchase or provide access to digital information. It is clear that research librarians need to turn more of their attention, effort, and resources to managing the new digital information system.

The fundamental structure of how scholarly information is published has yet to be altered in any significant way. Authors still submit their manuscripts, now more often than not in electronic form, to publishers. Publishers take ownership of the manuscripts, turn them into both print and electronic books and articles, and sell them to individuals and libraries.

Research librarians and faculty members are loath to give up their print collections and journal subscriptions until digital products are more stable and mature and are able to be archived successfully. In fact, many publishers still require that libraries purchase a print version along with their electronic product. One collection development expert, Robert Sewell, recently described the current electronic environment as one where a myriad of different interfaces exist; search engines crash; local loading, remote access, and operating systems have regular and recurring problems; radically different terms and conditions are found in licensing agreements; and wide fluctuations in the pricing of similar electronic products are found. He believes, however, that most research libraries have become extraordinarily adaptive in this chaotic and formative period.

At this point the digital information system is simply too immature for it to become a trusted and reliable medium for the collection and preservation of the record of scholarship. Despite its imperfections, the digital information system has and will continue to have a profound effect on scholarly communication. Several studies have appeared in this decade that demonstrate the magnitude and significance of any fundamental changes in scholarly communication as well as the great potential offered to the community of research and scholarship by developments in information technology.

Fundamental changes in scholarly communications are certainly in store. The traditional book and journal as organizing frames for scholarship will likely change as will basic production, distribution, and archiving. Odlyzko believes the new digital information system will allow scholars to become their own publishers and archivists. According to Odlyzko, "Publishers and librarians have been the middlemen between the scholars as producers of information and the scholars as consumers, and are likely to be largely squeezed out of this business."

Integration of Digital Resources

The nature and structure of scholarly archives need to be changed to manage better the growing quantity, specialization, and cost of scholarship. Rather than a highly decentralized system as exists today, with duplicative print collections spread across the country, digital technology has the potential to provide more centrally organized information storage and highly distributed, quick, and cost-effective access.

Digital technology can also foster the integration of the various components and sources of scholarly publication. In the future researchers will no doubt use hyperlinks to move quickly online from index or bibliographic citations to abstracts to full multimedia documents with the click of a mouse.

Such integration is already happening on the Web platform and through the efforts of library and scientific information services. The ability to use hyperlinks to integrate scholarship and to make possible interdisciplinary research online is an extraordinary feature, one with which a print format cannot compete.

Research librarians are just beginning to make broad, organizational changes in their management of the products of scholarship. Librarians are starting to provide more access to digital information not from files stored in their own libraries or on their own campuses, but from servers that are networked to publishers, government agencies, universities, and scholarly societies that can be located anywhere around the world. Rather than selecting scholarly resources on an item by item basis, librarians are turning into "aggregators," who are developing their collections at a macro and integrated level.

Collection builders will evolve into knowledge prospectors. "The creation of validated collections of digital materials and their relationship to validated nondigital materials will offer a significant added value to the serious information seeker, while allowing other linkages to be developed and used." Reference tools, electronic journals, and digital archives of historical materials now come in a variety of bundled packages.

A strategy that counters the bundling of publications that most publishers use emerged when California State University's (CSU) librarians and a high level university committee from the 21 campuses of CSU sent out a request for proposal for someone to build a customized database that would offer full-text access to 1,279 journals selected by Cal State. This imaginative proposal moved the responsibility for selecting titles back into the hands of the institutions and their libraries and was welcomed by many as an alternative to the growing model of "all or none" site licensing of an entire publisher's journal output.

What these new organizational developments in libraries have in common is the strategy of using digital information services to gain economies of scale, end unnecessary duplication, and provide faculty and students with more information at less cost. This pattern of networked, integrated access to central stores of electronic scholarly material seems inevitable in a new digital scholarly communication system.

At last the limitations of print collections may be overcome: self-sufficiency was never really possible in the traditional campus or departmental library, and, at the same time, there was always waste in the form of underutilized material in these decentralized archives. The elusive but ultimate goal of cooperative collection development to coordinate the collection of the entire record of scholarship may have a new lease on life in the digital information system.

Print Collections in the Digital Age

The new is also affecting the old. Research librarians, running out of stack space in prime campus real estate for their library's collections and seeing new access opportunities through improvements in document delivery services, are beginning to consolidate their print archives both on and off campus.

Regional storage facilities are in operation or under construction both in the United States and Canada. Scholars accustomed to browsing complete open-stack main library collections or separate discipline-based library collections in their school or department buildings are finding it disconcerting to see this convenient approach to library collection organization coming to an end.

The high cost of maintaining decentralized archives, however, combined with the development of new digital approaches to access are making the complete main library and the traditional departmental library a convenience of the past. Direct delivery of articles to the individual's computer and electronic browsing of titles and tables of contents may help to make up for traditional shelf browsing.

Still, in any large research library there are a variety of print collections that will continue to require access and preservation in traditional ways. Music libraries offer a good example of how the traditional and new formats are used regularly. Any music library of strength will contain, in addition to books on music, musical scores and parts, from which performers play-and probably will continue to play into the foreseeable future.

Even as students and professors use printed scores and parts to study and perform, they also use computers to compose, analyze, and listen to music. Similar scenarios exist in other kinds of departmental and special libraries, where users require a variety of media for their research, including film, slides, photographs, maps, rare books, manuscripts, and artifacts of all kinds.

Print collections, of course, are not likely to disappear from research libraries in the near or far future. The sheer amount of information in printed form from the past would be difficult to discard or to reformat. In current acquisitions, as well, print material still far exceeds digital material in any research library's collection development program.

Proper storage and preservation of print collections will continue to be a challenge for research librarians. Off-site and consortial storage arrangements and digital reformatting will provide new tools and options for managing this challenge. The J-STOR project is an excellent model of how new technology and cooperative support can be used to provide new options for access to and storage of scholarly journal backfiles. Digital reformatting and archiving are still problematic, however.

Ownership issues and their effect on the control and cost of information in the digital environment are serious concerns for research librarians. Libraries are usually thought of as places, collections, and services. Underlying this construct, however, is an economic model for funding and sharing information that is often taken for granted.

In the print world, libraries buy books and journals that can be borrowed any number of times or that can be copied within the limits of copyright law and fair use guidelines. This traditional library model for the central funding and communal sharing of information may or may not work in the new digital environment.

Both access to and control over information take on powerful new dimensions in the digital age. The development of firewalls, encryption techniques, authentication devices, and cybercash, has made the Internet a much more secure environment today for commerce and publishing.

In fact, controls on the use of information can be much more powerful in the digital world than they were in the print world. Tighter control over access to information along with the commercialization of scientific publishing that has resulted in higher subscription prices has, some believe, begun to disrupt the free flow of scholarship at the end of this century. This situation may only be exacerbated as publishers exert more ownership over their digital products in the 21st century.

Future of Digital Library Collection

Innovation in scholarly communication is forging ahead in a variety of arenas now that digitization and the World Wide Web allow informal distribution of information. Discipline-based servers dedicated to research fields or specific concepts are becoming essential platforms for scholars. These are sources for preprint and peer-reviewed articles, primary research, and an interactive exchange of ideas and even materials.

SPARC and JSTOR are examples of cooperation between libraries and publishers to maintain the values of academe in the publishing and distribution of, and access to, scholarly resources in the new digital landscape. Data collection capabilities from digital collections are far more sophisticated, reliable, and precise than from print collections, providing abundant opportunities for research on usage and user behaviour.

In response to the digitization movement, libraries are changing the ways they manage budgeting, staffing, and roles or work functions. Drexel University is an example of an early adopter of digital collections. Carol Montgomery described Drexel's move from a collection of 100 e-journals and 1,850 print journals in 1998 to a collection of 5,000 e-journals and 953 print journals in 2000. She described this transition's impact on staffing, shifting workloads, and new job functions. Administration, management, and computer network infrastructure all saw increases in responsibility.

Technical services functions—including e-journal acquisitions, cataloguing, and catalogue maintenance--all required increased staffing. In addition to obvious reductions in staff to check-in, claim, and bind printed journals, fewer staff were needed for reshelving and stack maintenance. Montgomery believes that building and maintaining a digital library collection is far more complex than doing the same for a print collection due to the price and license negotiations that are required.

All the presentations acknowledged to some degree that the economics of scholarly communication are changing rapidly. In 1989, ARL commissioned an economics consulting firm to analyze scholarly publishing trends. Their report pointed to the lack of competition in this market as a major contributing factor to spiraling costs. SPARC was created in 1997 by ARL to inject competition into the scholarly publishing market by facilitating the start-up of low-cost/high-quality academic publications.

SPARC has demonstrated remarkable impact already with a variety of new publications and outreach programs that have raised understanding of these complex issues across the nation. Further, library demand for scholarly publications creates a unique market environment. In other words, unlike most markets involving differentiated products, it is not appropriate to model demand as a discrete choice process. Rather, the typical library attempts to provide access to as many STM journals as possible through a combination of subscriptions and inter-library exchanges."

As commercial publishers analyzed the demand structure of libraries, they came to understand the profitability of acquiring more titles through mergers. As a few publishers gained greater market power they were able to increase the price of individual titles within the portfolios they had to offer. McCabe concludes that these three factors—inelasticity of demand, library acquisition by portfolio within broad subject areas, and publisher mergers—all contributed to a higher rate of journal price inflation over the last several years than can be explained by the improved quality or increased publishing costs of the journals themselves.

In short, users are going to the World Wide Web for their information, in many cases bypassing the library. What does this mean for the role of the library in the future? Traditionally, libraries have maintained the authoritative record of scholarship and made that record broadly available. Libraries must communicate the actual costs of digitizing collections to a wider audience and digitization must be understood not as a cost saver but as a value-added service.

The Library is a central cultural institution. The mission of the Library is: to collect, preserve and give access to recorded knowledge, in all documentary forms, for the benefit of all engaged in research and learning, or with other information needs.

In Australia, Wales, the fundamental nature of the Library's work was determined by the Royal Charter that established the Library's existence in 1907. The current wording of the Charter gives as the Library's functions: the collection, preservation and maintenance of manuscripts, printed matter, maps, photographs, visual and audiovisual material relating to Wales and the Celtic peoples and similar material which furthers the aims of higher education and literary and scientific research.

The Charter is the basis for several key features of the Library:

— its emphasis on material of Welsh (and Celtic) interest

— its wider collecting responsibilities (these are based on legal deposit and purchase)

— the fact that it collects material in such a wide variety of media

— its mission to support researchers and those in higher education

Wales' National Library is an Assembly-Sponsored Public Body, and receives Grant-in-Aid annually from the National Assembly for Wales. The relationship between the Library and the National Assembly is defined by a Management statement and financial memorandum.

Valuable pointers to the future of the Library were provided in 1999 by the many responses to Choosing the future, the first large-scale public consultation exercise ever conducted by the Library. Individuals and organisations expressed clearly and at length their strong views on how they think the Library should evolve. Among the consistent themes to have emerged from the responses were:

— universal support for the established 'core functions' of the Library

— general support for new developments within these core functions: opening up the Library, its buildings and contents to a wider range and a larger number of users developing new services for those in higher (and further) education making the collections and services more relevant to all learners, not only those in universities and colleges the use of remote, especially electronic services, and specifically digitisation, to further these aims building partnerships with other organisations, public and private

The existence and work of the Library depend on certain principles and values, shared by those who govern it, work in it and use it. They are seen as complimentary to the values and principles of the National Assembly in guiding the Library's work.

The Library has a vital role as a collector and guardian of the intellectual record of the life of Wales and the Welsh people. This is important in itself, and is also an important element in defining the cultural identities of the country. The new political status of Wales is a product of, and will itself contribute to, a renewed concern with cultural identities. The Library is likely to have an important part to play in reflecting, recording and even forming those identities.

This intellectual record is not confined to any particular medium, format, period or language. From its beginning the Library has been more than what is conventionally recognised as a 'library', that is, a collection of printed works. It stores a wide - and still widening - range of formats capable of carrying intellectual content. Among these are: books and periodicals, manuscripts and archives, pictures, photographs and maps, sound and moving images, and electronic material.

This record of the 'matter of Wales' (and of the other Celtic countries) is, however, part of a wider, indeed world-wide, domain of recorded knowledge, produced in many languages and over many centuries, which the Library attempts to represent in its collections for the benefit of its users.

The Library's wider collections, mainly acquired in print form through legal deposit, are essential to its ability to support study and learning, not only in Welsh or Celtic domains, but also in a very wide range of other subjects.

The Library's collections and services exist to meet the needs of all those who can benefit from them. The Library is proud of the fact that it is a public library, in the sense that any adult is able and welcome to use its collections for reference with little formality and without charge.

Among the groups that make use of the Library at present for consultation and reference are academic and personal researchers, students and other learners, businesses, the media, and visitors from Britain and overseas. This right of unrestricted access is part of the democratic rights of citizens in pursuit of information, knowledge and enlightenment, and contributes to the promotion of 'social inclusion'.

The Library has a duty not merely to 'hold its doors open', but to encourage awareness and use of its collections and services, by all the means at its disposal. The Library has an important function, as by far the largest and most significant institution of its kind in Wales, in leading, co-ordinating and supporting the development of library and archive services in Wales. This is not an optional part of its mission, but an essential role in a country where library and archive services tend to be small and scattered.

In its turn the National Library is part of a wider, interlocking structure of library, information and archive institutions in the United Kingdom and throughout the world. It co-operates with them to make the best use of the resources that are available to all. The National Library seeks to do everything it does - whether providing answers to enquiries, publishing books, mounting exhibitions, or any other relevant activity - to the highest possible standard, with excellence as a constant ideal in mind.

In short, as a thriving, relevant and well-regarded cultural and information resource for the people of Wales and the world. These will be among the defining characteristics of the Library:

— all of the Library's central functions will remain relevant, although how they are performed will change over time. In particular, more information and services will be delivered through the internet and will therefore be capable of reaching a much larger number of people. Among these will be: detailed information about items in the collections; digitised copies of many items; and transactional services, such as the sale of goods from the shop and reprographic services.

— many more people, and a wider range of people, will make use of the Library's services than in the past.

— as well as continuing to serve researchers and learners wishing to study the collections, the Library will welcome many more visitors interested in exploring the history and culture of Wales through the collections.

— a range of information services will be developed to satisfy the needs of specific groups of users, including those interested in family and community history.

— the systematic collection of electronic material, published and archival, will become a major element of the Library's activity, especially as web archiving becomes established, and if the law of legal deposit is extended to embrace electronic publications. The Library may gain the status of a 'Trusted Digital Repository' for the whole of Wales.

— the Library's services to readers and visitors will be backed up by a strong and well-organised series of collection, technical and administrative services.

— the Library's already well-developed partnerships with other organisations will be further strengthened.

The degree to which the Library will be able to realise this vision will depend on a number of factors:

— the availability of sufficient resources to maintain existing functions and fund new developments

— the speed and ease with which new technical systems and tools can be harnessed to the achievement of our objectives othe success with which the Library can nurture innovation and adaptive thinking among its own staff.

The essence of what the Library does is contained in its five 'core functions'. These set the minimum boundaries of its policies and practice. The core functions are defined below, with in each case an indication of the chief means by which they are performed.

To collect materials by legal deposit, purchase, donation, bequest, exchange and deposit, in accordance with agreed collection development policies. This function is carried out through:

— assembling as complete a collection as possible, in all media, of published material relating to Wales, including printed publications and sound and moving image material

— maintaining (mainly through legal deposit and purchase) the most comprehensive collection in Wales of printed material published in the United Kingdom and Ireland, and of research material from other countries

— developing collections of unpublished materials relating to or deriving from Wales, including archives and artistic works

— accessioning, processing, cataloguing and storing material acquired

To preserve and conserve materials in the collections. This function is carried out through:

— ensuring environmental, storage and handling conditions favourable to the continued preservation of materials

— intervening to conserve materials and hence arrest deterioration or repair damage

— transferring, in some cases, information to more suitable preservation formats

To provide satisfactory access for users of the Library to its building, collections and services, and adequate information about them. This function is carried out through:

— providing access to public spaces, collections and facilities within the Library's building

— providing document delivery, enquiry and information services to those wishing to use the Library, in person or remotely

— providing easy access to catalogues and lists of the Library's collections, and surrogates of selections from them

To raise awareness and disseminate knowledge of the Library's collections. This function is carried out through:

— issuing guides, leaflets and other publicity material

— publishing printed monographs and serials

— mounting material on the Library's website

— staging exhibitions derived from the collections

— arranging lectures and seminars

To collaborate with, and where appropriate give leadership to, related professional and other bodies in the fields of library and information services, archives, museums and galleries. This function is carried out through:

- — acting as a focal point for library and archive bodies in Wales
- — working with bodies in Wales, in Britain and beyond to pursue co-operative initiatives and partnerships, and advance professional practice

The Library underpins the performance of these five core functions through the following 'supporting functions':

- — management and development of its human resources
- — budgeting, control and accountability of its financial resources, and income generation
- — maintenance and development of the Library's information and communication technology infrastructure
- — maintenance and development of the Library's building and its facilities
- — continuing investigation, monitoring and analysis of user needs

Many of the Key Objectives below belong to the two major development initiatives of the Library: the Digital Library Initiative and the Open Library Initiative. These are priorities for increased funding

Browsing subject terms

For each collection with item-level bibliographic records, a browsable alphabetical list of all formal subject headings has been compiled. These subject headings typically include names of people and places, terms describing the genre and format of the original item, and topical descriptors.

Searching full text

For text collections, users can search the full text of documents. INQUERY is used for indexing and retrieval and the ranked list of hits is subdivided in the same way as for bibliographic searches. Each title in the result list acts as a link to an HTML presentation of the corresponding document.

Full-text search is the primary access tool for Life Histories gathered during the Federal Writers' Project, a project of the Works Progress Administration (WPA) in the 1930s, since there are no individual bibliographic records. For text collections with bibliographic records or SGML versions of the documents, there are corresponding links from the HTML version of the full text.

Limitations

The computer offers rapid access to an array of resources, but its screen is less convenient than a large table for studying images and than a book for skimming through indexes and pages of text to determine its relevance. The images the Library has disseminated to date have been sized for display on today's computer screens, usually between 500 and 1200 pixels wide.

For photographs and page images, these "reference" images are satisfactory for many uses, although many researchers and publishers will still want to see the original or take advantage of a high- resolution version at the cost of time to download (not currently supported).

However, if maps and large posters are scaled to fit on a screen, too much detail may be lost for all but the most cursory scanning. The Library hopes that other organizations will develop approaches allowing users to zoom in on selected areas with progressively higher resolution. A promising line of research is the application of wavelet transformations to a browsing model for large images at the Alexandria Project at the University of California, Santa Barbara.

Visitors to the Prints and Photographs reading room can explore image collections by skimming quickly through a folder full of similar images. They can pick out those that catch their eye and lay them out on the table. This is particularly valuable for comparing similar images. One approach to providing equivalent functionality is to display many thumbnail images in a grid.

Although an increasing volume of primary textual materials is available online, there is no consensus on how best to present long documents in a way that supports convenient use. The challenge is to support rapid navigation without losing the sense of context provided by a physical book. Most of the books, papers, and pamphlets in the historical collections have been coded in SGML with embedded links to images of the original pages, illustrations, and tables.

The SGML representation (using a document type definition based on the guidelines of the Text-Encoding Initiative) captures features of documents that provide great potential for both convenient presentation and effective searching, but the potential has not yet been fully exploited. American Memory resources must also be accessible to the widest possible audience, and convenient for use in the classroom.

Today, users of MS Windows who are comfortable with the technology can download a free SGML viewer. This free viewer can present a structured table of contents derived from chapter and section headings. Headings act as direct links to corresponding sections of a document. However, the internal search feature of Panorama Free does not take advantage of the structural information encoded in the SGML format.

The book-length works are somewhat clumsy in their HTML form, but this format does allow any user to download or print the text of the entire work reasonably conveniently -- absolutely necessary for use in schools where equipment for access to the Internet is, at best, a scarce resource. The problem of networked access to book-length works is not unique to the Library of Congress.

As an increasing array of documents are available in SGML format, the Library hopes that a more powerful SGML viewer will become widely available or that WWW browsers will be extended to handle SGML. Meanwhile, the Library will be experimenting with other options, such as Adobe's PDF format, the use of frames within HTML, and the development of viewer modules using the Java programming language.

Meanwhile, a variant approach using HTML will be taken for the Country Studies/Area Handbook Program. These studies have been prepared by the Library's Federal Research Division for over 60 countries around the world. Currently, contractors deliver files to the Library on CD-ROM. As for many other imaging projects, the highest-resolution images have been stored offline to save disk space.

Compressed files for on-line delivery of images are loaded onto disk drives attached to the WWW servers. The CD-ROMs serve as an archival copy for the uncompressed versions. As the size of the archive grows, these CD-ROMS require formal inventory control.

Ensuring the continuing usability of the archival files is also important since the accumulated effort involved in their creation will be valued in millions of dollars. The need to manage vast archives of computer files is not unique to libraries; solutions are appearing from the commercial sector.

To address the estimated need for 50 terabytes of managed storage by the year 2000, the Library will be installing a commercial hierarchical storage management system over the coming months. Storage management software will transfer files automatically between high- performance disk drives and less expensive storage media from which retrieval will take longer.

Typically, the location is based on time since last access, but more complex rules can be enforced. Since the highest resolution images will be accessed only occasionally, they will usually be resident on the slower medium. The allocation is transparent to applications accessing the files; "stub" files left in the logical file hierarchy point to the physical location of files that have been relegated to another "layer" of storage. For its second layer of storage, the Library has chosen high capacity magnetic tape cartridges under robotic control.

The tape unit has been installed and is already in use for regular backup and restore operations (associated with any computer system). Generation (and periodic regeneration) of archival copies of collections on tape cartridges is also possible for preservation of the digital materials.

The hierarchical storage management software will be installed on individual computers over the next few months, in conjunction with system upgrades. Direct access to the archival digital reproductions will also support other functions. Online access to high-resolution images could facilitate digital reproduction as an alternative to the Library's current service that provides users with photographic copies of graphical materials for a fee.

The expectations of users in the Prints and Photographs reading room have already been raised. After identifying the images they need in a few minutes, some users express dismay that photoduplication requests may take several weeks. In US, the National Digital Library Program also plans to disseminate materials in other forms, perhaps supplying source files to companies or organizations that will assemble subsets and tailor them to particular markets.

Providing source files will be easier and more reliable with on-line access than by manual sorting through CD-ROMs and copying large numbers of files. The hierarchical storage management system will address issues related to physical storage of files, but there is also a need for more formal management of the collections and objects themselves than can be provided by the Unix file system.

The organization of collections is currently through the relationships between naming schemes and Unix directories. There is no automatic enforcement of naming conventions. If a digital item has several component files, there is no way to treat that item reliably as a unit. One of the custodial divisions keeps track of directories on charts posted on an office wall.

While the number of collections is small, this approach is feasible, but the Library recognizes that it will need enforcement of unique names, more automatic adjustment of all pointers when files are relocated, and a structure that recognizes key relationships between items and their component files, and between collections and the items they comprise. Since no adequate system has emerged from the commercial marketplace to support effective access to multimedia resources of this complexity, the Library has begun work with collaborators to design and build two prototype "repositories" as experiments in this area.

A preliminary set of attributes or fields has been developed for use in both repositories, a set that is limited to metadata relating to the "physical" digital object, and its creation, modification, retrieval, and display. This "physical" metadata includes the logical name, access privileges, the digital format, key structural relationships, and administrative data such as the unit or person responsible for the item, date created, and number of times accessed.

In US, one prototype repository is under development with the Corporation for National Research Initiatives (CNRI). This repository will also be used for the CORDS project in the Copyright Office. The repository provides a secure environment from which the items in the collections and their metadata can be accessed together or separately. This permits negotiation over access terms and conditions for a digital object to be an integral part of every access, access which must be possible through many protocols, such as HTTP and Z39.50.

The repository will allow for an essentially limitless range of formats and for objects from the repository to be transformed before dissemination into a format which may be very different from the stored form. The implementation of the repository uses modern concepts of distributed objects. For interaction with other systems, it uses CORBA (the Common Object Request Broker Architecture) implemented through Xerox's Inter- Language Unification (ILU) system.

IBM is currently developing a program that will load the images already scanned into the VisualInfo repository. This program will integrate data from three sources: database records, created at scan time, that contain logical names and values for certain physical metadata fields; information recorded automatically in the TIFF header of image files; and the image data files. The development of these prototype repositories is at an early stage, and design details will probably change in the light of practical experience, and as the strengths of each approach become clear.

The prototype stage is important in testing the Library's model which separates the storage of primary descriptive information (bibliographic records and finding aids, which may describe intellectual items of which only one manifestation is digital) from the digital representation of the items described. The Library's model allows for multiple repositories, but all repositories must coordinate with independent external indexes and support standard external access protocols.

One important aspect of tests is to explore how well the different approaches scale, as the number of objects grows and additional formats must be supported. The repositories will also support experiments in the handling of access restrictions. Restrictions may be necessary for some items not only to comply with copyright law, but also because of conditions set by donors and the general legal concerns of privacy and publicity.

References

Bishop, Ann Peterson. "Document Structure and Digital Libraries: How Researchers Mobilize Information in Journal Articles." *Information Processing and Management* 35 May 1999.

Borgman, Christine L. *From Gutenberg to the Global Information Infrastructure: Access to Information in the Networked World.* Cambridge, MA: The MIT Press, 2000.

Kessler, Jack, *Internet digital libraries: the international dimension,* Boston and London: Artech House.

Rowlands, Ian, and David Bawden. "Building the Digital Library on Solid Research Foundations." *Aslib Proceedings* 51, September 1999.

4

Information Architecture

The information architects focus on the design of organisation, indexing, labeling, and navigation systems to support browsing and searching throughout the web site.

The designers are responsible for the graphic design and page layout that defines the graphic identity or look of the web site. They strive to create and implement a design philosophy that balances form and function.

Editors focus on the use of language throughout the web site. Their tasks may involve proofreading and editing copy, massaging content to ensure a common voice for the site, and creating new copy.

The technical designers and programmers are responsible for server administration and the development or integration of site production tools and web site applications. They advise the other teams regarding technology-related opportunities and limitations.

The project manager keeps the project on schedule and within budget. He or she facilitates communication between the other teams and the clients or internal stakeholders. The success of a web site design and production project depends on successful communication and collaboration between these specialised team members. A linear, black-box, throw-it-over-the-wall methodology just won't work. Everyone needs to understand the goals, perspectives, and approaches of the other members of the team. For example, while the marketing specialist may lead the audience analysis process, he or she needs to anticipate the types of questions about the audience that the specialists will have.

Otherwise, each will need to start from scratch in learning about that audience, wasting substantial time and resources. For the information architect, communication is a special challenge because of the intangible nature of the work. Anyone who has played Pictionary knows that it is much harder to draw an abstract concept such as science than a physical object such as moon. As an information architect, you face the daunting challenge of helping others visualise such abstract concepts as a metaphor-based architecture and indexing systems.

The information architect has to identify both the goals of the site and the content that it will be built on. This means getting the people who drive the business, whether bosses or clients, to articulate their vision of the site and who its users are. Once you've collected the data and developed a plan, you need to present your ideas for an information architecture and move the group toward consensus. All in all, this significantly burdens the architect to communicate effectively.

Design and production storm ahead without any unifying principle to guide the site's development. A web site essentially can be anything you want it to be and could cost millions of dollars, take years to complete, and cost thousands of lives to develop. To avoid such overkill, it will need to be defined somehow: it will need a definition. That's the main job of the information architect, who:

— Clarifies the mission and vision for the site, balancing the needs of its sponsoring organisation and the needs of its audiences.
— Determines what content and functionality the site will contain.
— Specifies how users will find information in the site by defining its organisation, navigation, labeling, and searching systems.
— Maps out how the site will accommodate change and growth over time.

Although these sound obvious, information architecture is really about what's not obvious. Users don't notice the information architecture of a site unless it isn't working.

Elements of Information Architecture

The elements of information architecture—navigation systems, labeling systems, organisation systems, indexing, searching methods, metaphors—are the glue that holds together a web site and allows it to evolve smoothly. To a novice, this terminology is not very clear. These elements are extremely difficult to measure, and therefore even harder to compare. You really have to spend time using a site and get a feel for it before you can confidently talk about a site's information architecture.

How many of the likes and dislikes are not related to technical issues, copy editing, or graphic design? Remaining issues are probably tied to information architecture. Although perhaps indirectly, a poorly planned information architecture will adversely affect those other areas. Well-planned information architectures greatly benefit both consumers and producers. Accessing a site for the first time, consumers can quickly understand it effortlessly. They can quickly find the information they need, thereby reducing the time wasted on both finding information and not finding information.

Producers of web sites and intranets benefit because they know where and how to place new content without disrupting the existing content and site structure. Perhaps most importantly, producers can use an information architecture to greatly minimise the politics that come to the fore during the development of a web site.

Perspectives

Consumers, or users as we more commonly refer to them, want to find information quickly and easily. Contrary to what you might conclude from observing the architectures of many large, corporate web sites, users do not like to get lost in chaotic hypertextual webs. Poor information architectures make busy users confused, frustrated, and angry. Because different users have varying needs, it's important to support multiple modes of finding information. Some users know exactly what they're looking for. They know what it's called, and they know it exists. They just want to find it and leave, as quickly and painlessly as possible. This is called known-item searching.

Other users do not know what they're looking for. They come to the site with a vague idea of the information they need. They may not know the right labels to describe what they want or even whether it exists. As they casually explore your site, they may learn about products or services that they'd never even considered. Iteratively, through serendipity and associative learning, they may leave your site with knowledge that they hadn't known they needed. These modes of finding information are not mutually exclusive.

In a well-designed system, many users will switch between known-item searching and casual browsing as they explore the site. If you care about the consumer, make sure your architecture supports both modes. While attractive graphics and reliable technologies are essential to user satisfaction, they are not enough.

Since few organisations are completely altruistic, they usually want to know the return on their investment for information architecture design. In other words, what's in it for them? First, a disclaimer. Buying information architecture services is not like investing in a mutual fund. You can't calculate hard and fast numbers to show the exact benefit of your investment over time.

Nonetheless, you can demonstrate the value to the organisation through less scientific means. Depending upon the goals and nature of your site, you may even be able to defend your investment with some not-so-hard numbers. Consideration of value to the producer takes us back to the consumer. If you're producing an external web site, this involves actual and prospective customers, investors, employees, and business partners, not to mention the media and senior executives within your organisation.

Do you really want to frustrate any of these people? What is the value of quickly and easily helping them find the information they need? If you're producing an intranet, the employees of your organisation are the consumers. What is the cost of their time spent to find the information they need? What is the cost when employees don't find the information they need? Finally, we need to consider the actual costs of designing and implementing the architecture. A well-designed, diplomatic architecture can prevent costly political battles that can stop a project in its tracks.

The cost of time spent by high-level executives arguing over which department's information belongs on the main page can skyrocket if you're not careful. A well-designed scaleable architecture can prevent doing it all over a year later. Far too many architectures are crushed under the weight of their own content. Redesign of the information architecture impacts all other aspects of the web site, from graphical navigation bars to the content itself, and it can be a very costly adventure. Let's illustrate with a real-life example. Recently, we met with about ten members of a large client's web site development team.

Because we were in the early stages of the planning process, we had just reviewed the client's likes and dislikes, and were determining their web design philosophy. Now we were ready to begin defining what their site would be. In discussing the site's likely users, around seven or eight audiences were suggested. Five or six major goals of the site were determined. Finally, we talked about the main areas of content and functionality that the site would include. This wish list included thirty or forty items.

Many site designers would happily dive in head first. Their work would be a site headed by a main page that included thirty or forty items and links, tried to please seven or eight different audiences, and ultimately failed at achieving its five or six goals. This is what happens when the big picture of a site is ignored.

Consider what happens to a site with a single designer who sees only the trees, not the forest. Now add an order of magnitude: large organisations, rife with complex goals and messy politics, often have sites designed by ten individuals with their own vision of the site, their own deadlines and goals to meet, and their own politics to play. Is it any wonder that these sites often work so poorly, even when huge investments of time and money are made in them?

Succinctly, information architecture is about understanding and conveying the big picture of a web site. Some even expressed concern that we shouldn't even bother wading into this swamp and instead should start doing something, like gathering together the site's content, pushing forward on the graphic design, and so on.

Having exposed so much frustration, we were obviously on the right track. Because these thorny and confounding issues of information architecture must be resolved during the design process, before the site is built. If we were to avoid answering these questions and the site's development was to proceed, these issues wouldn't go away. Instead, the burden would be on the site's users to understand how to use and find information in a confusing, poorly-designed web site.

Of course, we know that a frustrated user will click and leave with a bad memory of the site, likely to never return. Without a clear information architecture, the site's maintainers wouldn't know where to locate the new information that the site would eventually include; they'd likely begin to quarrel over whose content was more important and deserved visibility on the main page, and so on.

The information architect of a large, complex web site should be two things: someone who can think as an outsider and be sensitive to the needs of the site's users, and at the same time is enough of an insider to understand the site's sponsoring organisation, its mission, goals, content, audiences, and inner workings.

In terms of disciplinary background, the information architect should combine the generalist's ability to understand the perspectives of other disciplines with specialised skills in visualising, organising, and labeling information. As it's very difficult for someone to retain all of these characteristics, you'll have to make some compromises, but it's important to consider them as you search for that elusive information architect.

Because information architecture is largely about the big picture view of the organisation, its goals, and its politics, a logical choice for the architect role is a senior person who knows the organisation as a whole and who isn't involved exclusively within the activities of one department. A senior person can often think like an outsider even though being on the inside, and has enough clout to enlist other departments' resources when necessary. One drawback to choosing a senior level manager is that he or she may have so many other responsibilities that the work gets delegated out to staff, thereby negating the original goal of using a single, organisationally savvy person.

Another approach is bringing in a true outsider: a new hire or a consultant. The great thing about outsiders is that they can get away with asking naive questions considered suicidal by insiders, such as "Why does your organisation have two completely separate order fulfillment departments? The web site will confuse users if they can order products in two different, unresolved ways. Are there any politics going on here that we can get past to improve the site's design?"

The drawbacks of bringing in a true outsider are that they can be expensive and can lack sufficient knowledge of the organisation to do the job, thus delaying the project's progress. As many organisations can't afford to outsource information architecture services or move a head honcho into the role, the responsibility often goes to an insider who is not a senior level manager. Sometimes this is ideal; it's the people in the trenches who often know the most about an organisation's processes, and how to get things done within that organisation.

The problem with a lower-level person is that his or her knowledge may be too specific. Additionally, such a person often lacks the political base required to mobilise cooperation from others in the organisation. A possible solution is to make information architecture this person's only job responsibility. This could allow him or her to step away from original duties and focus on the broader needs of the organisation and the users of its site.

Since information architecture is a relatively new field, you can't just post a job description and expect a flock of interested, competent, and experienced candidates to show up on your doorstep. Instead, you'll need to actively recruit, outsource, or perhaps become the information architect for your site. If you are looking for someone else, you might consider the disciplines listed below as potential sources. If you're on your own, it might be worthwhile to learn a little bit about each of these disciplines yourself. Or, if possible, find someone knowledgeable about them to work with you and complement your own expertise. In either case, remember that no single discipline is the obvious source for information architects; each presents its own strengths and weaknesses.

Graphic Design

Most people who have written about and practice information architecture are graphic designers by training. This is not surprising; as mentioned, graphic design is much more than creating pretty pictures. It is geared more toward creating relationships between visual elements and determining their effective integration as a whole. On a page, printed or HTML, these elements include white space and typography as well as images. So graphic designers traditionally have been focused on the architectures of individual pages of information, which can be a weakness when building a web site.

Information and Library Science

Backgrounds in information science and librarianship have proven very useful in dealing with the relationships between pages and other elements that make up a whole site. By definition, librarians deal with organisation of and access to information within information systems and are trained to work with searching, browsing, and indexing technologies. Forward-looking librarians see that their expertise applies in new arenas unrelated to providing access to printed information stored in traditional libraries. So librarianship is an important discipline to turn to for information architecture expertise. Just remember that librarians are also prone to get lost in details, a weakness that can distract from determining the big picture of a web site.

Journalism

Journalists, like librarians, are trained at organising information, but in a different setting. If your web site delivers highly dynamic information, like a news wire or a push technology-based service, someone with a journalism background might have a great sense of how to best organise and deliver this information. Because of their writing experience, journalists are also good candidates for architecting sites that will have high levels of edited content. Occasionally, journalists who move into information architecture find themselves intellectually constrained by their experience in organising information for print and other traditional media.

Usability engineers are experts at testing and evaluating how systems work. For information systems, they measure such criteria as how long it takes users to learn how to use a system, how long it takes them to find information in a system, and how many errors they make along the way. Of all the disciplines we list, usability engineering is probably the most scientific in its view of users and the quality of their experiences with information systems. Keep in mind that usability engineers concentrate on measuring a system's performance, not in designing or redesigning a system.

Marketing specialists are expert at understanding audiences and communicating a message effectively to different audiences. This skill is especially valuable not only in designing externally oriented web sites, but also for intranets, which often have multiple audiences with very different needs. Marketing expertise can ensure that the message is presented in a user-oriented manner and not buried in organisational jargon. If your site is geared especially toward selling products and building brand-awareness, someone from your organisation's marketing department might do the trick.

The drawback to marketing-based approaches is the danger that they are more geared toward selling rather than helping users, and so may not be appropriate for certain types of web sites and audiences.

Computer Programs

Programmers and computer specialists bring an important skill to information architecture, especially to architecting information from the bottom up. For example, often a site requires a database to serve the content; this minimises maintenance and data integrity problems. Computer scientists have the best skills for modeling content for inclusion in a database.

However, unlike librarians or usability engineers, computer scientists aren't necessarily trained in user-centered approaches to designing information systems.

So, an information architect might come from one of many different disciplines. He or she will certainly need to know at least a little about every type of expertise involved in the entire web site design and development process, because his or her work will affect every part of the process. The architect also needs to be the keeper of the big picture as this process unfolds and the details of design and production become the main focus of all involved. Perhaps the most important quality in an information architect is the ability to think outside the lines, to come up with new approaches to designing information systems.

The Web provides many opportunities to do things in ways that haven't been done before. Many sites are pushing the envelope of design, architecture, and technology. While it's tempting to create a site that mirrors the same old things that an organisation already does in other media, this approach could severely damage your site's chances for success. If a site doesn't rise to the occasion for its users, it won't fare well in head-to-head competition with other sites. This medium is more competitive than any other.

Whomever you do use as an information architect, remember: everyone is biased by their disciplinary perspective. If possible, try to ensure that other disciplines are represented on your web site development team to guarantee a balanced architecture. Also, no matter your perspective, the information architect ideally should be solely responsible for the site's architecture, and not for its other aspects. It can be distracting to be responsible for other, more tangible aspects of the site, such as its graphic identity.

In this case, the site's architecture can easily, if unintentionally, get relegated to secondary status because the architect is concentrating, naturally, on the tangible stuff. However, with smaller organisations, limited resources mean that all or most aspects of the site's development--design, editorial, technical, architecture, and production--are likely to be the responsibility of one person. Our best advice for someone in this position is obvious but worth mentioning: 1) find a group of friends and colleagues who are willing to be a sounding board for your ideas, and 2) practice a sort of controlled schizophrenia in which you make a point to look at your site from different perspectives; first from the architect's, then from the designer's, and so on.

Collaboration and Communication

The information architect must communicate effectively with the web site development team. This is challenging, since an information architecture is highly abstract and intangible. Besides communicating the architecture verbally, documents must be created in ways that can be understood by the rest of the team regardless of their own disciplinary backgrounds.

In the early days of the Web, web sites were often designed, built, and managed by a single individual through sheer force of will. This webmaster was responsible for assembling and organising the content, designing the graphics. The only prerequisites were a familiarity with HTML and a willingness to learn on the job. People with an amasing diversity of backgrounds suddenly became webmasters overnight, and soon found themselves torn in many directions at once. One minute they were information architects, then graphic designers, then editors, then programmers.

Then companies began to demand more of their sites and, consequently, of their webmasters. Simple home pages quickly evolved into complex web sites. People wanted more content, better organisation, greater function, and prettier graphics. Increasingly, webmasters and their employers began to realise that the successful design and production of complex web sites requires an interdisciplinary team approach. An individual cannot be an expert in all facets of the process. Rather, a team of individuals with complementary areas of expertise must work together.

The composition of this team will vary, depending upon the needs of a particular project, available budget, and the availability of expertise. However, most projects will require expertise in marketing, information architecture, graphic design, writing and editing, programming, and project management.

The marketing team focuses on the intended purposes and audiences for the web site. They must understand what will bring the right people to the web site and what will bring them back again.

Technology in Public Libraries

The biggest changes in public libraries over the coming years will arise from the development of information technology (IT). The introduction of information and communication technologies presents a challenge and opportunity for the United Kingdom as great as the industrial revolution in the nineteenth century.

However, many citizens and communities will need help to meet the new demands of the emerging information society. Individual access to information and communications networks will be impeded by cost. And even as prices fall and ownership of suitable systems spreads, the intellectual challenge of obtaining access will remain, requiring skills development and support in information-handling for all citizens.

Public libraries are the ideal vehicle to provide this access and support, and to foster the spread of vital new technological skills among the population. Well over half the population already use libraries, and librarians have an unrivalled reputation for helping the knowledge-seeker. Tomorrow's new library will be a key agent in enabling people of all ages to prosper in the information society - helping them acquire new skills for employment, use information creatively, and improve the quality of their lives.

Libraries will play a central role in the University for Industry, in lifelong learning projects, and in support of any individual who undertakes self-development. The library is an enormously powerful agent for change: accountable to and trusted by people, and integral to education, industry, government and the community.

A UK-wide information network made available through libraries and implemented on the basis of a high-specification central core could do more to broaden and encourage the spread of information and communication technology skills among the population - especially the young - than any other measure the government could introduce. These developments will bring benefits - including export opportunities - throughout the UK economy, and not least for its software and graphics industries.

Renewed and reinvigorated by technology investment, libraries will become very different places. They will retain their spaces for books, study, exhibitions and events, but they will gain new learning spaces - interactive spaces - new uses and new users. The rapid spread of high-performance communications will mean that even the most remote rural library will offer access to the same facilities as a large urban library, providing a means to draw in those people who, through geography, are furthest removed from the opportunities offered by the Information Age.

Librarians will add new skills to their current capabilities. They will help people overcome their anxieties about the new world of networked and digitised information, and assist them to navigate through it. This development of an information society and the introduction of the UK Public Library Network - the people's network - will require the library service itself to change.

The UK Public Library Network will have enormous potential to deliver resources for information and learning to citizens across the whole country, through 4,200 static library sites and other library outlets. Access to the network will also allow every citizen to communicate interactively between libraries, with museums, galleries and the media, with local and national government, with public services, and with agencies in the voluntary and private sectors.

Moreover, there will also be the capability for communication within and between communities, whether they be local or global, founded on geography or on a common purpose. Public libraries are already used by 58 per cent of the population. They are a first stop for information, they are widely used by children and young people as an adjunct to formal learning, and their reputation for supporting the knowledge-seeker is unparalleled.

Their unique combination of resources, services and personal support attracts some 1.3 million visitors every working day, and 10 million users visit frequently - at least once a fortnight. Library staff respond to over 50 million enquiries each year, on a universal range of topics. In the information society, making information and communication networks accessible to every citizen will be vital to generate the energy for success. In exploiting new technologies through the networked library, priority must be given to:

a. enhancing education and lifelong learning opportunities for children and adults;

b. supporting training, employment and business, to foster economic prosperity;

c. nurturing social cohesion through fostering a politically and culturally informed society.

The new and growing range of resources and facilities which networking can deliver, combined with the existing assets of the public library system, will form the core of a powerhouse of knowledge, enabling the smallest and most isolated local library to offer the same range, depth and quality of information as a large centra central library, providing equal access to the global and the local.

The principal strands of content and services which will pervade the networked public library are:

a. education and lifelong learning;

b. citizens information and facilities for participation in society;

c. business and the economy, training and employment;

d. community history and community identity;

e. the National Digital Library.

Public libraries complement formal education provision by providing a resource base and a platform for people of all ages to participate in lifelong learning. They will therefore form an integral part of the National Grid for Learning and the Unversity for Industry, and implementation of the network should consider this a priority. Helping young people learn how to is an essential function of the public library.

Support for children and young people in acquiring basic skills, building their personal knowledge-base, and developing competence in information searching and analysis will complement the formal learning in their place of study. Rich multimedia resources provided after school, in a safe, culturally creative environment, will help overcome the inequality of opportunity experienced by those who do not have access to new technology at home.

Several studies have indicated that children can benefit both educationally and socially from having well-managed access to various forms of information and communication technology (ICT) from an early age. The early introduction to independent learning in the library will promote a more rounded education, while also imparting the skills needed to learn independently in later years.

Knowledge is power - and universal access to information is a hallmark of freedom in a democracy but knowledge is also discovery, excitement, personal growth and self-confidence. The use of existing services demonstrates that there is no limit to the type of information which people seek every day in libraries.

Digital communications in the information society will bring new resources in unprecedented quantity, making available the equivalent of millions of pages of words and pictures. The library as an entry point to the information superhighway will bring unprecedented opportunities to learn for leisure, to find out for fun, and to experience the personal fulfilment of discovery.

Through the networked public library, existing library resources will be newly opened up to more people. The catalogues of public library collections currently accessible only locally will be linked to create a UK-wide library system. This rich collective resource will be available at any local library.

Eventually, catalogues will be enhanced with requesting systems so that remote users can locate and order the items they need. Cross-sectoral access (public/FE/HE) will introduce the flexibility of access to resources inherent in the concepts of open and distance learning.

Such a wealth of resources will make digital discovery an awesome and exciting experience, but many people will need the support of a trusted and accountable intermediary - not only in accessing but also in interpreting and evaluating what is available. With library staff providing this support, the unique role of the library as 'the people's university' will be immeasurably enhanced.

The accessibility of public libraries, enhanced by networking technologies, will ensure that people with mobility problems will find it easy to exploit the new opportunities. At the same time, as systems develop on the back of current research, services will be adapted for use by people with impaired sight or hearing. People with disabilities have the same desires to find out and learn as others: the information society must not be one in which they experience exclusion. In this area, content to be delivered will include:

a. multimedia learning resources geared to national curricula;

b. self-training packages for core skills;

c. networked encyclopaedic databases;

d. specialist resources on topics for leisure and learning;

e. access to World Wide Web sites;

f. networked electronic journals;

g. digitised collections of images, film, and video and sound recordings;

h. all UK public library catalogues;

i. the digital collections of major libraries.

Services in support of educational and lifelong learning will include:

a. access to the National Grid for Learning;
b. support in accessing and searching global resources;
c. guidance on the reliability of databases;
d. access to and participation in special-interest Internet communities;
e. access to specialist libraries and collections, and to virtual visits to exhibitions;
f. information and guidance on educational and learning opportunities;
g. interactive communications with educational institutions;
h. access to local education authorities and information on finance for learning, grants, awards, etc.;
i. online application facilities;
j. Ofsted reports on schools and colleges;
k. access to the library network and networked resources from home, school or the workplace.

Network Communication

The UK Public Library Network will also be a gateway for citizen communications - an opening to the networked society which will promote a healthy democracy and social cohesion. In recent times disillusion with political, legal and social institutions has generated an atmosphere of cynicism and alienation.

People - particularly young people - have distanced themselves from a system which they see as irrelevant to their circumstances. A public library network of access points, open to every citizen, for the delivery of information on government and government services - both local and UK-wide - and, especially, for enabling interactive communications with government and others, will help bring a sense of belonging and renew the potential for participation in society.

Such a network will stimulate the production of digital information and interactive services for citizens which has already been explored by some government departments and local authorities. Many public agencies now have Internet Web sites; these will be further developed to meet the increased expectation of citizens using the library network.

Easier two-way transfer of information and documentation between people and providers will also allow faster and more efficient routine transactions with government and public services, leaving more time for citizen and public servant to interact face to face on individual issues of greater sensitivity.

A healthy society must also communicate with itself, and the UK Public Library Network will not only provide access to the centres of administration but will enable people to interact with all manner of voluntary organisations and interest groups. Individuals will be able to become better informed and to promote their views in the interests of wider community development.

When citizens are openly and freely in communication with government, democracy can be said to have 'grown up'. Those groups generally regarded as 'minorities' are, together, the majority; ensuring improved access for those with a minority or special interest will also enhance the quality of life for the whole of society. In this area, content to be delivered will include:

a. information on local authority services - education, health, welfare and social services, planning and leisure, for example;
b. information on local authority performance and budget deployment;
c. information on local and regional development;
d. online government publications and reports of proceedings;
e. information on European government, legislation and citizens' rights;
f. information on interest/action/pressure groups and voluntary organisations;
g. legislation and legal publications;
h. party-political information, policy and contacts.

The successful business already exploits information as an organisational resource. However, the majority of businesses in the UK are small and medium-sized enterprises - around 73 per cent of companies employ fewer than ten people - and such companies, and the 3 million self-employed, do not have the capacity to employ information specialists or to acquire expensive collections of data to inform their marketing and development activities.

Public libraries - especially the major city libraries - have variously developed enormous print-based resources to support business; the UK

Public Library Network will allow still larger amounts of information to be available to even the smallest and most remote local library through access to remote databases on trade and commerce. The technology will allow greater cooperation to inform and support the UK's industrial, commercial and financial enterprise.

The library has always been a resource for learning, and has a specially important role to play in learning in order to update or acquire job skills. A recent DTI study revealed that 52 per cent of UK companies think their employees have insufficient training in ICT, but at the same time 35 per cent of UK companies give no ICT training at all. As part of a return-to-work plan, skills development or reskilling for a different job, the UK Public Library Network will provide information and learning resources for independent study in a supported environment.

Citizens are also consumers, and thus the ultimate generators of national wealth. The consumer needs ready and reliable access to information on products, services and producers, as well as access to legal and commercial information - all of which the UK Public Library Network will provide. The IT for All initiative aims to raise awareness of ICT, provide access, and develop the ICT skills of individual citizens, and specifically adults.

Inherent within the capability of networking technologies is the capacity to reconstitute the visual into the virtual and to deliver it from its custodial home to the widest community in local libraries - and indeed elsewhere. The significant collections in public libraries - photographs, rare books, maps - as well as their sister collections in museums and galleries, will be converted to create online collections which are accessible not only to researchers but to all citizens, supporting cultural awareness and identity.

More imaginatively, multimedia exhibitions - images, narrative, background - which can be visited on-screen in local libraries will give everyone the opportunity for the 'guided tour' as opposed to the 'passive walkabout'. In addition to the value of giving the tax-payer greater direct access to publicly funded collections, such technology will also allow the development of new approaches to the visual arts and their promotion; projected through networks to an international audience, this will create the ultimate marketing tool in promoting the UK's cultural heritage to the peoples of the world. This will foster and support the tourism industry.

In this area, content to be delivered will include:

a. the unique visual and cultural assets of the national libraries;

b. the same in regard to the holdings of other significant libraries and of museums and galleries;
c. the ability to bring together related material from separate collections;
d. virtual visits to exhibitions and special programmes in museums, galleries and centres of culture;
e. transmissions in video of film, theatre and musical productions;
f. digitised collections of archives and record offices;
g. interactive learning resources on arts, culture and the media;
h. 'what's on' information in the arts and heritage.

Services in support of the National Digital Library will include:

a. informed, guided tours of virtual exhibitions;
b. access to supported virtual visits to libraries, records offices, museums and galleries;
c. interactive access to expertise;
d. partnership networks with advice and information specialists within or outside the public library sector.

Public Library Networking

Public libraries have already demonstrated their capacity to guide beginners in using information and communication technologies and to help individuals develop their 'computeracy'. Integral to public library networking will be provision for training/learning in the new technology. At an introductory level this may be provided by library staff, who will encounter the uninitiated on a daily basis, but learning organisations and private companies will be enthusiastic to collaborate with library service providers in developing strategies for public training/learning provision.

As trusted intermediaries, public libraries can span the present and the technological future, ensuring no citizen is left behind, providing a safety net against alienation and social exclusion from technological advance - a route to universal access and opportunity. Networking public libraries will take the UK's public library system through a period of substantial change into the new era of the information society.

During the transition years, and for the foreseeable future in some areas, the demand for books and other non-networked resources will continue; meanwhile a UK-wide lead and financial support will be necessary to generate the range of electronic resources and services which users will expect of their networked local library.

The range of resources and services envisaged will depend on a UK-wide initiative involving unprecedented collaboration, planning and investment, and we recommend that an agency be established to direct and manage the development process.

In UK, the National Digital Library envisaged in the plan will depend on the conversion of special and rare collections into digital format. A major project to identify and prioritise appropriate collections of items will be needed; it should look across all sectors to locate opportunities for partnership with collections in museums, galleries and the national libraries.

A range of services will exist to allow library users to discover both free and commercial resources on the Internet. It is important that all development work proceeds within a common framework of information standards and best practice. The British Library and the Joint Information Systems Committee of the Higher Education Funding Council are investigating the establishment of a National Agency for Resource Discovery to advise the library community in this area.

The public library is an important focal point in the community. There is a feeling that its position has been eroded, that it does not currently present a compelling reason to go there and that it is lagging behind the times rather than moving ahead. Though there is a tremendous amount of goodwill for the public library service among users, there is a significant opportunity to revitalise libraries, stimulate greater usage, broaden the appeal, and make a big difference in people's lives.

New technology and networked libraries are essential if libraries are to gain status in the new world of networked information, knowledge and learning. IT could be a big step forward in encouraging learning - making it seem more fun and motivating, especially to those who currently feel that libraries are not for them.

People really value the quiet learning space provided by the library at the moment, and any development needs to be complementary to this. There were some indications from our research that new uses would add value to the library in an exciting way, but that they would require separate spaces.

The future of librarians will be to enable and facilitate. The overall purpose of the job will be essentially the same, but the skills needed will be different. Librarians will have to think about their role, management skills, delivering services and 'customer care', and this may require a cultural shift in attitude for some. More librarians have to come out from behind the desk and be more outward-going.

The development of IT in public libraries was regarded as essential if libraries are to play an integral role in the new world of networked information, knowledge and learning. Respondents were impressed by what the information technology network could potentially deliver, and a large majority reacted very favourably.

The most enthusiastic were the better informed - aware of the Internet capabilities, and conscious of the fact that, if libraries did not go ahead with public library networking and be part of the global network, they would get left behind. The applications of networking libraries that aroused most enthusiasm tended to concern education and support for lifelong learning, while levelling the playing-field for those unlikely to be able to afford to buy the new technology themselves.

People perceived the library as the natural place for self-learning and training in appropriate skills. The librarian was seen to have an important role to play in helping and coaching people in IT. The presence of the librarian was also necessary to maintain a 'human feel' - especially to encourage those people with 'techno-fear', worried about the 'coldness' and inaccessibility of IT.

Digital Libraries and Lifelong Learning

The library was regarded as a good place to go to pursue self-education with more personal goals, or leisure interests and hobbies. Primarily it provided a quiet study space and reference materials that people could use in their own time - provided the library was open. Longer opening hours were obviously a particular issue here.

The majority thought that IT skills were necessary in a world in which technology-based employment is growing, and some had already taken steps to acquire these skills through public libraries. Others showed enthusiasm at the possibility of acquiring these skills at the library.

The concept of open learning in a library environment was appealing to many, though a minority felt they would personally prefer to have the greater social interaction from attending a course. The greatest barrier for some would initially be that they would need to acquire basic computer skills and to overcome some kind of 'techno-fear' in order to do this. A few more socially minded females recognised the value in encouraging literacy among people disadvantaged by a culture/language who they felt would be less likely to enrol into formal education.

Basic computer skills training was particularly appealing, though it seemed more appropriate for adults than for younger groups, who were already taught such skills at school. The idea of an introductory session to the Internet created strong interest in all groups. Centres where people could improve interpersonal communication skills generated interest and appeal across all groups, and overall the library was felt to be an appropriate place to house them.

The opportunities presented by videoconference links had broad appeal. As well as education-related use, the most relevant general application was as a way to access support groups in health matters. The relevance of the subject-matter would encourage people to use unfamiliar technology and to acquire basic skills. The idea of shared learning experiences through this channel had mixed appeal. The prospect of being able to 'attend' a lecture or consult an expert remotely was very motivating for a few, though the majority of the people we talked to were uninterested in this possibility.

Learning a language was of interest to a few, as was the benefit of being able to have a tutorial if doing a correspondence course. Access to advanced services, such as virtual reality, was especially motivating for younger male audiences, who were very enthusiastic at the prospect and thought it appropriate as long as the ideas were information- or communication-related. It was seen as a way for the library to move ahead and provide a unique service in allowing people to try out and use the latest new technology.

People were passionate about books, about being surrounded by books in peace and quiet, able to browse and find the unexpected - all important library values people do not want to lose. There was a general consensus that initial trial of IT services, and basic instruction, should be free. Access from home was seen as a convenience for the slightly 'better off' who had their own equipment, and as such could be more acceptably charged for.

Digital Reference Services

In the past, reference service has involved on-site service and local telephone support, designed to instruct and assist library users in their research endeavours. Now, digital reference is becoming an important remote service, as ever growing numbers of library users are learning and researching at a distance. McConnel Funding project addressed this trend by piloting a real-time, chat-based reference platform to meet the learning.

The short definition of digital reference is the provision of reference service over the Internet. The term for digital reference has taken many forms: digital, virtual, chat, on-line and real-time, to mention a few of the more popular names. More recently, distributed reference services, captures best the notion that the modern day library, to a great degree, is a web-based learning environment.

The lines between on and off-campus students and courses are blurring as technology is incorporated into all aspects of education. To expand the boundaries of current reference service, from the Library's point of view, is a natural outcome of both our commitment to digital resources and remote access, as well as the University's commitment to distributed learning.

In recent years, the Library has explored various means of providing web based assistance and instruction to our users, and has offered an email (asynchronous) reference service since the fall of 1999. The McConnell project involved the provision of a digital reference service by offering personal assistance in real-time (synchronous) through the use of web based interactive software.

This new chat service is called Ask a Librarian Live. Digital reference differs from traditional reference in two fundamental ways. First, there is a disconnect between the user and the physical space of the library. Second, digital reference creates artifacts of the exchange between librarian and user. That is, the transaction can be recorded in terms of the content of the interaction, the resources used, the time it took, the time of day it took place, the librarian involved, the general location of the user and a number of other quantifiable variables.

On many library Web sites, the user is hard-pressed to identify the staff, whose names, if they're there, are five levels down. The human factor is still important. Although the Library turnstile counts and circulation figures have shot up from last year, many students opt to do much of their research away from the Library or campus. The Library's considerable investment in electronic resources, as well as the growth in size of distance and web-based learning methods, has meant a steady increase in the use of our licensed databases, library catalogue and other resources, from home, office, student residences and the labs.

The culture created by the pervasive use of the Web is one of convenience and speed. Coupled with an increasingly computer savvy student body, our users both welcome and expect services delivered on-line. To address these realities, the Library has developed a number of proactive, innovative and flexible approaches to providing reference services. In addition to email reference, the Library offers online library research tutorials, web-based subject guides, an FAQ page, and a telephone call centre.

The launch of the Library's chat-based reference service, Ask a Librarian Live, gave us the opportunity to revamp our Ask a Librarian page with the help of the Digital Media Projects Office (DMP).

After some deliberation and exploration, the Library decided on acquiring software that provided the highest level of interaction with our users and resources. The buzz in the digital reference world is about providing "high tech with high touch." The software acquired is in fact not considered chat but web call centre software and it differs from chat platforms in a number of ways.

The most significant difference is the ability to co-browse web pages while conversing (chatting) via text with the user. The librarians considered this feature important because it gives us the ability to assist users "inside" licensed databases. The software acquired is called VRD - Virtual Reference Desk, and is a product of the company Library Systems and Services Incorporated (LSSI).

LSSI is unusual in the web based call centre business in that it is a company made up of librarians and has supported the library community for the past 20 years in the provision of automation based products and services. While web call centre software is a relatively new activity for the company, the product has become tremendously popular in the library community.

LSSI's VRD is the software of choice for many of the synchronous digital reference services currently being offered in North America. Of the ten digital reference initiatives in Canadian universities, six are running on LSSI. Ryerson was the first Canadian library to sign with LSSI. The software features are as follows:

— Private, secure communications between users and librarians
— Complete session transcripts, including URLs, emailed to both the users and the librarians at the end of each session
— Queuing features which let users and librarians know how many people are waiting to be helped
— "Push" technologies allowing librarians to send Web pages directly to users' desktops.
— Co-browsing capabilities allowing users and librarians to follow each other's progress through a database or Web site
— "Meeting room" features allowing for group instruction
— Customization of the software
— Statistical reports
— Secure protected access to session transcripts and patron information
— Operate on the library's current hardware configurations and require no special technologies on the users' end.
— On-site training for librarians

LSSI licenses the use of the VRD software on a per "seat" basis, at a cost of $6,000 U.S. per year for one seat. The Library acquired one seat which means that one librarian at a time is able to service the Ask a Librarian Live "desk." The Library acquired the VRD software in the spring of 2001. The librarians were trained in May on site by an LSSI trainer. Testing and service considerations were worked through during the summer.

An official launch date in September was moved back to October when software and network problems surfaced. Problems continued into October and had stabilized by the end of the month. What became clear is that moving to the Interact version of the software - which would allow the co-browsing of licensed databases - would have to be placed on hold for what turned out to be the duration of the pilot.

These issues changed both the time frame and the nature of the pilot project. The initial pilot project was to span the fall term. The McConnell working group decided to extend the pilot until the end of March in order to collect enough data to make a useful evaluation. The software was relatively stable for the duration of the pilot and the evaluation and assessment were done in the spring of 2002, rather than the winter.

Because of the focus on software and reference service provision, making significant inroads into web-based classroom environments, while an expressed goal of the McConnell proposal, was postponed until the fall of 2002. The software has a "meeting room" capability which was hoped could provide library group instruction on-line. This will be tested in the fall of 2002 with the commitment of one professor for a course on research methods in the School of Disability Studies.

Hours were based on current availability of staff and resources and not on what we considered were the ideal hours for our digital reference service. Privacy is an important consideration in a service of this type. A policy outlining what sort of information is collected and how it may be used, etc. was devised. The software notifies the librarian with a single bell sound when a patron has signed on. Besides the evening librarian, whose hours were three hours for each day the service was open, the rest of the librarians worked approximately 2 hours per week in addition to their regular reference desk hours.

The interesting training tension in a new area like digital reference are the dual concerns of technical training on the one hand and quality concerns regarding the provision of reference service on the other. A librarian who has effectively worked in reference for 10 years, will automatically be able to put all the same skills and knowledge to good use in the digital reference arena. While the training provided by LSSI covered this ground, to some extent, in their manual and in the session provided, over the next year as we move into our second year of service, more attention will be paid to process and quality outcome measures.

References

Blandford, Ann, and George Buchanan. "Usability of Digital Libraries: A Source of Creative Tensions with Technical Developments." *TCDL Bulletin*, Summer 2003.

Doty, Philip, "Policy Analysis and Networked Information: 'There Are Eight Million Stories'..." in *Evaluating Networked Information Services : Techniques, Policy, and Issues.* Medford, N.J.:Information Today, 2001.

Liu, Ying, and Anita S. Coleman. "Communicating Digital Library Services to Scientific Communities." *LIBRES* 14, no. 1, 2004.

Michelle Q. Wang Baldonado and Steve B. Cousins. Addressing heterogeneity in the networked information environment. *New Review of Information Networking*, 2:83-102, 1996

Saracevic, Tefko. "Digital Library Evaluation: Toward an Evolution of Concepts." *Library Trends* 49, Fall 2000.

5

Managing Access to Digital Library

Managing access to on-line information is a broad problem, which occurs in a wide range of different applications. Managers of on-line information wish to implement policies about who can access the information, under what terms and conditions.

Libraries often need to restrict access to parts of their collections for various reasons, including restrictions imposed by donors, concerns about privacy or obscenity, licensing arrangements, and other agreements with copyright owners.

Independent of terminology, it is important to view access management from the perspective of the manager of the information. In a digital library, information is obtained from a variety of sources, for example by license from a publisher, or by a donation with restrictions on use. In drawing up its access management policies, the library will reflect agreements with publishers and other third parties. There may also be relevant laws that must be embodied in the policies. However, with digital materials as with physical items, the library is responsible for managing access to its collections.

Cost of Access to Information

Libraries are expensive and research libraries are particularly expensive. Even in the United States, few people can afford good access to primary scientific, medical, legal and scholarly information. Members of major universities have excellent library services. So do people who work in teaching hospitals, or for drug companies or rich law firms. Others have access to information only through the tedious, inefficient system of interlibrary lending. In less affluent countries the situation is worse; even the best universities cannot afford good libraries. Must access to scientific and professional information always be expensive, or is it possible that digital libraries might change this sad situation?

The costs of a conventional research library fall into three main categories: facilities (which include buildings), library materials and staff. In digital libraries, the facilities costs are small, since digital libraries avoid the need for expensive buildings. Digital libraries require computers and networks, but these are relatively inexpensive, and the costs to users are shared with other services, such as electronic mail and word processing.

To build digital libraries that are inexpensive for users requires dramatic reductions in the costs of materials and of staff. Progress is being made in reducing material costs. Open access materials on the Internet are making many primary materials available at no cost. Some open access materials are identical to those that are available commercially. Others provide an acceptable substitute, such as Amazon.com as an alternative to *Books in Print*. For several disciplines, the open access materials are already good enough to support research.

Big libraries are labor-intensive. Although salaries are low, staff costs are the largest item in most budgets, typically about half. The libraries at Harvard employ a thousand people and the Library of Congress more than four thousand. If professional and research information is to be available more widely, either users must bypass libraries, or libraries will have to employ fewer people. Over the past thirty-five years, libraries have automated routine clerical tasks, such as circulation or filing catalog cards. Is it possible that, at some future date, computers might assume the skilled tasks that now require professional librarians?

The term "automated digital library" can be used to describe a digital library where all tasks are carried out automatically. Computer programs substitute for the intellectually demanding tasks that are traditionally carried out by skilled professionals. These tasks include selection, cataloguing and indexing, seeking for information, reference services, and so on. The common theme is that these activities require considerable mental activity, the type of activity that people are skilled at and computers find difficult. Automated digital libraries should not be confused with library automation, which uses computing to reduce routine tasks in conventional libraries.

Quality of service in automated digital libraries will not come from replicating the procedures of classical librarianship. More likely, automated libraries will provide users with equivalent services that are fundamentally different in the way that they are delivered. For example, within the foreseeable future, computer programs are unlikely to be much good at applying the Anglo American Cataloguing Rules to monographs. But cataloguing rules are a means to an end, not the end itself. They exist to provide services to users, notably information discovery. Automatic methods for information discovery may not need traditional cataloguing rules. The criterion for evaluating the new methods is whether the users find what the information that they require.

Consider the contrast between web search engines and conventional abstracting and indexing services or library catalogs. Almost everything that is best about a library catalog is done badly by a web search service. The selection of which materials to index by a web search engine relies on arbitrary considerations, the indexing records are crude at best, authority control is non-existent, and the elimination of duplicates leaves much to be desired. On the other hand, web search services are strong in ways that catalogs are weak. While cataloguing is expensive, indexing the web is cheap. The leading web search engines index several hundred million web pages every month, more than the total number of MARC records that have ever been created. It is wrong to claim that conventional catalogs or indexes are superior because of their quality control, and it is equally wrong to claim that the web search services are superior because of their coverage and currency. The value to users depends on what the user wants to achieve.

For medical research, no web search engine can approach the National Library of Medicine's Medline service. Medline has over 11 million references and abstracts. It is built by a team of indexers who have knowledge of bio-medical research, using indexing rules and MeSH subject headings that have been developed laboriously over decades. In contrast, web search services such as Google℠ are entirely automated. The indexes are built by a team of computers with no knowledge of what they are indexing. Google has the advantage over Medline of indexing hundreds of millions of web pages, and doing so repeatedly every month. It is quite useful for finding general information on medical topics, but it does not index the major scientific journals, its indexing records are crude, it has no understanding of medical terminology, and makes no attempt to separate sound medicine from quackery. It is a long way from being a substitute for Medline.

On the other hand, consider the trade-off between Google and Inspec, which is the leading abstracting and indexing service for computing. In many areas of computing, Google's restriction to open access web materials is relatively unimportant, since almost every significant result first appears on a web site and only later reaches the printed journals, if ever. Google is more up to date than Inspec, its coverage is broader and its indexIn computing, substantially the same information is often available from several sources. Google provides a direct link to an open access version. Inspec references a formally published version, which is usually printed or online with restricted access.

Serving the User

The people whom libraries are to serve are making increasing use of the new information technology of computers and electronic storage, in addition to the old information technology of pen, paper, and photocopier. The new tools provide powerful options for working with data, text, sound, and images. As examples, consider the reduction in labor now required for sending an message or text to distant collaborators, for the compilation of concordances, for complex simulations and calculations, for image enhancement, and for the analysis of large sets of numeric data.

There is, predictably, an increasing departure in information handling from the simple pattern of read, think, then write. Computers are used for so much more than the traditional notion of "computing." Since library services are provided for people to use, two relationships become important: How will changes in the provision of library services affect library users and what they do, and how should changes in the tasks and work habits of library users affect the provision of library services?

The change from the Paper Library to the Automated Library has been primarily a matter of computerising the library's internal procedures. There has been little impact on library users and little reason for there to be much, until the on-line catalog began to replace the card catalog. Before that time, users may have noticed improved circulation procedures and, perhaps, better-produced lists of various kinds, but the impact of the move to the Automated Library was mainly internal to the library and independent of changes among library users' working habits. The on-line catalog has two quite kinds of impact. For all who visit the library it is a different sort of catalog, with a keyboard, screen, and a new way of searching to be learned in the place of passive trays of cards.

A different impact has been on the growing proportion of library users whose work habits and working environment have changed to include routine use of computers. For these people the option of remote access to the library's catalog has constituted an important new extension of library service. Not since library catalogs were printed and distributed in book form in the nineteenth century has this kind of catalog access been possible. The fact is that this enhancement of service through the automation of the catalog is of benefit only to those who had the technology to use it.

This second, selective impact--an enhancement of service primarily for those whose work habits and equipment enable them to benefit--is a major characteristic of the shift from the Automated Library to the Electronic Library. The ability of the library to provide access from within the library to materials stored electronically and to generate copies on paper is clearly a useful extension of service. It can be symbolised by the provision of printouts of the results of bibliographic searches performed by librarians for library users. However, the ability of the library to arrange for access from outside the library to materials stored electronically, such that users with suitable equipment and skills can use these resources by themselves, constitutes a much more substantial extension of library service.

Extensive use of the Electronic Library depends on a change in the work habits and working environment of library users. In many work environments, especially in universities and corporations, and among professionals, administrative employees, and writers generally, it is common to find widespread and increasing use of computers and telecommunications. People who have moved to a personal computing environment for their work they need the provision of an Electronic Library because the effective conduct of their work is based on access to electronic records.

For these reasons the shift from the Automated Library to the Electronic Library should be associated with and paced by the parallel shift in the "task environment" of the people that the library is to serve. Once library users work electronically they are held back by the lack of remote access to an on-line catalog and by lack of access to materials in electronic form. The Electronic Library will be useful but the benefits are not fully achieved until the library users work electronically.

The old information technology of pen, paper, and, latterly, photocopier did not encourage much departure from library use as "read, think, write." In contrast, the new information technology is transforming the use of library materials, with computer-based techniques for identifying, locating, accessing, transferring, analysing, manipulating, comparing, and revising texts, images, sounds, and data. This close coupling of library development with changes in users' work-styles requires a new perspective among those responsible for library services. It is sad to have observed that "dial-in" access to on-line catalogs has often been slow in coming, limited in extent, or losing transmission the internal structure (fields) of the catalog record.

Extensive Connectivity

It now seems foolish not to assume for library planning purposes that a significant and increasing proportion of those to be served use a computer and that telecommunications are in place to support extensive connectivity between computers, the library, and databases. It is not difficult to outline what needs to be done: The starting point would be the principle that the kinds of services provided in the Paper Library should be made available for use by those who now use the new information technology. Hence from a computer anywhere a library user should be able:

1. To search the library catalog, including all cataloged holdings, without need to refer to additional catalogs on card or on microfiche. The library "catalog" is best seen as a series of concentric circles that include the holdings of the local library, of nearby, and of distant libraries. Within each catalog category, the searcher should have the option of expanding a search to associated files: circulation records, incompletely cataloged materials, and files of materials that are on order.
2. To search in bibliographies and also to be able to find the items listed, whether on paper, on microform, or on-line.
3. To search in directories and reference works.
4. To search for numeric data in social, technical, economic, and scientific databases--and to retrieve conveniently whichever datasets are needed.
5. To search for images and moving images--pictures currently on slides, movies, photos, videotapes--and to retrieve copies for use.
6. To search for texts, whether texts that were already known or those discovered in a catalog or bibliography.

These resources should be available for library users at their place of work using the tools with which they normally work, which implies copying in electronic form into personal storage, printing, or ordering a copy of printed material. These resources should suit the user's convenience by being available when needed, requiring minimal effort or formality, blend smoothly with personal computing practices. They should allow for convenient movement from one file or function to another and for integration of computerised with nonautomated procedures.

The Electronic Library will involve a heterogeneous hardware and software environment that requires a heavy emphasis on compatibility, linking, and interoperability through standardised protocols. The technical complexities of providing such service should be invisible to the library user.

Service to Self-service

The potential use of library service greatly exceeds the actual use, which is known to be sensitive to convenience. On the one hand, use of the Electronic Library depends on a technical infrastructure that is increasingly in place, at least as far as the users of university and corporate library services are concerned. On the other hand, the Electronic Library appears to remove many of the constraints of the Paper Library, such as the effective limitation to local collections, the tendency for desired books to be unavailable, limited opening hours, and, especially, the need to go to the library in order to use it. With these constraints removed or moderated there is the prospect of a dramatic increase in library use.

With so much more service possible in the Electronic Library, expanded use of library service seems likely to depend more and more on facilitating self-service than on ever more one-on-one service by library staff, even though the latter will remain necessary and desirable and even though the tasks facing the library users are becoming more complex. Funding for a corresponding increase in library staffing seems unlikely and, even if it were provided, with the Automated Library and, even more with the Electronic Library, an ever increasing proportion of the use of library services will be from outside the library.

A strategic shift from the direct provision of service one-on-one to the design and provision of library services intended for self-service seems inevitable, even though library services are becoming more powerful and more complex. Where there is increasing complexity, problems arise when the user's expertise is inadequate for the task. Different sorts of response are possible:

1. *User education:* Expertise can be increased.
2. *Advice:* The system could possibly be designed to offer helpful guidance or prompts.
3. *Simplification*: If the complexity facing the user could be reduced, then the user's expertise would become more adequate relative to the task;
4. *Mediation:* Providing an expert human intermediary to provide assistance--a reference librarian, for example--is an obvious course of action.
5. *Delegation:* It may be possible to shift some of the task complexity inside the system: Make the system itself smarter, more capable of determining what should be done next.

These different sorts of responses are not mutually exclusive. Which, or which combination, would be most cost-effective in any given case may vary greatly.

Forms of Assistance

Difficulties arise both because library users' needs are so extensive and so varied and because the sources of information are too complex, too imperfect, and too incomplete for self-service to be adequate. It is inherently unreasonable to assume that the provision of unaided library "self-service" will be satisfactory. Assistance is needed of three overlapping kinds: reference service, library instruction, and referral.

Reference Service

In addition to answering questions on almost every conceivable topic, reference librarians provide assistance on research projects, explain the use of complex bibliographic tools, arrange computerised searches of many different data bases, conduct on-line information searches, and offer both formal and informal instruction in the use of library services. Some requests can be answered with simple, factual information, but others may take hours or even days of investigation.

The library's first significant task, from the standpoint of the user, is to help with the identification and location of needed material. For many types of materials, the bibliographic tools available for this task are complex or incomplete, and the user is unlikely to be successful in finding the material needed without help. Librarians are therefore needed to assist users in interpreting such tools, and to insure that all suitable possible sources of information are made known to the reader.

The advent of computerised services for searching machine-readable data bases has also added a new dimension to reference and information services. Many of the major abstracting and indexing services, such as Chemical Abstracts and the Readers' Guide, are now searched on-line as well as on paper. Increasingly bibliographies are available not only from on-line search services but also as optical digital disks (CD-ROMs) that can be searched inside the library and as files mounted on on-line library catalogs. The commands to use these systems differ and the on-line version may not be the same as the paper version where both exist.

Library Instruction

There are various ways in which instruction in using libraries can be given. At the simplest level, there is the familiar "orientation" technique, or guided tour, the main purpose of which is to familiarise students with the layout of the library building and the location of various resources and services. At a more specific level, there are also "point-of-use" instructions, including printed guides on basic techniques in using the resources of the library; brochures on how to use bibliographic tools, such as indexing and abstracting services; video-tape, audio tape and slide-tape presentations; and personal guidance by reference librarians in methods of pursuing research in particular fields.

A third type of instruction has also gained increasing support in academic libraries: the formal course in bibliographic and research methods, offered for academic credit, and particularly designed for undergraduate students. The major objective of such classes is to impart skills for continuing self-education on the part of the student.

Library instruction can be expensive and labor-intensive, but the prospect of a major increase in self-service makes it an important and a more plausible investment. Library service can be characterised by reaching out to teach. It is unsatisfactory for all parties for there to be frustrated, unsuccessful users.

Referral

A third form of assistance is referral to other sources. This might be a difficult question being referred to another, more specialised library, librarian, or other expert or referring a library user to another more appropriate source. In both cases it is necessary to know to whom or to where a referral can be made with a reasonable chance of success. The development of detailed knowledge of resources is necessary for referral to work effectively.

Library use and bibliographic research are complex and becoming more so. A greater investment in user education will be needed to ensure that effective use is made of library resources, all the more so as any library's resources comes to include the resources of all cooperating libraries. Such an investment is needed if library users are to achieve a return on the greater investment in the creation of Paper, Automated, and Electronic Libraries.

Organisation and Implementation

Whatever scheme for service might be designed, implementation is unlikely to be, or to remain, successful unless there is a proper political and economic structure of governance, authority, resource allocation, and accountability. Failure to develop satisfactory governance and organisational structures can have very serious consequences. Nevertheless, for three reasons, this area will not be examined in any detail beyond the noting of a few general guidelines:

First, organisational structures and governance tend to be situational: They need to be compatible with the culture and traditions of the larger organisation or community that the library serves. Arrangements which might be acceptable in one situation might not be acceptable in another.

Secondly, flexibility and adaptability are important. The characteristics of the Automated Library are different enough from those of the Paper Library to indicate changes in organisation. The Electronic Library, in turn, will have its own characteristics which can be expected to lead to additional changes in the management and organisation of libraries.

Thirdly, organisation and governance should, in a sense, be the last aspect to be considered. This assertion is not meant to diminish their importance but is, rather, a tactical consideration. Different organisational structures lend themselves to different sorts of activities. Manufacturing organisations, for example, tend to function differently from service organisations.

In manufacturing, differences have been found in the organisational structures suited for small batch production, for large batch production, and for continuous process production. In service activities, differences have been found in organisational structures between routine services and professional services.

For these reasons any existing structure or any specific structure that might be designed will necessarily be more suitable for some activities and circumstances than for others. In this way "organisational technology" shares the attributes of any other technology: Each approach offers different constraints in terms of the activities for which it is suited.

Given the importance of compatibility between activities and administrative structure, to start by assuming or prescribing any given organisational structure is to impose the constraints and limitations of that organisational structure. It would, ideally, seem better to defer administrative considerations and to concentrate initially on the needs of library users and on the potential of available information technology.

After that has been accomplished, then political and economic realities will have to be considered. By deferring that consideration the desired design for service will have been less inhibited, and there would be a better basis for evolving organisational structures consistent with what one is trying to achieve. That might seem the best course of action in theory, but the show has to go on: Governance and organisational structure cannot be suspended.

The organisational structure of a library tends to be relatively complex because it reflects a mixture of technologies: Technical services resemble continuous-process manufacturing; circulation and shelving are routine-service activities; and reference work is a professional-service activity. For more general discussion reference should be made to general management texts. Important basic guidelines include:

— Responsibility should be matched by authority and resources
— Authority should be matched by accountability.
— Accountability depends on effective dissemination of information and on mechanisms for decision-making.
— Any structure needs to be compatible with and acceptable to parent organisations.

— Cooperative and exchange arrangements should be mutually beneficial.

— Flexibility and the ability to adapt enable an organisation to evolve.

Good planning is a process that leads to consistent anticipatory decision-making. Planning that does not influence decisions is futile. Decision making should be anticipatory in that plans should be ready for events as events occur. Decisions should be consistent with the mission of the organisation and with each other.

Bad planning or, more commonly, an absence of planning is reflected in decisions that are taken too late and that are inconsistent: Any good resulting from one decision is liable to be undone by the next. A plan in the form of a document is not strictly necessary for good planning since planning can be done in the mind. A written plan is a tool usually designed for a specific purpose: to establish consensus, to generate approval, to communicate, or to obtain resources.

With technological change there is often unfortunate confusion between "research and development" and "innovation." Research and development have to do with the identification of feasible new options and is a matter of inquiry, investigation, and testing. Innovation is a matter of selecting or rejecting available options and is a management activity. These are quite different activities. Failure to recognise the difference between them leads to the development of options that are not properly considered or to the adoption of impractical or unsuitable innovations.

The management of research and development, the implementation of change, and effective planning are important and widely underestimated skills.

Elements of Access Management

An obvious reason for controlling access is economic. When publishers expect revenue from their products, they permit access only to users who have paid. It might be thought that access management would be unnecessary except when revenue is involved, but that is not the case; there are other reasons to control access to materials in a digital library.

Materials donated to a library may have conditions attached, perhaps tied to external events such as the lifetime of certain individuals. Organisations may have information in their private collections that they wish to keep confidential, such as commercial secrets, police records, and classified government information. The boundaries of art, obscenity, and the invasion of privacy are never easy to draw. Even when access to the collections is provided openly, controls are needed over the processes of adding, changing, and deleting material, both content and metadata. A well-managed digital library will keep a record of all changes, so that the collections can be restored if mistakes are made or computer files are corrupted.

Uncertainty is a fact of life in access management. People from a computing background sometimes assume that every object can be labeled with metadata that lists all the rights, permissions, and other factors relevant to access management. People who come from libraries, and especially those who manage historic collections or archives, know that assembling such information is always time consuming and frequently impossible. Projects, such as the American Memory project at the Library of Congress, convert millions of items from historic collections. For these older materials, a natural assumption is that copyright has expired and there need be no access restrictions, but this is far from true.

For published materials, the expiration of copyright is linked to the death of the creator, a date which is often hard to determine, and libraries frequently do not know whether items have been published. Access management policies that are based on these laws are subject to this fuzziness. As the boundaries become clarified through new laws, treaties, or legal precedents, policies have to be modified accordingly.

Users need to be authenticated and their role in accessing materials established. Digital material in the collections must be identified and its authenticity established. Access is expressed in terms of permitted operations. When users request access to the collections, each request passes through an access carry out specified operations.

The responsibility for access lies with whoever manages the digital material. The manager may be a library, a publisher, a Webmaster, or the creator of the information. Parts of the responsibility may be delegated. If a library controls the materials and makes them available to users, the library sets the policies and implements them, usually guided by external restraints, such as legal restrictions, licenses from publishers, or agreements with donors. If a publisher mounts materials and licenses access, then the publisher is the manager, but may delegate key activities, such as authorisation of users, to others.

Users

When a user accesses a computer system, a two-step process of identification usually takes place. The first is authentication which establishes the identify of the individual user. The second is to determine what a user is authorised to do. A wide variety of techniques are used to authenticate users; some are simple but easy to circumvent, while others are more secure but complex. The techniques divide into four main categories:

— What does the user know? A standard method of authentication is to provide each user with a login name and a password. This is widely used but has weaknesses. Passwords are easily stolen. Most people like to select their own password and often select words that are easy to remember and hence easy to guess, such as personal names, or everyday words.

— What does the user possess? Examples of physical devices that are used for authentication include the magnetically encoded cards used by bank teller machines, and digital smart-cards that execute an authentication program. Smart-cards are one of the best systems of authentication; they are highly secure and quite convenient to use.

— What does the user have access to? A common form of authentication is the network address of a computer. Anybody who has access to a computer with an approved intellectual property address is authenticated. Data on many personal computers is unprotected except by physical access; anybody who has access to the computer can read the data.

— What are the physical characteristics of the user? Authentication by physical attributes such as voice recognition is used in a few esoteric applications, but has had little impact in digital libraries.

Policies for access management rarely specify users by name. They are usually tied to categories of users or the role of a user. An individual user can have many roles. At different times, the same person may use a digital library for teaching, private reading, or to carry out a part-time business. The digital library may have different policies for the same individual in these various roles. Typical roles that may be important include:

— *Membership of a group:* The user is a member of the Institute of Physics. The user is a student at the U.S. Naval Academy.

— *Location:* The user is using a computer in the Carnegie Library of Pittsburgh. The user is in the USA.

— *Subscription:* The user has a current subscription to Journal of the Association for Computing Machinery. The user belongs to a university that has a site license to all JSTOR collections.

— *Robotic use:* The user is an automatic indexing program, such as a Web crawler.

— *Payment:* The user has a credit account with Lexis. The user has paid $10 to access this material.

Most users of digital libraries are people using personal computers, but the user can be a computer with no person associated, such as a program that is indexing Web pages or a mirroring program that replicates an entire collection. Some sites explicitly ban access by automatic programs.

Digital Material

For access management, digital materials must be clearly identified. Identification associates some name or identifier with each item of material. This is a major topic in both digital libraries and electronic publishing. Authentication of digital materials assures both users and managers of collections that materials are unaltered. In some contexts this is vital. In one project, we worked with a U.S. government agency to assemble a collection of documents relevant to foreign affairs, such as trade agreements and treaties.

In most digital libraries, the accuracy of the materials is not verified explicitly. Where the level of trust is high and the cost of mistakes are low, no formal authentication of documents is needed. Deliberate alterations are rare and mistakes are usually obvious. In some fields, however, such as medical records, errors are serious. Digital libraries in these areas should seriously consider using formal methods of authenticating materials. To ensure the accuracy of an object, a digital signature can be associated with it. A digital signature ensures that a file or other set of bits has not changed since the signature was calculated.

A group of methods that are related to authentication of materials are described by the term watermarking. They are defensive techniques used by publishers to deter and track unauthorised copying. The basic idea is to embed a code into the material in a subtle manner that is not obtrusive to the user, but can be retrieved to establish ownership. A simple example is for a broadcaster to add a corporate logo to a television picture, to identify the source of the picture if is copied. Digital watermarks can be completely imperceptible to a users, yet almost impossible to remove without trace.

Digital material attributes

Access management policies frequently treat different material in varying ways, depending upon properties or attributes of the material. These attributes can be encoded as administrative metadata and stored with the object, or they can be derived from some other source. Some attributes can also be computed. Thus the size of an object can be measured when required. Some examples are given below:

— *Division into sub-collections:* Collections often divide material into items for public access and items with restricted access. Publishers may separate the full text of articles from indexes, abstracts and promotional materials. Web sites have public areas, and private areas for use within an organisation.

— *Licensing and other external commitments:* A digital library may have material that is licensed from a publisher or acquired subject to terms and conditions that govern access, such as materials that the Library of Congress receives through copyright deposit.

— *Physical, temporal, and similar properties:* Digital libraries may have policies that depend upon the time since the date of publication or physical properties, such as the size of the material. Some newspapers provide open access to selected articles when they are published while requiring licenses for the same articles later.

— *Media types:* A digital library may have access policies that depend upon format or media type, for example treating digitised sound differently from textual material, or computer programs from images.

Attributes need to be assigned at varying granularity. If all the materials in a collection have the same property, then it is convenient to assign the attribute to the collection as a whole. At the other extreme, there are times when parts of objects may have specific properties. The rights associated with images are often different from those associated with the text in which they are embedded and will have to be distinguished. A donor may donate a collection of letters to a library for public access, but request that access to certain private correspondence be restricted. Digital libraries need to offer flexibility, so that attributes can be associated with entire collections, sub-collections, individual library objects, or elements of individual objects.

Operations

Access management policies often specify or restrict the operations and the various actions that a user is authorised to carry out on library materials. Some of the common categories of operation include:

— *Computing actions:* Some operations are defined in computing terms, such as to write data to a computer, execute a program, transmit data across a network, display on a computer screen, print, or copy from one computer to another.

— *Extent of use:* A user may be authorised to extract individual items from a database, but not copy the entire database.

These operations can be controlled by technical means, but many policies that an information manager might state are essentially impossible to enforce technically. They include:

— *Business or purpose:* Authorisation of a user might refer to the reason for carrying out an operation. Examples include commercial, educational, or government use.

— *Intellectual operations:* Operations may specify the intellectual use to be made of an item. The most important is the rules that govern the creation of a new work that is derived from the content of another. The criteria may need to consider both the intent and the extent of use.

Systems for access management have to consider both direct operations and subsequent use of material. Direct operations are actions initiated by a repository, or another computer system that acts as a agent for the managers of the collection. Subsequent use covers all those operations that can occur once material leaves the control of the digital library. It includes all the various ways that a copy can be made, from replicating computer files to photocopying paper documents.

Intellectually, it can include everything from extracting short sections, the creation of derivative works, to outright plagiarism. When an item, or part of a item, has been transmitted to a personal computer it is technically difficult to prevent a user from copying what is received, storing it, and distributing it to others.

This is comparable to photocopying a document. If the information is for sale, the potential for such subsequent use to reduce revenue is clear. Publishers naturally have concerns about readers distributing unauthorised copies of materials. At an extreme, if a publisher sells one copy of an item that is subsequently widely distributed over the Internet, the publisher might end up selling only that one copy. As a partial response to this fear, digital libraries are often designed to allow readers access to individual records, but do not provide any way to copy complete collections. While this does not prevent a small loss of revenue, it is a barrier against anybody undermining the economic interests of the publisher by wholesale copying.

A Framework for Access Management

The final branch of Figure 1 is the unifying concept of a policy, on the left-hand side of the figure. An informal definition of a policy is that it is a rule, made by information managers that states who is authorised to do what to which material. Typical policies in digital libraries are:

— A publication might have the policy of open access. Anybody may read the material, but only the editorial staff may change it.

— A publisher with journals online may have the policy that only subscribers have access to all materials. Other people can read the contents pages and abstracts, but have access to the full content only if they pay a fee per use.

— A government organisation might classify materials, e.g., "top secret", and have strict policies about who has access to the materials, under what conditions, and what they can do with them.

Policies are rarely as simple as in these examples. For example, while D-Lib Magasine has a policy of open access, the authors of the individual articles own the copyright. The access policy is that everybody is encouraged to read the articles and print copies for private use, but some subsequent use, such as creating a derivative work, or selling copies for profit requires permission from the copyright owner. Simple policies can sometimes be represented as a table in which each row relates a user role, attributes of digital material, and certain operations.

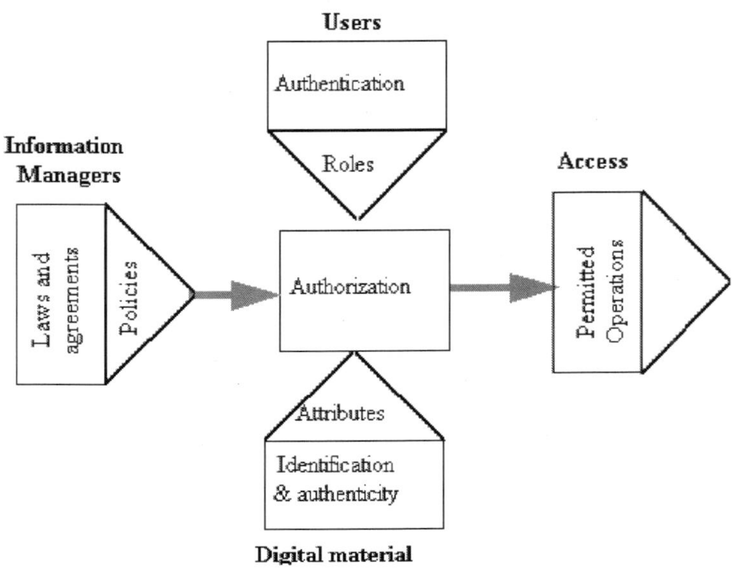

Figure 1. A framework for access management

Because access management policies can be complex, a formal method is needed to express them, which can be used for exchange of information among computer system. The Digital Property Rights Language, which he developed, is a language for expressing the rights, conditions, and fees for using digital works. The purpose of the language is to specify attributes of material and policies for access, including subsequent use. The manager of a collection can specify terms and conditions for copying, transferring, rendering, printing, and similar operations.

The language allows fees to be specified for any operation, and it envisages links to electronic payment mechanisms. The notation used by the language is based on Lisp, a language used for natural language processing. Some people have suggested that, for digital libraries, a more convenient notation would use XML, which would be a straightforward transformation. The real test of this language is how effective it proves to be when used in large-scale applications.

Access management is not simply a question of developing appropriate policies. Information managers want the policies to be followed, which requires some form of enforcement. Some policies can be enforced technically. Others are more difficult. There are straightforward technical methods to enforce a policy of who is permitted to change material in a collection, or search a repository. There are no technical means to enforce a policy against plagiarism, or invasion of privacy, or to guarantee that all use is educational. Each of these is a reasonable policy that is extremely difficult to enforce by technical means. Managing such policies is fundamentally social.

There are trade-offs between strictness of enforcement and convenience to users. Technical method of enforcing policies can be annoying. Few people object to typing in a password when they begin a session, but nobody wants to be asked repeatedly for passwords, or other identification. Information managers will sometimes decide to be relaxed about enforcing policies in the interests of satisfying users.

Satisfied customers will help grow the size of the market, even if some revenue is lost from unauthorised users. The publishers who are least aggressive about enforcement keep their customers happy and often generate most total revenue. If technical methods are relaxed, social and legal pressures can be effective. The social objective is to educate users about the policies that apply to the collections, and coax or persuade people to follow them. This requires policies that are simple to understand and easy for users to follow. Users must be informed of the policies and educated as to what constitutes reasonable behavior.

One useful tool is to display an access statement when the material is accessed; this is text that states some policy. An example is, "For copyright reasons, this material should not be used for commercial purposes." Other non-technical methods of enforcement are more assertive. If members of an organisation repeatedly violate a licensing agreement or abuse policies that they should respect, a publisher can revoke a license. In extreme cases, a single, well-publicised legal action will persuade many others to behave responsibly.

Access Management at a Repository

Most digital libraries implement policies at the repository or collection level. Although there are variations in the details, the methods all follow the outline in Figure 1. Digital libraries are distributed computer systems, in which information is passed from one computer to another. If access management is only at the repository, access is effectively controlled locally, but once material leaves the repository problems multiply.

The issue of subsequent use has already been introduced; once the user's computer receives information it is hard for the original manager of the digital library to retain effective control, without obstructing the legitimate user. With networks, there is a further problem. Numerous copies of the material are made in networked computers, including caches, mirrors, and other servers, beyond the control of the local repository.

To date, most digital libraries have been satisfied to provide access management at the repository, while relying on social and legal pressure to control subsequent use. Usually this is adequate, but some publishers are concerned that the lack of control could damage their revenues. Therefore, there is interest in technical methods that control copying and subsequent, even after the material has left the repository. The methods fall into two categories: trusted systems and secure containers.

Digital Library Security

Security begins with the system administrators, the people who install and manage the computers and the networks that connect them. Their honesty must be above suspicion, since they have privileges that provide access to the internals of the system. Good systems administrators will organise networks and file systems so that user have access to appropriate information. They will manage passwords, install firewalls to isolate sections of the networks, and run diagnostic programs to search for problems. They will back-up information, so that the system can be rebuilt after a major incident whether it is an equipment breakdown, a fire, or a security violation.

The Internet is basically not secure. People can tap into it and observe the packets of information traveling over the network. This is often done for legitimate purposes, such as trouble-shooting, but it can also be done for less honest reasons. The general security problem can be described as how to build secure applications across this insecure network.

Since the Internet is not secure, security in digital libraries begins with the individual computers that constitute the library and the data on them, paying special attention to the interfaces between computers and local networks. For many personal computers, the only method of security is physical restrictions on who uses the computer. Other computers have some form of software protection, usually a simple login name and password. When computers are shared by many users, controls are needed to determine who may read or write to each file. The next step of protection is to control the interface between local networks and the broader Internet, and to provide some barrier to intruders from outside. The most complete barrier is isolation, having no external network connections.

A more useful approach is to connect the internal network to the Internet through a special purpose computer called a firewall. The purpose of a firewall is to screen every packet that attempts to pass through and to refuse those that might cause problems. Firewalls can refuse attempts from outside to connect to computers within the organisation, or reject packets that are not formatted according to a list of approved protocols. Well-managed firewalls can be quite effective in blocking intruders.

Managers of digital libraries need to have a balanced attitude to security. Absolute security is impossible, but moderate security can be built into networked computer systems, without excessive cost, though it requires thought and attention. Universities have been at the heart of networked computing for many years. Despite their polyglot communities of users, they have succeeded in establishing adequate security for campus networks with thousands of computers. Incidents of abusive, anti-social, or malicious behavior occur on every campus, yet major problems are rare.

With careful administration, computers connected to a network can be made reasonably secure, but that security is not perfect. There are many ways that an ill-natured person can attempt to violate security. In universities, most problems come from insiders: disgruntled employees or students who steal a user's login name and password. More sophisticated methods of intrusion take advantage of the complexity of computer software. Every operating system has built-in security, but design errors or programming bugs may have created gaps.

Some of the most useful programs for digital libraries, such as Web servers and electronic mail, are some of the most difficult to secure. For these reasons, everybody who builds a digital library must recognise that security can never be guaranteed. With diligence, troubles can be kept rare, but there is always a chance of a flaw.

Encryption

Encryption is the name given to a group of techniques that are used to store and transmit private information, encoding it in a way that the information appears completely random until the procedure is reversed. Even if the encrypted information is read by somebody who is unauthorised, no damage is done. In digital libraries, encryption is used to transmit confidential information over the Internet, and some information is so confidential that it is encrypted wherever it is stored. Passwords are an obvious example of information that should always be encrypted, whether stored on computers or transmitted over networks. In many digital libraries, passwords are the only information that needs to be encrypted.

The basic concept of encryption is shown in Figure 2. The data that is to be kept secret, X, is input to an encryption process which performs a mathematical transformation and creates an encrypted set of data, Y. The encrypted set of data will have the same number of bits as the original data. It appears to be a random collection of bits, but the process can be reversed, using a reverse process which regenerates the original data, X. These two processes, encryption and decryption, can be implemented as computer programs, in software or using special purpose hardware.

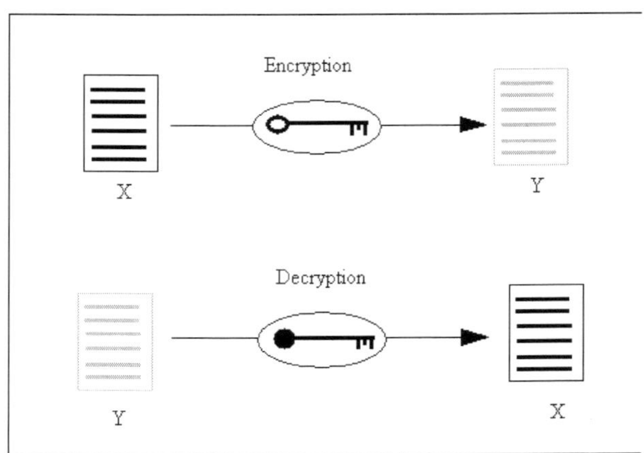

Figure 2. Encryption and decryption

The commonly used methods of encryption are controlled by a pair of numbers, known as keys. One key is used for encryption, the other for decryption. The methods of encryption vary in the choice of processes and in the way the keys are selected. The mathematical form of the processes are not secret. The security lies in the keys. A key is a string of bits, typically from 40 to 120 bits or more. Long keys are intrinsically much more secure than short keys, since any attempt to violate security by guessing keys is twice as difficult for every bit added to the key length.

Historically, the use of encryption has been restricted by computer power. The methods all require considerable computation to scramble and unscramble data. The methods are excellent for encrypting short message, such as passwords, or occasional highly confidential messages, but the methods are less suitable for large amounts of data where response times are important.

Private Key Encryption

Private key encryption is a family of methods in which the key used to encrypt the data and the key used to decrypt the data are the same, and must be kept secret. Private key encryption is also known as single key or secret key encryption.

The Data Encryption Standard (DES)The Data Encryption Standard (DES) is a method of private key encryption originally developed by IBM. It has been a U.S. standard since 1977. The calculations used by DES are fairly slow when implemented in software, but the method is fast enough for many applications. A modern personal computer can encrypt about one million bytes per second.DES uses keys that are 56 bits long. It divides a set of data into 64 bit blocks and encrypts each of them separately.

From the 56 bit key, 16 smaller keys are generated. The heart of the DES algorithm is 16 successive transformations of the 64 bit block, using these smaller keys in succession. Decryption uses the same 16 smaller keys to carry out the reverse transactions in the opposite order. This sounds like a simple algorithm, but there are subtleties. Most importantly, the bit patterns generated by encryption appear to be totally random, with no clues about the data or the key.Fanatics argue that DES with its 56 bit keys can be broken simply by trying every conceivable key, but this is a huge task. For digital library applications it is perfectly adequate.

Private key encryption is only as secure as the procedures that are used to keep the key secret. If one computer wants to send encrypted data to a remote computer it must find a completely secure way to get the key to the remote computer. Thus private key encryption is most widely used in applications where trusted services are exchanging information.

When using private key encryption over a network, the sending computer and the destination must both know the key. This poses the problem of how to get started if one computer can not pass a key secretly to another. Dual key encryption permits all information to be transmitted over a network, including the public keys, which can be transmitted completely openly. For this reason, it has the alternate name of public key encryption. Even if every message is intercepted, the encrypted information is still kept secret. The RSA method is the best known method of dual key encryption. It requires a pair of keys.

The first key is made public; the second is kept secret. If an individual, A, wishes to send encrypted data to a second individual, B, then the data is encrypted using the public key of B. When B receives the data it can be decrypted, using the private key, which only B knows. This dual key system of encryption has many advantages and one major problem. The problem is to make sure that a key is genuinely the public key of a specific individual. The normal approach is to have all keys generated and authenticated by a trusted authority, called a certification authority. The certification authority generates certificates, which are signed messages specifying an individual and a public key. This works well, so long as security at the certificate authority is never violated.

Digital Signatures

Digital signatures are used to check that a computer file has not been altered. Digital signatures are based on the concept of a hash function. A hash is a mathematical function that can be applied to the bytes of a computer file to generate a fixed-length number. One commonly used hash function is called MD5. The MD5 function can be applied to any length computer file. It carries out a special transformation on the bits of the file and ends up with an apparently random 128 bits.

If two files differ by as little as one bit, their MD5 hashes will be completely different. Conversely, if two files have the same hash, there is an infinitesimal probability that they are not identical. Thus a simple test for whether a file has been altered is to calculate the MD5 hash when the file is created; at a later time, to check that no changes have taken place, recalculate the hash and compare it with the original. If the two are the same then the files are almost certainly the same.

The MD5 function has many strengths, including being fast to compute on large files, but, as with any security device, there is always a possibility that some bright person may discover how to reverse engineer the hash function, and find a way to create a file that has a specific hash value.

A hash value gives no information about who calculated it. A digital signature goes one step further towards guaranteeing the authenticity of a library object. When the hash value is calculated it is encrypted using the private key of the owner of the material. This together with the public key and the certificate authority creates a digital signature. Before checking the hash value the digital signature is decrypted using the public key. If the hash results match, then the material is unaltered and it is known that the digital signature was generated using the corresponding private key.

Digital signatures have a problem. While users of a digital library want to be confident that material is unaltered, they are not concerned with bits; their interest lies in the content. For example, the Copyright Office pays great attention to the intellectual content, such as the words in text, but does not care that a computer system may have attached some control information to a file, or that the font used for the text has been changed, yet the test of a digital signature fails completely when one bit is changed. As yet, nobody has suggested an effective way to ensure authenticity of content, rather than bits.

Since the basic mathematics of public key encryption are now almost twenty years old, it might be expected that products based on the methods would have been widely deployed for many years. Sadly this is not the case. One reason for delay is that there are significant technical issues. Many of them concern the management of the keys, how they are generated, how private keys are stored, and what precautions can be taken if the agency that is creating the keys has a security break-in. However, the main problems are policy problems.

A more serious problem has been interference from U.S. government departments. Agencies such as the CIA claim that encryption technology is a vital military secret and that exporting it would jeopardise the security of the United States. Police forces claim that public safety depends upon their ability to intercept and read any messages on the networks, when authorised by an appropriate warrant.

The export argument is hard to defend when the methods are widely published overseas, and reputable companies in Europe and Japan are building products that incorporate them. The public safety augment is more complicated, but it is undercut by the simple fact that the American public does not trust the agencies, neither their technical competence nor their administrative procedures. People want the ability to transmit confidential information without being monitored by the police.

The result of these policy problems has been to delay the deployment of the tools that are needed to build secure applications over the Internet. Progress is being made and, in a few years time we may be able to report success.

References

Rothenberg, J. Ensuring the Longevity of Digital Information. *Scientific American,* 272(1):24-9. 1995.

Rowlands, Ian, and David Bawden. "Building the Digital Library on Solid Research Foundations." *Aslib Proceedings* 51, September. 1999.

Schatz, Bruce R. "Information Retrieval in Digital Libraries: Bringing Search to the Net." *Science*, 17 January. 1997.

Schwartz, Candy. "Digital Libraries: An Overview." *The Journal of Academic Librarianship* 26, November. 2000.

Thibodeau, K. *Overview of Technological Approaches to Digital Preservation and Challenges in Coming Years*. In: The State of Digital Preservation: An International Perspective.Conference Papers and Documentary Abstracts, http://www.clir.org/pubs/reports/pub107/thibodeau.html

6

Electronic Preservation

Today, information technologies that are increasingly powerful and easy to use, especially like those that support the World Wide Web, have unleashed the production and distribution of digital information. Such information is penetrating and transforming nearly every aspect of our culture. If we are effectively to preserve for future generations the portion of this rapidly expanding corpus of information in digital form that represents our cultural record, we need to understand the costs of doing so and we need to commit ourselves technically, legally, economically and organizationally to the full dimensions of the task.

Preserving or archiving digital information is not a new one and has been explored at a variety of levels over the last five decades. Archivists responsible for governmental and corporate records have been acutely aware of the difficulties entailed in trying to ensure that digital information survives for future generations. Far more than their library colleagues, who have continued to collect and organize published materials primarily in paper form, archivists have observed the materials for which they are responsible shift rapidly from paper objects produced on typewriters and other analog devices to include files created in word processor, spreadsheet and many other digital forms.

Early attention to the difficulties in preserving digital information focused on the longevity of the physical media on which the information is stored. Even under the best storage conditions, however, digital media can be fragile and have limited shelf life. Moreover, new devices, processes and software are replacing the products and methods used to record, store, and retrieve digital information on breathtaking cycles of 2- to 5- years. Given such rates of technological change, even the most fragile media may well outlive the continued availability of readers for those media.

Efforts to preserve physical media thus provide only a short-term, partial solution to the general problem of preserving digital information. Indeed, technological obsolescence represents a far greater threat to information in digital form than the inherent physical fragility of many digital media. In the face of rapid technological obsolescence and to overcome the problem of media fragility, archivists have adopted the technique of "refreshing" digital information by copying it onto new media.

Copying from medium to medium, however, also suffers limitations as a means of digital preservation. Refreshing digital information by copying will work as an effective preservation technique only as long as the information is encoded in a format that is independent of the particular hardware and software needed to use it and as long as there exists software to manipulate the format in current use. Otherwise, copying depends either on the compatibility of present and past versions of software and generations of hardware or the ability of competing hardware and software product lines to interoperate.

In respect of these factors- backward compatibility and interoperability- the rate of technological change exacts a serious toll on efforts to ensure the longevity of digital information. Digital information today is produced in highly varying degrees of dependence on particular hardware and software. Moreover, it is costly and difficult for vendors to assure that their products are either "backwardly compatible" with previous versions or that they can interoperate with competing products.

Jeff Rothenberg, for example, has recently suggested that there may be sufficient demand for entrepreneurs to create and archive emulators of software and operating systems that would allow the contents of digital information to be carried forward and used in its original format. Refreshing digital information by copying it from medium to medium and the possibility of maintaining a complex set of emulators describe two distinct points on a continuum of approaches to preserving digital information. However, neither refreshing nor emulation sufficiently describes the full range of options needed and available for digital preservation.

Instead, a better and more general concept to describe these options is migration. Migration is the periodic transfer of digital materials from one hardware/software configuration to another, or from one generation of computer technology to a subsequent generation. The purpose of migration is to preserve the integrity of digital objects and to retain the ability for clients to retrieve, display, and otherwise use them in the face of constantly changing technology. Migration includes refreshing as a means of digital preservation but differs from it in the sense that it is not always possible to make an exact digital copy or replica of a database or other information object as hardware and software change and still maintain the compatibility of the object with the new generation of technology.

Even for information that is encoded in a contemporary standard form, forward migration of the information to a new standard or application program is, as anyone knows who has witnessed or participated in such a process, time-consuming, costly and much more complex than simple refreshing. Compounding the technical challenges of migrating digital information is the problem of managing the process in a legal and organizational environment that is in flux as it moves to accommodate rapidly changing digital technologies.

Consider, for example, the barriers to decisive preservation action caused by widespread uncertainty about legal and organizational requirements for managing the intellectual property that digital information represents. Addressing and resolving the legal and practical questions of migrating intellectual property in digital form necessarily involves a complex set of interested parties, including the creators and owners of intellectual property, managers of digital archives, representatives of the public interest, and actual and potential users of intellectual property.

In addition, the parties who represent, for example, owners and users of different kinds of intellectual property (e.g., text and other document-like objects, photographs, film, software, multimedia objects) each operate under very different organizational regimes, with different experiences and expectations. Adding to these complexities is the deep uncertainty that these groups face in confronting an increasingly digital world. Owners of intellectual property are unsure about how to price access to their information and worry, given the ease of copying, that the first digital copy of a work they sell may be the only copy they sell.

Users of intellectual property are unsure about what rights are conveyed with the use of a particular digital information object and about how much such use is worth. Government representatives seek in the public interest to manage the powerful changes that accompany digital technologies, but are unsure about what levels of influence are available to them and how to generate appropriate public policy. The state of the copyright law, which was generated and developed in an analog world but is applied in an increasingly digital universe, is itself confusing and uncertain.

And all of these concerns are exacerbated by the fact that bits know no borders. The costs and the technical, legal and organizational complexities of moving digital information forward into the future raise our greatest fear about the life of information in the digital future: namely, that owners or custodians who can no longer bear the expense and difficulty will deliberately or inadvertently, through a simple failure to act, destroy the objects without regard for future use. Repeated anecdotes about the loss of land use information, satellite imagery or census data, even when false or misleading, feed our general anxiety about the future of the cultural record we are accumulating in digital form.

And uncertainty and lack of confidence about our will and ability to carry digital information forward into the future exert a major inhibiting force in our disposition to fully exploit the digital medium to generate, publish and disseminate information. But how well does the evidence really support our fears, anxieties and inhibitions regarding digital information? Even after more than forty years of growth, the digital world of information technology and communication is still relatively young and immature in relation to the larger information universe, parts of which have been under development for centuries.

Viewed developmentally, the problem of preserving digital information for the future is not only, or even primarily, a problem of fine tuning a narrow set of technical variables. It is not a clearly defined problem like preserving the embrittled books that are self-destructing from the acid in the paper on which they were printed. Rather, it is a grander problem of organizing ourselves over time and as a society to manoeuvre effectively in a digital landscape. It is a problem of building-almost from scratch-the various systematic supports, or deep infrastructure, that will enable us to tame anxieties and move our cultural records naturally and confidently into the future.

Foundation for Digital Preservation

The vision of creating digital libraries that will be able to preserve our heritage currently rests on technological quicksand. There is as yet no viable long-term strategy to ensure that digital information will be readable in the future. Not only are digital documents vulnerable to loss via media decay and obsolescence, but they become equally inaccessible and unreadable if the software needed to interpret them—or the hardware on which that software runs—is lost or becomes obsolete.

Digital Longevity

Documents, data, records, and informational and cultural artifacts of all kinds are rapidly being converted to digital form, if they were not created digitally to begin with. This rush to digitise is being driven by powerful incentives, including the ability to make perfect copies of digital artifacts, to publish them on a wide range of media, to distribute and disseminate them over networks, to reformat and convert them into alternate forms, to locate them, search their contents, and retrieve them, and to process them with automated and semi-automated tools. Yet the longevity of digital content is problematic for a number of complex and interrelated reasons. It is now generally recognised that the physical lifetimes of digital storage media are often surprisingly short, requiring information to be "refreshed" by copying it onto new media with disturbing frequency. The technological obsolescence of these media poses a different and equally urgent threat.

Moreover, most digital documents and artifacts exist only in encoded form, requiring specific software to bring their bit streams to life and make them truly usable; as these programs become obsolete, the digital documents that depend on them become unreadable—held hostage to their own encoding. This problem is paradoxical, given the fact that digital documents can be copied perfectly, which is often naively taken to mean that they are eternal. In addition to the technical aspects of this problem, there are administrative, procedural, organisational, and policy issues surrounding the management of digital material. Digital documents are different from traditional paper documents in ways that have significant implications for the means by which they are generated, captured, transmitted, stored, maintained, accessed, and managed.

Paramount among these differences is the greatly reduced lifetime of digital information without some form of active preservation. This mandates new approaches to accessioning and saving digital documents to avoid their loss. These approaches raise nontechnical issues concerning jurisdiction, funding, responsibility for successive phases of the digital document life cycle, and the development of policies requiring adherence to standard techniques and practices to prevent the loss of digital information. However, few of these nontechnical issues can be meaningfully addressed in the absence of a sound, accepted technical solution to the digital longevity problem.

Preservation constitutes one leg of a tripod that supports informational institutions such as libraries, the other legs being access and the development and management of collections. Without preservation, access becomes impossible, and collections decay and disintegrate. Informational artifacts include documents, data, and records of all kinds, in all media, which can be refered to as "documents" for simplicity. The essence of preserving informational artifacts is the retention of their meaning. This requires the ability to recreate the original form and function of a document when it is accessed, for example, to establish its authenticity, validity, and evidential value and to allow the document's users to understand how its creator and original viewers saw it, what they were able to infer from it, what insights it may have conveyed to them, and what aesthetic value it may have had for them.

Let us focus on digital documents, which we mean informational artifacts, some or all aspects of whose intended behavior or use rely on their being encoded in digital form. The term "digital" in this context denotes any means of representing sequences of discrete symbolic values—each value having two or more unambiguously distinguishable states—so that they can, at least in principle, be accessed, manipulated, copied, stored, and transmitted entirely by mechanical means, with high reliability. The preservation of digital documents involves a number of distinctive requirements. In particular, all such documents possess a unique collection of core digital attributes that must be retained. These attributes include their ability to be copied perfectly, to be accessed without geographic constraint, to be disseminated at virtually no incremental cost, and to be machine-readable so that they can be accessed, searched, and processed by automated mechanisms that can modify them, reformat them, and perform arbitrary computations on their contents in all phases of their creation and distribution. Furthermore, new inherently digital document forms, such as dynamic, distributed, interactive hypertext and hypermedia, must retain their unique functionality, including their ability to integrate information from disparate traditional sources, such as books, periodicals, newspapers, mail, phone messages, data, imagery, and video.

In response to the difficulty of saving digital documents it is sometimes suggested that they be printed and saved in hard-copy form. This is a rear-guard action and not a true solution. Printing any but the simplest, traditional documents results in the loss of their unique functionality, and printing any document makes it no longer truly machine-readable, which in turn destroys its core digital attributes. Beyond this loss of functionality, printing digital documents sacrifices their original form, which may be of unique historical, contextual, or evidential interest.

Proposed alternatives to printing digital documents include translating digital documents into standard forms or extracting their contents without regard to their original nature. Though these approaches have traditional analogues, they are fraught with danger. The meaning of a document may be quite fragile, since meaning is in the eye of the beholder: what may be a trivial transformation to a casual reader may be a disastrous loss to a scholar, historian, or lawyer. Examples of loss of meaning abound in our daily experience of converting digital documents from their native form into that of some other software application in order to read them. At its best, such conversion often sacrifices subtleties; at its worst, it leaves out entire segments or produces meaningless garbage.

While it is often useful to create contemporary vernacular transcriptions of historical documents, society places a high value on retaining the originals so that we may verify that content has not been lost in transcription, as well as for scholarly and aesthetic purposes. For digital documents, retaining an original may not mean retaining the original medium, but it should mean retaining the functionality, look, and feel of the original document.

Scope of the Problem

The preservation of digital documents is a matter of more than purely academic concern. In its short history, computer science has become inured to the fact that every new generation of software and hardware technology entails the loss of information, as documents are translated between incompatible formats. The most serious losses are caused by paradigm shifts (such as those between networked, hierarchical, and relational databases), which often require the complete redesign of documents to migrate to the new paradigm. Whenever this happens, documents that are not in continuing use may well be orphaned by the demise of their original formats, that is, they may be abandoned to save the cost of migration, while each document that does migrate may be turned into something unrecognisably different from its original, which is generally lost.

Even when migration does not involve a major paradigm shift, it can result in subtle losses of context and content. Yet aside from this ad hoc migration process, there exists no proven strategy for preserving (or translating) documents over time. The scope of this problem extends beyond the traditional library domain, affecting government records, environmental and scientific baseline data, documentation of toxic waste disposal, medical records, corporate data (such as the documentation of drug trials for pharmaceutical companies or of geologic survey data for petrochemical companies), electronic-commerce transactions, and electronic records needed to support forthcoming digital government initiatives.

The library and archives communities have identified at least some critical aspects of this problem and have recognised that preserving digital documents may require substantial new investments and commitments by institutions and government agencies. Showing admirable foresight, these communities have begun to discuss alternative economic and administrative policies for funding and managing digital preservation and have begun to develop conceptual frameworks for metadata that are not restricted to the print medium. Yet the lack of any long-term technical solution to the problem of digital preservation limits the efficacy of such explorations, since attempting to allocate responsibilities and assess costs for a nonexistent process is of questionable value.

Need for Triage

The practical problem of digital preservation can be viewed at three different time scales. In the short term, many organisations are faced with an urgent need to save digital material that is in imminent danger of becoming unreadable or inaccessible, or to retrieve digital records that are already difficult to access. Yet the often heroic efforts needed to save or retrieve such material may not be generally applicable to preserving digital documents far into the future, and the techniques employed may not even be generalisable to solve similar urgent problems that may arise in the future.

These short-term efforts therefore do not provide much leverage, in the sense that they are not replicable for different document types, though they may still be necessary for saving crucial records. In the medium term, organisations must quickly implement policies and technical procedures to prevent digital records from becoming vulnerable to imminent loss in the near future. For the vast bulk of records—those being generated now, those that have been generated fairly recently, or those that have been translated into formats and stored on media that are currently in use—the medium-term issue is how to prevent these records from becoming urgent cases of imminent loss within the next few years, as current media, formats, and software evolve and become obsolete.

In the long term, it is necessary to develop a truly long-lived solution to digital longevity that does not require continual heroic effort or repeated invention of new approaches every time formats, software or hardware paradigms, document types, or recordkeeping practices change. Such an approach must be extensible, in recognition of the fact that we cannot predict future changes, and it must not require labor-intensive translation or examination of individual records. It must handle current and future records of unknown type in a uniform way, while being capable of evolving as necessary.

Types of Digital Information Affected

Though most early digital documents have consisted largely of text, the generation of multimedia records has increased rapidly in recent years, to include audio recordings, graphical charts, photographic imagery, and video presentations, among others. In the digital domain, all of these media can be combined into hypermedia records, whose impact and expressivity can be expected to stimulate their increased use. Whereas the bulk of existing digital documents may be textual, multimedia and hypermedia records are likely to become ever more popular and may well become dominant in the near future. Any solution to digital preservation that is limited to text will therefore quickly become obsolete. A true long-term solution should be completely neutral to the form and content of the digital material it preserves.

Contextual issues

The preservation and management of digital records involves interrelated technical, administrative, procedural, organisational, and policy issues, but a sound technical approach must form the foundation on which everything else rests. Preserving digital records may require substantial new investments and commitments by organisations, institutions and agencies, forcing them to adopt new economic and administrative policies for funding and managing digital preservation. Yet it is impossible to allocate responsibilities or assess costs for an undefined process: until a viable technical approach to digital longevity has been identified and developed, it is premature to spend much effort attempting to design the administrative and organisational environment that will embed whatever technical approach is ultimately adopted.

Technical Dimensions

Digital media are vulnerable to loss by two independent mechanisms: the physical media on which they are stored are subject to physical decay and obsolescence, and the proper interpretation of the documents themselves is inherently dependent on software.

Physical Decay and Obsolescence

There is reasonably widespread awareness of the fact that digital storage media have severely limited physical lifetimes. The National Media Lab has published test results for a wide range of tapes, magnetic disks, CD-ROMs, and other media, showing that a tape, disk, or even CD that is picked at random is unlikely to have a lifetime of even five years. Vendors and media scientists may argue vehemently about such numbers, but accurate estimates are ultimately largely irrelevant, since the physical lifetime of media is rarely the constraining factor for digital preservation.

Even if archival quality media were introduced in the market, they would probably fail, since they would quickly be made obsolete—despite their physical longevity—by newer media having increased capacity, higher speed, greater convenience, and lower price. This is a natural outgrowth of the exponential improvement in storage density, speed, and cost that has characterised digital media development for the past several decades: the market makes older storage media obsolete as newer, better media become available. The short lifetimes of eight-inch floppy disks, tape cartridges and reels, hard-sectored disks, and seven-track tapes, among others, demonstrate how quickly storage formats become inaccessible.

Media obsolescence manifests itself in several ways: the medium itself disappears from the market; appropriate drives capable of reading the medium are no longer produced; and media-accessing programs (device drivers) capable of controlling the drives and deciphering the encodings used on the medium are no longer written for new computers. Upgrading to a new computer system therefore often requires abandoning an old storage medium, even if an organisation still has documents stored on that medium. The dual problems of short media lifetime and rapid obsolescence have led to the nearly universal recognition that digital information must be copied to new media (refreshed) on a very short cycle (every few years). Copying is a straightforward solution to these media problems, though it is not trivial: in particular, the copy process must avoid corrupting documents via compression, encryption, or changing data formats.

In addition, as media become more dense, each copy cycle aggregates many disks, tapes, or other storage units onto a single new unit of storage. This raises the question of how to retain any labeling information and metadata that may have been associated with the original media: since it is infeasible to squeeze the contents of the labels of 400 floppy disks to fit on the label of a single CD, label information must be digitised to ensure that it continues to accompany the records it describes. But whereas labels are directly human-readable, digitised information is not; labels and metadata must therefore be digitised in such a way that they remain more easily readable by humans than are the documents they describe. This may seem a relatively trivial aspect of the problem, but it has serious implications.

Software-dependency

Though media problems are far from trivial, they are but the tip of the iceberg. Far more problematic is the fact that digital documents are in general dependent on application software to make them accessible and meaningful. Copying media correctly at best ensures that the original bit stream of a digital document will be preserved. But a stream of bits cannot be made self-explanatory, any more than hieroglyphics were self-explanatory for the 1,300 years before the discovery of the Rosetta Stone. A bit stream can represent anything: not just text but also data, imagery, audio, video, animated graphics, and any other form or format, current or future, singly or combined in a hypermedia lattice of pointers whose formats themselves may be arbitrarily complex and idiosyncratic.

Without knowing what is intended, it is impossible to decipher such a stream. In certain restricted cases, it may be possible to decode the stream without additional knowledge: for example, if a bit stream is known to represent simple, linear text, deciphering it is amenable to cryptographic techniques. But in general, a bit stream can be made intelligible only by running the software that created it, or some closely related software that understands it. This point cannot be overstated: in a very real sense, digital documents exist only by virtue of software that understands how to access and display them; they come into existence only by virtue of running this software.

The only reliable way to access the meaning and functionality of a digital document is to run its original software—either the software that created it or some closely related software that understands it. Yet such application software becomes obsolete just as fast as do digital storage media and media-accessing software. And although we can save obsolete software as just another bit stream, running that software requires specific computer hardware, which itself becomes obsolete just as quickly. It is therefore not obvious how we can use a digital document's original software to view the document in the future on some unknown future computer. This is the crux of the technical problem of preserving digital documents. Any technical solution must also be able to cope with issues of corruption of information, privacy, authentication, validation, and preserving intellectual property rights. This last issue is especially complex for documents that are born digital and therefore have no single original instance, since traditional notions of copies are inapplicable to such documents. Finally, any technical solution must be feasible in terms of the societal and institutional responsibilities and the costs required to implement it.

Inadequacy of Most Proposed Approaches

Most approaches that have been proposed fall into one of four categories:

1) Reliance on hard copy,
2) Reliance on standards,
3) Reliance on computer museums, or
4) Reliance on migration.

Though some of these may play a role in an ultimate solution, none of them comes close to providing a solution by itself, nor does their combination.

Reliance on hard copy

It is sometimes suggested that digital documents be printed and saved as hard copy. This is not a true solution to the problem, since many documents cannot meaningfully be printed at all, or would lose many of their uniquely digital attributes and capabilities if they were printed. Even digital renditions of traditional documents lose their core digital attributes by being printed; that is, they sacrifice direct machine-readability, which means they can no longer be copied perfectly, transmitted digitally, searched or processed by computer programs, and so forth. Similarly, attempting to save digital documents by printing the 0s and 1s of their bit streams on paper sacrifices their machine-readability and the core digital attributes that it enables. Moreover, any such scheme destroys whatever interactive or dynamic functionality an inherently digital document may have, since the document's original software can no longer be run. For all of these reasons, saving digital documents by printing them does not offer a solution to the true problem of digital preservation.

Reliance on standards

On the face of it, reliance on standards appears to offer a solution by allowing digital documents to be represented in forms that will endure into the future and for which future software will always provide accessibility. One version of this argument offers the relational database (RDB) as a paradigmatic example of how this might work. This argument contends that since all relational database management systems (RDBMSs) are based on the same mathematical foundation, any RDB that is accessioned by an institution can be translated without loss into the specific RDB form recognised by the RDBMS used by that institution. Even if the institution later changes RDBMSs, all of its RDBs should be able to migrate to the new RDBMS without loss, since all RDBMSs support the same baseline functionality. While this argument appears convincing, it fails in several significant ways. First, precisely because the relational model legislates a standard baseline of functionality, real RDBMSs must distinguish themselves in the marketplace by introducing proprietary features that extend the relational model.

Any RDB that makes use of such proprietary features becomes at least somewhat nonstandard and will lose some of its functionality if translated into some other RDBMS. In this way standardisation sows the seeds of its own destruction by encouraging vendors to implement nonstandard features in order to secure market share. Users are motivated to use such features because they provide enhanced functionality, but using these features produces nonstandard databases that are likely to be orphaned by reliance on standards, since standards enforce strict limitations on what they can represent, and thereby preserve. In addition, far from being a paradigmatic example, the relational database is actually unique: no other kind of digital document rests on an underlying formal mathematical foundation that can serve as the basis for its standardisation.

Word-processing documents, spreadsheets, graphics and image files, hypermedia, animation, and audio and video formats are still evolving so rapidly that it is unrealistic to expect definitive standards for any of these forms to emerge in the near future. Though standards continue to be developed for many kinds of digital documents, they are almost always informal, ad hoc, and relatively short-lived. Moreover, since they lack a formal underpinning, they often compete with rival standards produced for different purposes or by different groups. The relational database example demonstrates a fundamental flaw in the standards-based approach. Just as the relational paradigm replaced earlier network and hierarchical database paradigms, it is currently under attack by the new object-oriented database (OODB) paradigm, which may well replace it or at least relegate it to the role of a low-level storage mechanism hidden beneath future object-oriented database management systems (OODBMSs). As was the case with previous database paradigm shifts, the transition from relational to object-oriented databases cannot be made simply by automatically translating RDBs into OODBs.

The paradigms are so different that such translation is typically meaningless: even when it is possible, the result is likely to possess neither the formal rigor of the original relational form nor the enhanced semantic expressiveness of the new object-oriented form. This illustrates the fact that even the best standards are often bypassed and made irrelevant by the inevitable paradigm shifts that characterise information science—and will continue to do so. Proponents of standards often argue that the way to deal with the problem of paradigm shifts is to force digital documents into current standard forms and then translate them, when current standards become obsolete, into whatever standards supplant the obsolete ones. This is analogous to translating Homer into modern English by way of every intervening language that has existed during the past 2,500 years.

The fact that scholars do not do this (but instead find the earliest original they can, which they then translate directly into the current vernacular) is indicative of the fact that something is always lost in translation. Rarely is it possible to recover the original by retranslating the translated version back into the original language. Not even character encodings last forever: ASCII (the venerable 7-bit American Standard Code for Information Interchange) is slowly giving way to Unicode (a newer 16-bit character set). Furthermore, the history of these encodings shows that successful standards do not always subsume their competitors, as exemplified by the ascendance of ASCII over EBCDIC (the 8-bit Extended Binary Coded Decimal Interchange Code long used by IBM) and the APL character set (designed for Iverson's "A Programming Language"), despite the fact that ASCII cannot represent all of their characters.

Nevertheless, standards should not be dismissed. Some standards have proven highly extensible and worthwhile within their limited scope. Since text is likely always to be a part of most documents, SGML provides a useful capability, even though it does not by itself solve the problems of nontextual representation or of representing dynamic, interactive documents. In fact, if SGML had been adopted as a common interlingua among word processing programs, it would have greatly relieved the daily conversion problems that plague most computer users; yet this has not occurred, implying that even well-designed standards do not necessarily sweep the marketplace. Nevertheless, converting digital documents into standard forms, and migrating to new standards if necessary, may be a useful interim approach while a true long-term solution is being developed.

Reliance on computer museums

To avoid the dual problems of corruption via translation and abandonment at paradigm shifts, some have suggested that computer museums be established, where old machines would run original software to access obsolete documents. While this approach exudes a certain technological bravado, it is flawed in a number of fundamental ways. It is unlikely that old machines could be kept running indefinitely at any reasonable cost, and even if they were, this would limit true access to the original forms of old digital documents to a very few sites in the world, thereby again sacrificing many of these documents' core digital attributes.

Furthermore, this approach ignores the fact that old digital documents will rarely survive on their original digital media. If an obsolete digital document and its software survive into the future, this will probably be because their bit streams have been copied onto new media that did not exist when the document's original computer was current. An old word processing file from a 1970s personal computer system will not still exist on the 8-inch floppy disk that was native to that system but will instead have migrated onto a 3.5 inch floppy, a CD-ROM, or perhaps a DVD. The obsolete document would therefore have to be read by an obsolete machine from a new medium for which that machine has no physical drive, no interface, and no device software. The museum approach would therefore require building unique new device interfaces between every new medium and every obsolete computer in the museum as new storage media evolve, as well as coding driver software for these devices, which would demand maintaining programming skills for each obsolete machine. This seems hopelessly labor-intensive and ultimately infeasible.

Computer chips themselves have limited physical lifetimes. Integrated circuits decay due to processes such as metal migration (the traces that define circuit connections on the chips migrate through the substrate over time) and dopant diffusion (the atoms that make semiconductors semiconduct diffuse away over time). Even if obsolete computers were stored carefully, maintained religiously, and never used, aging processes such as these would eventually render them inoperative; using them routinely to access obsolete digital documents would undoubtedly accelerate their demise. One role that computer museums might play in preservation is to perform heroic efforts to retrieve digital information from old storage media. If an old disk or tape is found that may indeed still have readable information on it, an obsolete machine in the museum could be used in a last-ditch attempt to tease the bits off the medium, as an alternative to electron microscopy or other equally extreme measures. A second role for computer museums might be in verifying the behavior of emulators, as discussed below. Beyond these limited roles, however, computer museums do not appear to be a serious option for the long-term preservation of digital documents.

Reliance on migration

The approach that most institutions are adopting is to expect digital documents to become unreadable or inaccessible as their original software becomes obsolete and to translate them into new forms as needed whenever this occurs. This is the traditional migration approach of computer science. While it may be better than nothing, it has little to recommend it. Migration is by no means a new approach: computer scientists, data administrators and data processing personnel have spent decades performing migration of data, documents, records, and programs to keep valuable information alive and usable. Though it has been employed widely, the nearly universal experience has been that migration is labor-intensive, time-consuming, expensive, error-prone, and fraught with the danger of losing or corrupting information.

Migration requires a unique new solution for each new format or paradigm and each type of document that is to be converted into that new form. Since every paradigm shift entails a new set of problems, there is not necessarily much to be learned from previous migration efforts, making each migration cycle just as difficult, expensive, and problematic as the last. Automatic conversion is rarely possible, and whether conversion is performed automatically, semiautomatically, or by hand, it is very likely to result in at least some loss or corruption, as documents are forced to fit into new forms. As has been proven repeatedly during the short history of computer science, formats, encodings, and software paradigms change often and in surprising ways.

Of the many dynamic aspects of information science, document paradigms, computing paradigms, and software paradigms are among the most volatile, and their evolution routinely eludes prediction. Relational and object-oriented databases, spreadsheets, Web-based hypermedia documents, e-mail attachments, and many other paradigms have appeared on the scene with relatively little warning, at least from the point of view of most computer users. Each new paradigm of this kind requires considerable conversion of programs, documents, and work styles, whether performed by users themselves or by programmers, data administrators, or data processing personnel. Even though some new paradigms subsume the ones they replace, they often still require a significant conversion effort.

Similarly, word processing subsumes simple text editing, but conversion of a document from a simple textual form into a specific word processing format requires that fonts, paragraph types, indentation, highlighting, and so forth, be specified, in order to make use of the new medium and avoid producing a result that would otherwise be unacceptably old-fashioned, if not illegible. One of the worst aspects of migration is that it is impossible to predict what it will entail. Since paradigm shifts cannot be predicted, they may necessitate arbitrarily complex conversion for some or all digital documents in a collection. In reality, of course, particularly complex conversions are unlikely to be affordable in all cases, leading to the abandonment of individual documents or entire corpora when conversion would be prohibitively expensive. As when refreshing media, there is a degree of urgency involved in migration. If a given document is not converted when a new paradigm first appears, even if the document is saved in its original form, the software required to access its now-obsolete form may be lost or become unusable due to the obsolescence of the required hardware, making future conversion difficult or impossible.

Though this urgency is driven by the obsolescence of software and hardware, rather than by the physical decay and obsolescence of the media on which digital documents are stored, it is potentially just as crucial. Therefore migration cannot generally be postponed without incurring the risk that it may become impossible in the future, and that the documents may be irretrievably lost. Worse yet, this problem does not occur just once for a given document but recurs throughout the future, as each form into which the document has migrated becomes obsolete in turn. Because the cycles of migration that must be performed are determined by the emergence of new formats or paradigms, which cannot be controlled or predicted, it is essentially impossible to estimate when migration will have to be performed for a given type of document—the only reliable prediction being that any given type of document is very likely to require conversion into some unforeseeable new form within some random number of years.

Since different format changes and paradigm shifts affect different types of documents, it is likely that some of the documents within a given corpus will require migration before others, unless the corpus consists entirely of a single type of document. This implies that any given corpus is likely to require migration on an arbitrarily short cycle, determined by whichever of the component types of any of its documents is the next to be affected by a new format or paradigm shift. Migration does not scale well. Because it is labor-intensive and highly dependent on the particular characteristics of individual document formats and paradigms, migration will derive little benefit from increased computing power. It is unlikely that general-purpose automated or semiautomated migration techniques will emerge, and if they do, they should be regarded with great suspicion because of their potential for silently corrupting entire corpora of digital documents by performing inadvertently destructive conversions on them. As the volume of our digital holdings increases over time, each migration cycle will face a greater challenge than the last, making the essentially manual methods available for performing migration increasingly inadequate to the task.

Problem in Preserving Digital Information

For digital preservation, the organizational effort-the process of building deep infrastructure-necessarily involves multiple, interrelated factors, many of which are either unknown or poorly defined. One of the biggest unknowns is the full impact on traditional information handling functions of distributed computing over electronic networks. The effort to meet the cultural imperative of digital preservation thus requires a complex iteration and reiteration of exploration, development and solution as the relevant factors and their interrelationships emerge and become clearer and more tractable.

And the first task in the effort is not to posit answers, but to frame questions and issues in such a way as to engage the many parties already working in various ways with digital information so that they can help us understand the relevant issues and, within the context of their work, help us identify, define and incorporate solutions that contribute to the larger, common goal of preserving our cultural heritage.

Digital archives are distinct from digital libraries in the sense that digital libraries are repositories that collect and provide access to digital information, but may or may not provide for the long-term storage and access of that information. Digital libraries thus may or may not be, in functional terms, digital archives and, in fact, much of the recent work on digital libraries is notably silent on the archival issues of ensuring long-term storage and access. Conversely, digital archives necessarily embrace digital library functions to the extent that they must select, obtain, store, and provide access to digital information. Many of the functional requirements for digital archives defined and thus overlap those for digital libraries.

Digital technologies increasingly serve to integrate information resources. Text, numeric data, images, voice, and video have heretofore resided in print or other analog media for storage and transmission. When they are encoded digitally, either by conversion or at the point of creation, these various kinds of resources share layers of technology-a common means of storage and transmission- that allows them to be brought together and used in both old and new ways.

Multimedia and hyperlinked objects on the World Wide Web represent some of the new kinds of information and new ways of knowing in the digital realm that bring together the traditional forms of information and transform their use. The application of computer hardware and software has also generated other new kinds of information objects, including the products of simulation, remote sensing, computer-aided design (CAD) and geographic information (GIS) systems. These objects come into being and exist as creatures of the digital environment; if nurtured well, digital technologies will certainly beget still other kinds of information objects, which we can now only anticipate.

The processes of preserving digital information will vary significantly with the different kinds of objects-textual, numeric, image, video, sound, multimedia, simulation and so on-being preserved. Whatever preservation method is applied, however, the central goal must be to preserve information integrity; that is, to define and preserve those features of an information object that distinguish it as a whole and singular work. In the digital environment, the features that determine information integrity and deserve special attention for archival purposes include the following: content, fixity, reference, provenance, and context.

What digital archives are trying to preserve after all is the intellectual substance contained in information objects. The notion of content, however, is itself a complex idea that operates at several different levels of abstraction. To preserve the integrity of objects in their charge, digital archives must decide at which level, or levels, of abstraction they are defining information content. At the lowest level of abstraction, all digital information objects consist of simple bitstreams of 0s and 1s. One can distinguish objects from one another merely by distinguishing the configuration of bits.

Preserving the integrity of an information object in this sense means preserving the bit configuration that uniquely defines the object. There are various well-established techniques, such as checksums and digests, for tracking the bit-level equivalence of digital objects and ensuring that a preserved object is identical to the original. Defining content as a collection of bits, however, is often too limited and simplistic to be useful. In the digital environment, as we have seen, ideas are typically embedded in particular formats and structures that are dependent on hardware and software technologies subject to rapid change.

Conceived at this higher level of abstraction-that is, in terms of format and structure-the definition of content poses considerable difficulties for managing information integrity in an archival context, and we are just beginning to come to terms with the expression of these problems in the digital environment. Text today is generally covered by a formal, international ASCII standard for representing character formats. Standard extensions exist for encoding diacritic characters in romance languages other than English and a new standard is slowly emerging to incorporate scripted languages under a new common encoding scheme (UNICODE).

Alternative encoding methods, however, abound. IBM maintains its own EBCDIC character encoding scheme and Apple and Intel-based personal computers differ in the ways that they support extended ASCII character sets. For documents in which any of these character codes can adequately represent the contents, the differences in encoding schemes may matter little and digital archives can manage object integrity by mapping character sets from one to the other. However, for works involving multiple languages or complex equations and formula, where character mapping is imperfect or not possible, character set format takes on considerably more significance over the long-term as a matter of content integrity.

In addition to character set issues, digital archives must also grapple with the means of representing and preserving textual content embedded in layout and structure. Markup systems, such as implementations of TeX and the Standard Generalized Markup Language (SGML), do exist as platform-independent mechanisms for identifying and tagging for subsequent layout and retrieval detailed structural elements of documents. The use of TeX and its variants, for example, is relatively common among scholars in some scientific disciplines such as mathematics and computer science, and the federal government and scholarly publishers are increasingly employing the SGML standard in documents that they produce and distribute electronically.

Beyond these relatively specialized segments, however, word processing and desktop publishing systems still dominate the market for the creation of documents with complex structure and layout, and the software for such use typically models and stores document structure and layout in proprietary terms. Although software may provide mechanisms for converting documents to common interchange formats, use of such mechanisms often results in the loss or inadequate rendering of content such as page structures and the layout of headers, footers and section headings.

The preservation of images comprises another example of the ways in which content, defined in terms of structure and format, poses integrity problems for digital archives. Image resolution, accuracy of color representation and compression for storage all require attention, but the interaction of these structural factors tends to pit judgments about the quality of content against the need for its efficient archival storage and use. In general, one can express the tradeoffs as follows: the higher the resolution and the richer the color register, the larger the file size and more costly the storage.

The use of compression technologies further complicates the equation because the application of some algorithms to reduce space needs may involve an irreversible loss of data. The popular JPEG algorithm, for example, supports “lossy” compression, whereby the greatest degree of compression requires the maximum settings for allowable loss. At the highest level of abstraction, digital archives define content in a way that transcends the limits of the hardware and software systems needed for reading and interpreting the bits of an information object and for rendering it for use in a specific format and structural representation; that is, they define content in terms of the knowledge or ideas the object contains.

Expressed in this way, the preservation challenge for digital archives is to migrate (or to enable the user to migrate) intellectual content using standard interchange algorithms and other appropriate migration strategies so that the ideas available in the end are identical to those contained in the original object. The measure of integrity in the preservation process thus turns, at least in part, on informed and skillful judgments about the appropriate definition of the content of an digital information object-about the extent to which content depends on its configuration of bits, on the structure and format of its representation, and on the ideas it contains-and for what purposes.

The process of identifying and preserving a digital information object as a whole and singular work goes well beyond considerations of content. It also depends, for instance, on the way that the content is fixed as a discrete object. If an object is not fixed, and the content is subject to change or withdrawal without notice, then its integrity may be compromised and its value as a cultural record would be severely diminished. Outside the digital landscape, business practices, editorial policies, and legal constraints, have created disciplines for fixing information in discrete objects. The acts of production and broadcast establish radio and television programs as discrete objects.

And the act of publication marks a specific version or edition of a literary work. In each of these cases, it is virtually impossible to change or withdraw the cultural record that the release of an information object establishes. On the digital landscape, by contrast, it is still relatively easy for a creator to alter or retract previously released information. Such actions can eliminate or overlay significant content and thereby corrupt the record. It is also relatively easy in an on-line environment-and equally confusing for purposes of preserving information integrity-for an author (or user) to make available concurrently multiple representations of what he or she considers to be the same work, providing no definition of a canonical version and viewing all representations as having equal quality and validity.

To address these problems, a wide range of cryptographic techniques, such as watermarking, already exist for various kinds of digital information objects. These could serve well to mark and identify specific, canonical versions and editions of textual, audio and visual works, and to establish trusted, protected channels of distribution for those objects. However, the standards and infrastructure and the policies and practices for applying such techniques to the creation of fixed versions of digital information objects still need considerable development. Absent such development and the fixity of information that would result, digital archives face considerable challenges in trying to preserve the integrity of digital objects.

Some kinds of digital objects present the problem of fixity of information in yet another way. An increasing number of networked information resources are better modeled, not in terms of versions or editions of works, but as continuously updated databases. The Human Genome Project supports such a database, which serves as a vehicle and record for a worldwide collaborative effort. The financial communities also depend on large, continuously updated databases. There is no natural way to fix these resources at the database level, no natural set of publication points for the objects as a whole. Their integrity, or singularity, as databases resides in the coherence of the database as a whole and in the continuousness of the updates.

To preserve the integrity of such information resources, the complete record of changes has to be built into the design of the database and fixed at the record level. Technology exists for constructing databases that maintain all previous versions of the records in the database as well as details about when new information is added or logically deleted. A database designed to a so-called time-travel specification, however, is expensive to construct and operate. In the absence of such a preservation-oriented design, digital archives may have no choice but to fix the database artificially in time and capture a series of snapshots of its state at periodic intervals as a way of preserving its integrity.

A third aspect of information integrity that bears crucially on the preservation process is that information objects must have a consistent means of reference. Information objects come into being and acquire their distinctiveness in relation to various other objects in an information space. For an object to maintain its integrity, its wholeness and singularity, one must be able to locate it definitively and reliably over time among other objects. Systems of citation, description and classification provide the necessary means of reference so that one can consistently discover, identify and retrieve relevant objects.

Such systems traditionally include bibliographies, catalogs, indices, data dictionaries, directory systems, finding aids and the like, all of which collect, assemble and organize references to bodies of work. Creators of these resources are already extending them with such innovations, for example, as the use of the 856 field in bibliographic records, to incorporate reference to digital objects. Moreover, in the electronic environment, there are also emerging sophisticated tools for automatically gathering and presenting in new kinds of products referential information from textual, image, sound, video and other kinds of digital objects.

To meet the test of consistent reference, however, citations to digital objects from these various manually and automatically generated sources must over time reliably identify the works to which they refer. One way of establishing confidence in a reference system is to generate citations in the first place- either manually or automatically-from the self-referential information that a work itself carries with it, perhaps in a header, a digital envelope or some other distinct part of the digital object. Unfortunately, except for documents marked up to the standard of the Text Encoding

Initiative, few digital objects today contain self-referential information that meets conventional citation quality.

Matching citation and digital work to meet the test of consistent reference thus is difficult. Moreover, reliably identifying multiple versions and editions of works in electronic form remains a persistent reference problem. Part of the general problem of identifying and consistently referring to variant digital works is the specific problem of resolving names and locations for them. Coordinated by such groups as the Internet Engineering Task Force (IETF), active research and development has led to an emerging consensus that several factors contribute to the unique identification of digital information objects.

Two of the most important factors are the Uniform Resource Name (URN) and the Uniform Resource Locator (URL). The URL refers to the specific place where a digital object resides and is currently the dominant method of object location on the World Wide Web. The weakness of the URL, however, is that it may frequently change, especially as an object migrates from one machine to the next. By contrast, a name, the URN, is supposed to apply uniquely and permanently to a distinct object and to designate it independently of its particular location at any point in time.

URNs today exist more in concept than in practice. Thus, resolving the name and location for variant digital works and thereby providing consistent reference to them means moving from a conceptual design of the relation between names and locations to an operational reality through the implementation of naming authorities, which assign URNs, and and the development of digital services that translate names into currently valid URLs. In order to provide a consistent means of reference for digital objects, systems of citation, description and classification will need to dispense more than name and location information.

The IETF framework provides a general category for additional reference information in what it calls Uniform Resource Characteristics (URCs). Among the kinds of information that a reference system might provide under this general category is information about the intellectual property rights governing the use of a particular object and its cost. For archival purposes, however, there are two other qualities of digital information objects that a reference system must take into account. These are the features of provenance and context.

Provenance has become one of the central organizing concepts of modern archival science. The assumption underlying the principle of provenance is that the integrity of an information object is partly embodied in tracing from where it came. To preserve the integrity of an information object, digital archives must preserve a record of its origin and chain of custody. For some information objects, the formal process of publication creates a trusted channel of distribution and serves to establish a sophisticated record of provenance, at least from the creator through the point of release.

In the digital environment, the problems of documenting provenance through a record of publication are bound up with the problems of fixity. Outside the path of publication, however, there are several other channels of information creation and distribution, including tracing the path of migration within their own organization, that digital archives need to document in order to preserve the integrity of digital objects in their custody.

First, there is a chain of provenance from individuals, a trail which has comprised a traditional concern of archivists. In the digital environment, as in other domains, individuals produce and accrete much information that relates to their private lives and to their public roles and responsibilities, including their means of livelihood. Among the kinds of information objects that may count as personal records in digital form are electronic mail, notes, manuscripts, journals, photographs or videos, and databases of personal finances. For objects of these kinds, which make their way into digital archives and which the custodian deems worth keeping as part of the historical record, the archival responsibility in establishing provenance is to establish, as unambiguously as possible, the identity of the individuals who are the source of the objects and to trace the chain of custody to arrival in the archives.

A second kind of digital information flow that requires special attention with respect to provenance are those mediated or governed by corporate information systems. The digital products of such systems may include databases of employment and financial records, contracts and other legal records, planning documents, FDA filings, technical reports and so on. The distinctive feature of such objects is that they are all best viewed not as the result of individual works but as proceeding from the business, governmental or other social practices that the information system organizes and instantiates. The archival challenge for establishing the provenance of such objects is to find ways to preserve an understanding of the corporate policies and processes and roles and responsibilities thus represented in the information system and its products.

Third, there is the chain of provenance that traces information, particularly scientific data, to a source in electronic instrumentation. In some cases, the instrumentation produces data in the service of individual experiments or of clinical practice; in other cases, remote sensors gather streams of observational data about physical systems in space or on earth. Of course, one ultimately accounts for the origin of the resulting data in the design and conduct of the experiment or clinical service, or in the character of the remote sensing program. However, the use of the instrumentation creates a special requirement to trace the provenance of the data to the design characteristics of the instrument itself. The data are a direct product of and derive their meaning and usefulness from the calibration, units of measure, sampling rate, conditions of recording and other relevant features embedded in the technology of the instrument.

Finally, a concern for provenance in preserving the integrity of digital information means that digital archives must document what happens to the information within their own organizations. They must keep a record of migration activity, and particularly of the transformations they make to keep information objects current with new technologies for use.

In the end, the investment that digital archives make in establishing the provenance of objects in their care serves to preserve the integrity of digital information in two distinct ways. First, a tracing of chain of custody from the point of creation helps to create the presumption that an object is authentic, that it is what it purports to be and that its content, however defined, has not been manipulated, altered or falsified. The second effect of establishing provenance through a chain of custody is to document, at least in part, the particular uses of the object by the custodians. In thus creating a record of use, the archival concern with provenance is intimately related to the notion of context as a matter of information integrity.

The fifth attribute of information integrity that bears on the preservation of digital information objects is their context, the ways in which they interact with elements in the wider digital environment. The context of digital information includes a technical dimension, a dimension of linkage to other objects, a communication dimension, and a wider social dimension.

Digital archives must be attentive to the ways in which each of these contextual dimensions affects the integrity of the objects in their care. First, to specify the technical context of digital information is to specify its hardware and software dependencies. Digital objects, by nature, require the use of computer hardware and software to create and use them.

As network-based objects, such as video and records of confidential transactions, make their way into digital repositories, an archival account of their integrity must include an account of the features of the network context that supports their existence. Finally, the wider social environment plays a significant contextual role that contributes to the integrity of digital information objects. Networked information, for example, depends on specific policy and implementation decisions that address the bandwidth, security and other qualities of the network and related technical infrastructure.

Electronic mail is subject to a variety of social distinctions when, in some contexts, it is used to convey highly personal messages among friends and, in other contexts, is a vehicle for formal communication among academic or business colleagues. One might account for digital business records, too, in the social context of the political and organizational regime in which they were generated. Indeed, the social context of digital information objects is an expression of what one might characterize in other terms as the interests of stakeholders in those objects. Digital information objects acquire the qualities of content, fixity, reference, provenance and context-and thereby their integrity-as they move through a life cycle in a series of relationships with parties, or stakeholders, who have specific interests in their creation, management, dissemination, use or retention.

Electronic Texts

Today the authors have tended to concentrate on those types of electronic text which, to a greater or lesser extent, represent a transcription of a non-electronic source, rather than the category of electronic texts which are primarily composed of digitised images of a source text. However, there are a growing number of electronic textual resources which support both these approaches; for example some projects involving the digitisation of rare illuminated manuscripts combine high-quality digital images with electronic text transcriptions. Creating and processing electronic texts was one of the earliest areas of computational activity, and has been going on for at least half a century.

When combined with an intimate knowledge of the non-electronic source material, readers should be able to decide for themselves which approach—and thus which combinations of hardware and software, techniques and design philosophy—will be most appropriate to their needs and the needs of any other prospective users. Although every functional aspect of computers is based upon the distinctive binary divide evidenced between 1's and 0's, true and false, presence and absence, it is rarely so easy to draw such clear distinctions at the higher levels of creating and documenting electronic texts. Readers should not assume that any course of action recommended here will necessarily be the 'best' approach in any or all given circumstances; however everything the authors say is based upon our understanding of what constitutes good practice—and results from almost twenty-five years of experience running the Oxford Text Archive. Conversely, if you are hoping to produce an electronic text that will have broad functionality and appeal, and the original source contains presentational features which might be considered worthy of note, then you should be attempting to create a very different object - perhaps one where visual fidelity is more important than the absolute accuracy of any transcription.

Deciding to create an electronic text is just like deciding to begin any other type of construction project. While the desire to dive right in and begin building is tempting, any worthwhile endeavour will begin with a thorough planning stage. In the case of digitised text creation, this stage is called document analysis. Document analysis is literally the task of examining the physical object in order to acquire an understanding about the work being digitised and to decide what the purpose and future of the project entails. The digitisation of texts is not simply making groups of words available to an online community; it involves the creation of an entirely new object. This is why achieving a sense of what it is that you are creating is critical. The blueprint for construction will allow you to define the foundation of the project. It will also allow you to recognise any problems or issues that have the potential to derail the project at a later point. Document analysis is all about definition - defining the document context, defining the document type and defining the different document features and relationships. At no other point in the project will you have the opportunity to spend as much quality time with your document. This is when you need to become intimately acquainted with the format, structure, and content of the texts.

One of the first tasks to perform in document analysis is to define the goals of the project and the context under which they are being developed. This could be seen as one of the more difficult tasks in the document analysis procedure, as it relies less upon the physical analysis of the document and more upon the theoretical positions taken with the project. This is the stage where you need to ask yourself why the document is being encoded. It is also important to take into consideration the external influences on the project. Often the bodies that oversee digitisation projects, either in a funding or advisory capacity, have specific conditions that must be fulfilled. They might for example have markup requirements or standards (linguistic, TEI/SGML, or EAD perhaps) that must be taken into account when establishing an encoding methodology.

Also, if you are creating the electronic text for scholarly purposes, then it is very likely that the standards of this community will need to be adhered to. Again, it must be remembered that the electronic version of a text is a distinct object and must be treated as such. Just as you would adhere to a publishing standard of practice with a printed text, so must you follow the standard for electronic texts.

The most stringent scholarly community, the textual critics and bibliographers, will have specific, established guidelines that must be considered in order to gain the requisite scholarly authority. Therefore, if you were creating a text to be used or approved by this community their criteria would have to be integrated into the project standards, with the subsequent influence on both the objectives and the creative process taken into account.

If the digitisation project includes image formats, then there are specific archiving standards held by the electronic community that might have to be met—this will not only influence the purchase of hardware and software, but will have an impact on the way in which the electronic object will finally be structured.

External conditions are easily overlooked during the detailed analysis of the physical object, so be sure that the standards and policies that influence the outcome of the project are given serious thought, as having to modify the documents retrospectively can prove both detrimental and expensive.

While you cannot satisfy each desire, trying to evaluate what information might be the most important to your audience will allow you to address the needs and concerns you deem most appropriate and necessary. Also, if there are specific objectives that you wish users to derive from the project then this too needs to be established at the outset. If the primary purpose for the texts is as a teaching mechanism, then this will have a significant influence on how you choose to encode the document.

Conversely, if your texts are being digitised so that users will be able to perform complex thematic searches, then both the markup of content and the content of the markup will differ somewhat. Regardless of the decision, be sure that the outcome of this evaluation becomes integrated with the previously determined project objectives.

You must also attempt to assess what tools users will have at their disposal to retrieve your document. The hardware and software capabilities of your users will differ, sometimes dramatically, and will most likely present some sort of restriction or limitation upon their ability to access your project. SGML encoded text requires the use of specialised software, such as Panorama, to read the work.

Even HTML has tagsets that early browsers may not be able to read. It is essential that you take these variants into consideration during the planning stage. There might be priorities in the project that require accessibility for all users, which would affect the methodology of the project. However, don't let the user limitations stunt the encoding goals for the document.

Hardware and software are constantly being upgraded so that although some of the encoding objectives might not be fully functional during the initial stages of the project, they stand a good chance of becoming accessible in the near future.

The first stage of document analysis is not only necessary for detailing the goals and objectives of the project, but also serves as an opportunity to examine the context of the document. This is a time to gather as much information as possible about the documents being digitised.

The amount gathered varies from project to project, but in an ideal situation you will have a complete transmission and publication history for the document. There are a few key reasons for this. Firstly, knowing how the object being encoded was created will allow you to understand any textual variations or anomalies. This, in turn, will assist in making informed encoding decisions at later points in the project.

The difference between a printer error and an authorial variation not only affects the content of the document, but also the way in which it is marked up. Secondly, the depth of information gathered will give the document the authority desired by the scholarly community. A text about which little is known can only be used with much hesitation.

While some users might find it more than acceptable for simply printing out or reading, there can be no authoritative scholarly analysis performed on a text with no background history. Thirdly, a quality electronic text will have a TEI header attached. The TEI header records all the information about the electronic text's print source. The more information you know about the source, the more full and conclusive your header will be—which will again provide scholarly authority.

Lastly, understanding the history of the document will allow you to understand its physicality. The physicality of the text is an interesting issue - and one on which very few scholars fully agree. Clearly, an understanding of the physical object provides a sense of the format, necessary for a proper structural encoding of the text, but it also augments a contextual understanding.

While the physical object has trained readers to follow a more linear narrative, the electronic document will provide you with an opportunity to develop the variant branches found within the text. Depending upon the decided project objectives, you are free to highlight, augment or furnish your users with as many different associations as you find significant in the text. Yet to do this, you must fully understand the ontology of the texts and then be able to delineate this textuality through the encoding of the computerised object. It is important to remember that the transmission history does not end with the publication of the printed document. Tracking the creation of the electronic text, including the revision history, is a necessary element of the encoding process. The fluidity of electronic texts precludes the guarantee that every version of the document will remain in existence, so the responsibility lies with the project creator to ensure that all revisions and developments are noted. While some of the documentation might seem tedious, an electronic transmission history will serve two primary purposes.

One, it will help keep the project creator(s) aware of what has developed in the creation of the electronic text. If there are quite a few staff members working on the documents, you will be able to keep track of what has been accomplished with the texts and to check that the project methodology is being followed. Two, users of the documents will be able to see what emendations or regularisations have been made and to track what the various stages of the electronic object were.

Defining the document type is a critical part of the digitisation process as it establishes the foundation for the initial understanding of the text's structure. At this point you should have an idea of what documents are going to be digitised for the project. Even if you not sure precisely how many texts will be in the final project, it is important to have a representative sample of the types of documents being digitised.

Examine the sample documents and decide what categories they fall under. The structure and content of a letter will differ greatly from that of a novel or poem, so it is critical to make these naming classifications early in the process. Not only are there structural differences between varying document types but also within the same type.

Deciding upon document type will give you an initial sense of the shape of the text. There are basic structural assumptions that come with classification: looking for the stanzas in poetry or the paragraphs in prose for example. Having established the document type, you can begin to assign the texts a more detailed structure. Without worrying about the actual tag names, as this comes later in the process, label all of the features you wish to encode.

For example, if you are digitising a novel, you might initially break it into large structural units: title page, table of contents, preface, body, back matter, etc. Once this is done you might move on to smaller features: titles, heads, paragraphs, catchwords, pagination, plates, annotations and so forth. One way to keep the naming in perspective is to create a structure outline. This will allow you to see how the structure of your document is developing, whether you have omitted any necessary features, or if you have labelled too much.

Once the features to be encoded have been decided upon, the relationships between them can then be examined. Establishing the hierarchical sequence of the document should not be too arduous a task—especially if you have already developed a structural outline. It should at this point be apparent, if we stick with the example of a novel, that the work is contained within front matter, body matter, and back matter.

Within front matter we find such things as epigraphs, prologues, and title pages. Within the paragraphs can be found quotations, figures, and notes. This is an established and understandable hierarchy. There is also a sequential relationship where one element logically follows another.

Using the above representation, if every body has chapters, paragraphs, and notes, then you would expect to find a sequence of <chapter> then <paragraph> then <note>, not <chapter>, <note>, then <paragraph>. Again, the more you understand about the type of text you are encoding, the easier this process will be. While the level of structural encoding will ultimately depend upon the project objectives, this is an opportune time to explore the form of the text in as much detail as possible.

Having these data will influence later encoding decisions, and being able to refer to these results will be much easier than having to sift through the physical object at a later point to resolve a structural dilemma. The analysis also brings to light any issues or problems with the physical document. Are parts of the source missing? Perhaps the text has been water damaged and certain lines are unreadable? If the document is a manuscript or letter perhaps the writing is illegible? These are all instances that can be explored at an early stage of the project.

While these problems will add a level of complexity to the encoding project, they must be dealt with in an honest fashion. If the words of a letter are illegible and you insert text that represents your best guess at the actual wording then this needs to be encoded. The beauty of document analysis is that by examining the documents prior to digitisation you stand a good chance of recognising these issues and establishing an encoding methodology.

The benefit of this is threefold: firstly, having identified and dealt with this problem at the start you will have fewer issues arise during the digitisation process; secondly, there will be an added level of consistency during the encoding stage and retrospective revision won't be necessary; thirdly, the project will benefit from the thorough level of accuracy desired and expected by the scholarly community.

This is also a good time to examine the physical document and attempt to anticipate problems with the digitisation process. Fragile spines, flaking or foxed paper, badly inked text, all will create difficulties during the scanning process and increase the likelihood of project delays if not anticipated at an early stage. This is another situation that requires examining representative samples of texts.

It could be that one text was cared for in the immaculate conditions of a Special Collections facility while another was stored in a damp corner of a bookshelf. You need to be prepared for as many document contingencies as possible. Problems not only arise out of the condition of the physical object, but also out of such things as typography. OCR digitisation is heavily reliant upon the quality and type of fonts used in the text.

OCR software is optimised for laser quality printed text. This means that the older the printed text, the more degradation in the scanning results. These types of problems are critical to identify, as decisions will have to be made about how to deal with them - decisions that will become a significant part of the project methodology.

The final stage of document analysis is deciding which features of the text to encode. Once again, knowing the goals and objectives of the project will be of great use as you try to establish the breadth of your element definition. You have the control over how much of the document you want to encode, taking into account how much time and manpower are dedicated to the project.

Once you've made a decision about the level of encoding that will go into the project, you need to make the practical decision of what to tag. There are three basic categories to consider: structure, format and content. In terms of structure there are quite a few typical elements that are encoded. This is a good time to examine the structural outline to determine what skeletal features need to be marked up.

In most cases, the primary divisions of text - chapters, sections, stanzas, etc.—and the supplementary parts—paragraphs, lines, pages—are all assigned tag names. With structural markup, it is helpful to know how detailed an encoding methodology is being followed. As you will discover, you can encode almost anything in a document, so it will be important to have established what level of markup is necessary and to then adhere to those boundaries.

Some of the common elements relate to attributes such as bold, italic and typeface. Then there are other aspects that take a bit more thought, such as special characters. Format issues also include notes and annotations (items that figure heavily in scholarly texts), marginal glosses, and indentations.

Elements of format are easily forgotten, so be sure to go through the representative documents and choose the visual aspects of the text that must be carried through to the electronic object.

The third encoding feature concerns document content. This is where you will go through the document looking for features that are neither structural nor format based. This is the point where you can highlight the content information necessary to the text and the user. Refer back to the decisions made about textual relationships and what themes and ideas should be highlighted.

If, for example, you are creating a database of author biographies you might want to encode such features as author's name, place of birth, written works, spouse, etc. Having a clear sense of the likely users of the project will make these decisions easier—and perhaps more straightforward. This is also a good time to evaluate what the methodology will be for dealing with textual revisions, deletions, and additions—either authorial or editorial.

Again, it is not so critical here to define what element tags you are using but rather to arrive at a listing of features that need to be encoded. Once these steps have been taken you are ready to move on to the digitisation process.

Process of Digitisation

Digitisation is quite simply the creation of a computerised representation of a printed analog. There are many methods of digitising and varied media to be digitised. Digitising other formats, audio and video for example, there are many thorough analyses of procedure. In other words, recommendations for digitising are constantly changing. As hardware and software develop, so does the quality of digitised output. The price cuts in storage costs allow smaller projects to take advantage of archival imaging standards. The digitisation chain is a concept expounded by Peter Robinson in his aforementioned publication. The idea is based upon the fundamental concept that the best quality image will result from digitising the original object. If this is not an attainable goal, then digitisation should be attempted with as few steps removed from the original as possible. Therefore, the chain is composed of the number of intermediates that come between the original object and the digital image - the more intermediates, the more links in the chain. Each link attains a level of importance so that if one piece of the chain were to break, the entire project would fail. Regardless of the technology utilised by the project, the results will depend, first and foremost, on the quality of the image being scanned. Scanning a copy of a microfilm of an illustration originally found in a journal is acceptable if it is the only option you have, but clearly scanning the image straight from the journal itself is going to make an immeasurable difference in quality.

This is one important reason for carefully choosing the hardware and software. If you know that you are dealing with fragile manuscripts that cannot handle the damaging light of a flatbed scanner, or a book whose binding cannot open past a certain degree, then you will probably lean towards a digital camera. If you have text that is from an 18th-century book, with fading pages and uneven type, you will want the best text scanning software available. Knowing where your documents stand in the digitisation chain will influence the subsequent imaging decisions you will make for the project. The first step in digitisation, both text and image, is to obtain a workable facsimile of the page. To accomplish this you will need a combination of hardware and software imaging tools. This is a somewhat difficult area to address in terms of recommending specific product brands, as what is considered industry (or at least the text creation industry) standard is subject to change as technology develops.

There are quite a few methods of image capture that are used within the humanities community. The equipment ranges from scanners (flatbed, sheetfed, drum, slide, microfilm) to high-end digital cameras. In terms of standards within the digitising community, the results are less than satisfactory. Projects tend to choose the most available option, or the one that is affordable on limited grant funding. However, two of the most common and accessible image capture solutions are flatbed scanners and high-resolution digital cameras. Flatbed scanners have become the most commonplace method for capturing images or text. Their name comes from the fact that the scanner is literally a flat glass bed, quite similar to a copy machine, on which the image is placed face down and covered. The scanner then passes light-sensitive sensors over the illuminated page, breaking it into groups of pixel-sised boxes. It then represents each box with a sero or a one, depending on whether the pixel is filled or empty.

The importance of this becomes more apparent with the discussion of image type below. As a result of their lowering costs and widespread availability, the use of quality flatbeds ranges from the professional digital archiving projects to the living rooms of the home computer consumer. One benefit of this increased use and availability is that flatbed scanning technology is evolving continually. This has pushed the purchasing standards away from price and towards quality. In an attempt to promote the more expensive product, the marketplace tends to hype resolution and bit-depth, two aspects of scanning that are important to a project but are not the only concerns when purchasing hardware. While it is not necessarily the case that you need to purchase the most expensive scanner to get the best quality digital image, it is unlikely that the entry-level flatbeds will provide the image quality that you need. However, while it used to be the case that to truly digitise well you needed to purchase the more high-end scanner, at a price prohibitive to most projects, the advancing digitising needs of users have pushed hardware developers to create mid-level scanners that reach the quality of the higher range. As a consumer, you need to possess a holistic view of the scanner's capabilities. Not only should the scanner provide you with the ability to create archival quality images but it should also make the digitisation process easier. Many low-cost scanners do not have high-grade lenses, optics, or light sources, thereby creating images that are of a very poor quality. The creation of superior calibre images relates to the following hardware requirements:

— the quality of the lens, mirrors, and other optics hardware;
— the mechanical stability of the optical system;
— the focal range and stability of the optical system;
— the quality of the scanning software and many other hardware and software features.

Also, many of the better quality scanners contain tools that allow you to automate some of the procedures. This is extremely useful with such things as colour and contrast where, with the human eye, it is difficult to achieve the exact specification necessary for a high-quality image. Scanning hardware has the ability to provide this discernment for the user, so these intelligent automated features are a necessity to decrease task time. One of the disadvantages of a flatbed scanner is that to capture the entire image the document must lie completely flat on the scanning bed. With books this poses a problem because the only way to accomplish this is to bend the spine to the breaking point. It becomes even worse when dealing with texts with very fragile pages, as the inversion and pressure can cause the pages to flake away or rip.

A solution to this problem, one taken up by many digital archives and special collections departments, is to digitise with a stand-alone digital camera. Digital cameras are by far the most dependable means of capturing quality digital images. The ability to digitise with variant lighting is a significant benefit as it won't damage the make-up of the work, a precaution which cannot be guaranteed with flatbed scanners. The high resolution and heightened image quality allows for a level of detail you would expect only in the original. As a result of these specifications, images can be delivered at great sise. A good example of this is the Early American Fiction project being developed at UVA's Electronic Text Center and Special Collections Department. The Early American Fiction project, whose goal is the digitisation of 560 volumes of American first editions held in the UVA Special Collections, is utilising digital cameras mounted above light tables. They are working with camera backs manufactured by Phase One attached to Tarsia Technical Industries Prisma 45 4x5 cameras on TTI Reprographic Workstations. This has allowed them to create high quality images without damaging the physical objects. As they point out in their overview of the project, the workflow depends upon the text being scanned, but the results work out to close to one image every three minutes.

While this might sound detrimental to the project timeline, it is relatively quick for an archival quality image. The images can be seen at such a high-resolution that the faintest pencil annotations can be read on-screen. There are a few tools that are commonly seen in use with many digitisation projects. Regardless of the brand of software purchased, the project will need text scanning software if there is to be in-house digitisation of text and an image manipulation software package if imaging is to be done. There are a wide variety of text scanning softwares available, all with varying capabilities. As this software is optimised for laser quality printouts, projects working with texts from earlier centuries need to find a package that has the ability to work through more complicated fonts and degraded page quality. While there is no standard, most projects work with Caere's OmniPage scanning software. In terms of image manipulation, there are more choices depending upon what needs to be done.

For image-by-image manipulation, including converting TIFFs to web-deliverable JPEGs and GIFs, Adobe Photoshop is the more common selection. However, when there is a move towards batch conversion, Graphic's DeBabelizer Pro is known for its speed and high quality. If the conversion is being done in a UNIX environment, the XV operating system is also a favourite amongst digitisation projects. Electronic text creation primarily involves the digitisation of text and images. Apart from re-keying, the best method of digitising text is Optical Character Recognition (OCR). This process is accomplished through the utilisation of scanning hardware in conjunction with text scanning software. OCR takes a scanned image of a page and converts it into text. Similarly, image capture also requires an image scanning software to accompany the hardware. However, unlike text scanning, image capture has more complex requirements in terms of project decisions and, like almost everything else in the digitisation project, benefits from clearly thought out objectives. The first decision that must be made regarding image capture concerns the purpose of the images being created. The reason for this is simple: the higher quality the image need be, the higher the settings necessary for scanning. There are four main types of images: 1-bit black and white, 8-bit greyscale, 8-bit colour and 24-bit colour. A bit is the fundamental unit of information read by the computer, with a single bit being represented by either a '0' or a '1'. A '0' is considered an absence and a '1' is a presence, with more complex representations of information being accommodated by multiple or gathered bits.

A 1-bit black and white image means that the bit can either be black or white. This is a rarely used type and is completely unsuitable for almost all images. The only amenable image for this format would be printed text or line graphics for which poor resulting quality did not matter. Another drawback of this type is that saving it as a JPEG compressed image—one of the most prevalent image formats on the web—is not a feasible option. 8-bit greyscale images are an improvement from 1-bit as they encompass 256 shades of grey. It is often used for non-colour images and provides a clear image rather than the resulting fuzz of a 1-bit scan. While greyscale images are often considered more than adequate, there are times when non-colour images should be scanned at a higher colour because the finite detail of the hand will come through distinctly.

Also, the consistent recommendation is that images that are to be considered preservation or archival copies should be scanned as 24-bit colour. 8-bit colour is similar to 8-bit greyscale with the exception that each bit can be one of 256 colours. The decision to use 8-bit colour is completely project dependent, as the format is appropriate for web page images but can come out somewhat grainy. Another factor is the type of computer the viewer is using, as older ones cannot handle an image above 8-bit, so it will convert a 24-bit image to the lower format. However, the factor to take into consideration here is primarily storage space. An 8-bit image, while not having the quality of a higher format, will be markedly smaller. If possible, 24-bit colour is the best scanning choice.

This option provides the highest quality image, with each bit having the potential to contain one of 16.8 million colours. The arguments against this image format are the size, cost and time necessary. Again, knowing the objectives of the project will assist in making this decision. If you are trying to create archival quality images, this is taken as the default setting. 24-bit colour makes the image look more photo-realistic, even if the original is greyscale. The thing to remember with archival quality imaging is that if you need to go back and manipulate the image in any way, it can be copied and adjusted. However, if you scan the image as a lesser format then any kind of retrospective adjustments will be impossible. While a 24-bit colour archived image can be made greyscale, an 8-bit greyscale image cannot be converted into millions of colours.

The second concern relates to the resolution of the image. The resolution is determined by the number of dots per inch (dpi). The more dots per inch in the file, the more information is being stored about the image. Again, this choice is directly related to what is being done with the image. If the image is being archived or will need to be enlarged, then the resolution will need to be relatively higher. If, when using an imaging software program, you click on the 'save as' function to finalise the capture, you will see that there are quite a few image formats to choose from. In terms of text creation there are three types fundamental to the process: TIFF, JPEG, and GIF. These are the most common image formats because they transfer to almost any platform or software system.

TIFF (Tagged Image File Format) files are the most widely accepted format for archival image creation and retention as master copy. More so than the following formats, TIFF files can be read by almost all platforms, which also makes it the best choice when transferring important images. Most digitisation projects begin image scanning with the TIFF format, as it allows you to gather as much information as possible from the original and then saves these data. This touches on the only disadvantage of the TIFF format - the size of the image. However, once the image is saved, it can be called up at any point and be read by a computer with a completely different hardware and software system. Also, if there exists any possibility that the images will be modified at some point in the future, then the images should be scanned as TIFFs.

JPEG (Joint Photographic Experts Group) files are the strongest format for web viewing and transfer through systems that have space restrictions. JPEGs are popular with image creators not only for their compression capabilities but also for their quality. While a TIFF is a lossless compression, JPEGs are a lossy compression format. This means that as a filesize condenses, the image loses bits of information. However, this does not mean that the image will markedly decrease in quality. If the image is scanned at 24-bit, each dot has the choice of 16.8 million colours - more than the human eye can actually differentiate on the screen. So with the compression of the file, the image loses the information least likely to be noticed by the eye. The disadvantage of this format is precisely what makes it so attractive - the lossy compression. Once an image is saved, the discarded information is lost. The implication of this is that the entire image, or certain parts of it, cannot be enlarged. Additionally, the more work done to the image, requiring it to be re-saved, the more information is lost. This is why JPEGs are not recommended for archiving - there is no way to retain all of the information scanned from the source. Nevertheless, in terms of viewing capabilities and storage size, JPEGs are the best method for online viewing.

GIF (Graphic Interchange Format) files are an older format that are limited to 256 colours. Like TIFFs, GIFs use a lossless compression format without requiring as much storage space. While they don't have the compression capabilities of a JPEG, they are strong candidates for graphic art and line drawings. They also have the capability to be made into transparent GIFs - meaning that the background of the image can be rendered invisible, thereby allowing it to blend in with the background of the web page. This is frequently used in web design but can have a beneficial use in text creation. There are instances, where it is possible that a text character cannot be encoded so that it can be read by a web browser. It could be inline images (a head-piece for example) or the character is not defined by ISOLAT1 or ISOLAT2.

TIFFs would not be used for online delivery, but if you want your images to have any future use, either for archiving, later enlarging, manipulation, or printing, or simply as a master copy, then there is no other format in which to store the images. In terms of online presentation, then

JPEGs and GIFs are the best method. JPEGs will be of a better calibre and smaller filesize but cannot be enlarged or they will pixelate. Yet in terms of viewing quality their condition will almost match the TIFF. How you use GIFs will depend on what types of images are associated with the project. However, if you are making thumbnail images that link to a separate page which exhibits the JPEG version, then GIFs are a popular choice for that task. Preservation imaging is defined as 'high-speed, 1-bit (simple black and white) page images shot at 600 dpi and stored as Group 4 fax-compressed files'. The results of this are akin to microfilm imaging. While this does preserve the text for reading purposes, it ignores the source as a physical object. Archiving often presupposes that the objects are being digitised so that the source can be protected from constant handling, or as an international means of accessibility.

However, this type of preservation annihilates any chance of presenting the object as an artefact. Archiving an object has an entirely different set of requirements. Yet, having said this, there is also a prevalent school of thought in the archiving community that the only imaging that can be considered of archival value is film imaging, which is thought to last at least ten times as long as a digital image. Nonetheless, the idea of archival imaging is still discussed amongst projects and funding bodies and cannot be overlooked. There is no set standard for archiving, and you might find that different places and projects recommend another model. However, the following type, format and resolution are recommended:

— *24-bit*: There really is little reason to scan an archival image at anything less. Whether the source is colour or greyscale, the images are more realistic and have a higher quality at this level. As the above example shows, the filesize of the subsequently compressed image does not benefit from scanning at a lower bit-size.

— *600 dpi*: This is, once again, a problematic recommendation. Many projects assert that scanning in at 300 or 400 dpi provides sufficient quality to be considered archival. However, many of the top international digitisation centres recommend 600 dpi as an archival standard - it provides excellent detail of the image and allows for quite large JPEG images to be produced.

  The only restrictive aspect is the filesize, but when thinking in terms of archival images you need to try and get as much storage space as possible. Remember, the master copies do not have to be held online, as offline storage on writeable CD-ROMs is another option.

— *TIFF*: This should come as no surprise given the format discussion above. TIFF files, with their complete retention of scanned information and cross-platform capabilities are really the only choice for archival imaging. The images maintain all of the information scanned from the source and are the closest digital replication available. The size of the file, especially when scanned at 24-bit, 600 dpi, will be quite large, but well worth the storage space. You won't be placing the TIFF image online, but it is simple to make a JPEG image from the TIFF as a viewing copy.

This information is provided with the caveat that scanning technology is constantly changing for the better. It is more than likely that in the future these standards will become passé, with higher standards taking their place. The goal of recognition technology is to re-create the text and, if desired, other elements of the page including such things as tables and layout. Refer back to the concept of the scanner and how it takes a copy of the image by replicating it with the patterns of bits - the dots that are either filled or unfilled. OCR technology examines the patterns of dots and turns them into characters. Depending upon the type of scanning software you are using, the resulting text can be piped into many different word processing or spreadsheet programs.

Caere OmniPage released version 10.0 in the Autumn of 1999, which boasts the new Predictive Optical Word Recognition Plus+ (POWR++) technology. As the OmniPage factsheet explains, POWR++ enables OmniPage Pro to recognise standard typefaces, without training, from 4 to 72 point sizes. POWR++ recognises 13 languages (Brazilian Portuguese, British English, Danish, Dutch, Finnish, French, German, Italian, Norwegian, Portuguese, Spanish, Swedish, and U.S English) and includes full dictionaries for each of these languages. However, OCR software programs (including OmniPage) are very up-front about the fact that their technology is optimised for laser printer quality text. The reasoning behind this should be readily apparent. As scanning software attempts to examine every pixel in the object and then convert it into a filled or empty space, a laser quality printout will be easy to read as it has very clear, distinct, characters on a crisp white background - a background that will not interfere with the clarity of the letters.

However, once books become the object type, the software capabilities begin to degrade. This is why the first thing you must consider if you decide to use OCR for the text source is the condition of the document to be scanned. If the characters in the text are not fully formed or there are instances of broken type or damaged plates, the software will have a difficult time reading the material. The implications of this are that late 19th and 20th-century texts have a much better chance of being read well by the scanning software. As you move further away from the present, with the differences in printing, the OCR becomes much less dependable. The changes in paper, moving from a bleached white to a yellowed, sometimes foxed, background creates noise that the software must sift through. Then the font differences wreak havoc on the recognition capabilities. The gothic and exotic type found in the hand-press period contrasts markedly with the computer-set texts of the late 20th century.

It is critical that you anticipate type problems when dealing with texts that have such forms as long esses, sloping descenders, and ligatures. Taking sample scans with the source materials will help pinpoint some of these digitising issues early on in the project. While the advantages of exporting text in different word processing formats are quite useful if you are scanning in a document to print or to compensate for an accidentally deleted file, there are a few issues that should take priority with the text creator. Assuming you are using a software program such as OmniPage, you should aim for a scan that retains some formatting but not a complete page element replication. In terms of text creation, and the long-term preservation of the digital object, you want to be able to control this markup. If possible, scanning at a setting that will retain font and paragraph format is the best option. Scanning at a mid-level of formatting will assist you if you have decided to use your own encoding.

Unfortunately for the text creator, there are still many situations where the documents or project preclude the use of OCR. If the text is of a poor or degraded quality, then it is quite possible that the time spent correcting the OCR mistakes will exceed that of simply typing in the text from scratch. The amount of information to be digitised also becomes an issue. Even if the document is of a relatively good quality, there might not be enough time to sit down with 560 volumes of texts (as with the Early American Fiction project) and process them through OCR. The general rule of thumb, and this varies from study to study, is that a best-case scenario would be three pages scanned per minute - this doesn't take into consideration the process of putting the document on the scanner, flipping pages, or the subsequent proofreading. If, when addressing these concerns, OCR is found incapable of handling the project digitisation, the viable solution is re-keying the text. Once you've made this decision, the next question to address is whether to handle the document in-house or out-source the work. Deciding to digitise the material in-house relies on having all the necessary hardware, software, staff, and time.

There are a few issues that come into play with in-house digitisation. The primary concern is the speed of re-keying. Most often the re-keying is done by the research assistants working on the project, or graduate students from the text creator's local department. The problem here is that paying an hourly rate to someone re-keying the text often proves more expensive than out-sourcing the material. Also, there is the concern that a single person typing in material tends to overlook keyboarding errors - and if the staff member is familiar with the source material, there is a tendency to correct automatically those things that seem incorrect. So while in-house digitisation is an option, these concerns should be addressed from the outset. Again, as with most steps in the text creation process, the answers to these questions will be project dependent. The decisions made for a project that plans to digitise a collection of works will be markedly different from those made by an academic who is creating an electronic edition. It reflects back, as always, to the importance of the document analysis stage. You must recognise what the requirements of the project will be, and what external influences will affect the decision-making process.

References

Beagrie, N. and Jones, M. *Preservation Management of Digital Materials: A Handbook*, London. 2001.

Fenton, E. & R. Schonfeld.. "Digital Preservation Library Periodicals Expenses: Variance between Non-Subscription Costs for Print and electronic Formats on a Life-Cycle Basis." Presented at the Fall 2003 CNI Task Force Meeting, Portland, OR, 8-9 December 2003.

Friedlander, A., 'The National Digital Information In frastructure Preservation Program,' *D-Lib Magazine*, 8.4, April 2002, http://www.dlib.org/dlib/april02/friedlander/04friedlander.html

OCLC/RLG Working Group on Preservation Metadata. "Preservation Metadata and the OAIS Information Model: A Metadata Framework to Support the Preservation of digital Objects." 2002.

7

Information Retrieval

As we move into the electronic era of digital objects it is important to know that there are new barbarians at the gate and that we are moving into an era where much of what we know today, much of what is coded and written electronically, will be lost forever. Enormous amounts of digital information are already lost forever.

Digital history cannot be recreated by individuals, and organisations cannot recreate a digital history because it was not archived or managed properly or it resides in formats that cannot be accessed because the information is on out-dated word-processor files, old database formats, or saved on unreadable media. Many large data-sets in governments and universities world-wide have been made obsolete by changing technologies and will either be lost or subject to expensive 'rescue' operations to save the information.

There will be a demographic bulge of electronic materials coming into libraries and archives as the Baby Boom generation of authors and academics begin to wind down their careers and begin off-loading their materials to various libraries and archives. These materials will come to libraries on a wide variety of storage devices, perhaps even in entire computer systems, and will probably have equally significant paper collections associated with them.

Information technologies are essentially obsolete every 18 months. This dynamic creates an unstable and unpredictable environment for the continuance of hardware and software over a long period of time and represents a greater challenge than the deterioration of the physical medium. Many technologies and devices disappear as the companies that provide them move on to new product lines, often without backwards compatibility and ability to handle older technologies, or the companies themselves disappear.

There is a proliferation of document and media formats, each one potentially carrying their own hardware and software dependencies. Copying these formats from one storage device to another is simple. However, merely copying bits is not suffi-cient for preservation purposes: if the soft-ware for making sense of the bits is not available, then the information will be, for all practical purposes, lost. Libraries will have to contend with this wide variety of digital formats.

Many digital library collections will not have originated in digital form but come from materials that were digitised for particular purposes. Those digital resources which come to libraries from creators or other content providers will be wildly heterogeneous in their storage media, retrieval technologies and data formats. Libraries which seek out materials on the Internet will quickly discover the complexity of maintaining the integrity of links and dealing with dynamic documents that have multimedia contents, back-end script support, and embedded objects and programming.

Financial resources available for libraries and archives continue to decrease and will likely do so for the near future. The argument for preserving digital information has not effectively made it into public policy. There is little enthusiasm for spending resources on preservation at the best of times and without a concerted effort to bring the issues into the public eye, the preservation of digital information will remain a cloistered issue.

The importance of libraries has been diminished in the popular press as the pressures from industry encourage consumers to see libraries as anachronistic while the Internet and electronic products such as Microsoft Encarta are promoted as inevitable replacements. Until this situation changes, libraries and archives will continue to be asked to do more with lessÑboth in terms of providing traditional library services, as well as new digital library services: preservation will have to encompass both kinds of collections.

Increasingly restrictive intellectual property and licensing regimes will ensure that many materials never make it into library collections for preservation. These will be corporate assets and will not be deposited into public collections without substantive financial and licensing arrangements that few libraries will be able to afford. From a positive perspective, this fact will allow libraries to essentially ignore the preservation question for many kinds of key information resources as these may be preserved by their corporate owners. The flip-side of this argument is whether corporate owners will develop a public-spirited interest in providing this archival role for future generations and whether the resources will be accessible to the public.

The archiving and preservation functions within a digital environment will become increasingly privatized as information continues to be commodified. Companies will be the place where the most valuable information is retained and preserved, and this will be done only insofar as there is a corporate recognition of the information as an asset. But companies have no binding commitment to making information available over a long term. Those librarians who suggest that legal deposit is the means for addressing this issue are not likely to be successful.

The first line of defense against the loss of valuable digital information rests with the creators, providers and owners of digital information. This fact is a critical one for preservation purposes as it strongly suggests that the role that librarians and archivists must play will be an increasingly public one. Preservation is a desktop issue, not merely an institutional one.

The role of preservationists must be to interact with users and to address preservation and information management issues on their desktops, not the archivists' desktop.

Standards will not emerge to solve fundamental issues with respect to digital information. The challenge in preserving electronic information is not primarily a technological one, it is a sociological one. The dynamism of the market for information technologies and products ensures the fundamental instability of hardware and software primarily because product obsolescence is often key to corporate survival in a competitive capitalist demo-cracy. Product differentiation manifests itself at the very level of the document standard. Proprietary systems provide commercial enterprises with profitable products whereas static formats do not create a continuing need for upgrading which software and hardware companies depend upon. This situation conspires against standards that create a stable nexus of hardware, software, and administration.

Libraries and archives will be required to continue their existing archival and preservation practices as the current paper publishing boom continues. Clearly, digital collections are not going to be a substitute for existing and future library collections and plans must be made to accommodate both. A significant concern of libraries and archives is that the financial resources necessary to address expensive IT upgrades, embark on data rescue operations, and undertake digital preservation will have detrimental impacts on other aspects of library and archival operations such as building collections and providing services for the public.

Document Formats

Mixed media and multiple document formats will continue to remain the fly-in-the-ointment of digital collections. Multiple formats may require maintaining multiple hardware/software platforms and will confound simple migration to new storage media.

Whether possible or even preferred, requiring that data be stored in a common format is unlikely for the foreseeable future. Similarly, existing translation software available for the migration and translation of document formats illustrates that the problems are significant and the results are often less than satisfactory. The simple case of conversion between the most popular document formats, MS-Word and WordPerfect, provide ample illustration of the challenges that are faced and argue for skepticism about claims for future systems which will make this task easier.

There will probably be no effective solution to this problem. If a library will be receiving electronic objects from content providers such as authors or publishers, they may want to specify a limited range of acceptable document formats. Working with creators to bring these problems to their attention and providing guidance on how to organise files and which formats to use for purposes of archiving will help. Once again, more research and effective communications with content and technology providers are required to address the issue of multiple formats.

Promoting the Importance of Preservation

Librarians and archivists must engage in a concerted effort to raise the profile of preservation. The Commission on Preservation and Access and Research Libraries Group (RLG) in the United States, the Joint Information Systems Committee (JISC) in the UK and PADI Working Group and National Library in Australia, among others, have all been active in framing the problems of digital preservation within their constituencies.

As a profession, librarians and archivists need to encourage critical thinking and be highly pragmatic about the nature of the new medium and the challenges of digital preservation. Although there are positive benefits to digitisation, particularly in providing remote and enhanced access to information, as Klaus-Dieter Lehmann, Director General of Die Deutsche Bibliothek warns, there is a danger here as well. The problem is that 'digitisation may come to be regarded as a panacea for all of the real and imagined problems libraries now face in connection with the preservation of physical collections: the growing need for storage space, the deterioration of books due to acid paper, and the rising costs of library operation.' Only by increasing public support and understanding of the issues of preservation, both digital and analog can we hope to address the shortfall in fiscal and human resources that continue to hinder preservation efforts and impact upon library services.

Digital Preservation as a Public Good

Librarians and archivists protect the public interest by making information available to the community and by asserting the importance of maintaining a record of our collective intellectual heritage. This task will be a continuing challenge because libraries and archives are too often considered to be competitors to publishers, document delivery services, and other private sector content providers. It is unlikely, unless a substantive ground-swell of public support is generated, that libraries will win in the battle against commodification of infor-mation resources or be able to generate the public support necessary to meet the challenges.

Despite the present lack of public interest in digital preservation, it is necessary to believe, perhaps as an article of faith, that the efforts of librarians and archivists will be appreciated in the future. The traces of information that we are able to save from our digital vellum will be valuable sources of information to the future. Even if the task of digital preservation remains thankless, it is a vital one and must still be undertaken. The objective is a noble and necessary one even as the many problems appear insurmountable.

Digital collections facilitate access, but do not facilitate preservation. Being digital means being ephemeral. Digital places greater emphasis on the here-and-now rather than the long term, just-in-time information rather than just-in-case. The research programme for digital preservation has only recently been initiated to develop strategies, guidelines, and standards. Although tremendous work has been undertaken in defining the problems and challenges, much more remains to be done, and the tough task of actually doing digital preservation remains ahead.

A critical appraisal of where we are vis-a-vis our digital culture, and what we want for the future something which may not be defined in technical terms at allÑis required both inside and outside of the library and archival professions. If history and cultural heritage are to be important, then it will likely fall to librarians and archivists, the monastic orders of the future, to ensure that something of the heady days of our 'digital revolution' remains for future generations. The challenges to digital preservation are considerable and will require a concerted effort on the part of librarians and archivists to rise up to these challenges and assert in public forums the importance of protecting a fragile digital heritage.

Durability of Books and Paper

Through the twentieth century, preservation methods focused initially on achieving permanence and durability for two core kinds of materials in library collections: the book and the newspaper. Technological innovations in the mid-nineteenth century had produced a less expensive kind of paper made from wood pulp, which made possible an explosion in printed materials that contributed to public literacy and to the organization of public libraries with print collections.

The unintended consequence of the new paper technology was the later "brittle book." The chemistry of paper and of paper processing was not fully understood at the time. Indeed the chemistry of paper was the subject of fairly substantial research in the early twentieth century. The new, cheaper books, which were a boon to literacy and libraries, turned out to deteriorate fairly quickly. Spofford and his contemporaries already had seen books begin to decay.

In 1897, his successor as the Librarian of Congress, John Russell Young, took note of the "grave questions arising out of the modern conditions in the manufacture of paper". Young presented a plan to Congress calling for materials presented for copyright protection to be printed on good-quality paper.

Late-nineteenth century librarians like Mr. Spofford could see that parts of their collections were crumbling but did not fully understand the scientific reasons. But by 1910, federal scientists had begun to explore the chemistry of paper and paper products, and these efforts continued. Some in the professional library community tried to stay abreast of the research. Nonetheless, for most librarians in Spofford's professional lifetime, binding and repair were conservators' primary preservation activities, along with managing library buildings protectively, training staff in the proper handling of materials, and trying to persuade patrons not to mark, abuse, or steal the books. Little systematic effort occurred in professional librarianship programs or in libraries themselves to address the source of the problem until the late 1950s and the 1960s.

In that period, the Council on Library Resources (CLR) made a number of grants to support preservation efforts. CLR sponsored research by W. J. Barrow into the causes of paper deterioration and the possibilities for development of a "permanent/durable" text paper. Barrow horrified the library world when he reported research indications that only three percent of the books published between 1900 and 1949 would last more than fifty years. In 1960, the Association of Research Libraries (ARL) appointed a Standing Committee on the Preservation of Research Library Materials, which recommended establishing a central federal agency to preserve a physical copy of every "significant written record" and to provide copies to other libraries as needed. Microfilming, in use in a few libraries as early as the 1930s, was endorsed as a method to preserve rare and endangered texts and to reduce use of fragile originals.

Televised images of the great floods in Florence of 1966 further increased awareness of preservation among research libraries and collections in the U.S., provoking research into preservation, conservation, and disaster recovery methods for books and other artifacts. Many preservation specialists went to Florence to help save materials and learned much about preservation techniques in the process.The 1960s also saw the inauguration by Chicago's Newberry Library of the first local conservation program, the organization of professional associations for conservation, the introduction of formal training programs for conservators and museum professionals, and more publications dealing with preservation and conservation in libraries and museums.

In 1972, the Library of Congress established a research laboratory, headed by John C. Williams, which spearheaded work on diethyl zinc de-acidification, work that continues to be important at the library. More recently, the Library of Congress awarded contracts to Pittsburgh-based Preservation Technologies, L.P. (PTLP) for de-acidification. Other preservation methods have been explored at the Barrow Laboratory and the Public Archives of Canada. Institutions of higher education such as Carnegie-Mellon University and the Rochester Institute of Technology set up centers for studying the chemistry and technology of paper, binding, paints, inks, and varnishes.

Realizing that the cycle of deterioration would not end unless alkaline paper was adopted in book manufacture, the library community worked with other concerned communities and standards-setting organizations to promote guidelines for and use of durable paper. The Council on Library Resources initiated work on production guidelines for book longevity in 1979. A committee, headed by Herbert Bailey of the Princeton University Press, made important studies of "permanent" paper and binding. And in 1981, the Z39 Committee of the American National Standards Institute drafted a standard for permanent paper for printed library materials.In the 1970s, major university libraries began to undertake large, cooperative preservation projects. An important by-product was that preservation departments became commonplace in research libraries.

Unfortunately, institutional preservation programs were not generally funded as a regular part of the research universities' budgets. Instead, many preservation efforts were made possible by external funding from the National Endowment for the Humanities (NEH) and private foundations, especially The Andrew W. Mellon Foundation.In the mid-1980s, both the book-preservation problem and the effort to address it took on new dimensions. CLR spun off the Commission on Preservation and Access to give brittle books special attention. The commission estimated that at least 3.3 million and possibly more than ten million books remained at risk in the U.S., and that de-acidification would cost between $250 million and $1 billion.

NEH expanded grant-making for preservation, setting a goal of helping research libraries microfilm at least three million of the most at-risk volumes. NEH also promoted standards and guidelines for microfilming so that individual library preservation activities would produce a decentralized but nationally accessible collection of works on durable microfilm. Book deterioration may be slower than was projected, but microfilming seemed essential at the time to ensure preservation of the content of millions of valuable texts that librarians feared would crumble on research library shelves.

Librarians also recognized the need to conserve unique paper artifacts in special collections.The biggest debate during the brittle books era focused on centralization. Patricia Battin, president of the Commission on Preservation and Access, believed that centralization would finally link preservation and access. She argued for the creation of a central repository for microfilm masters that would serve as an archives as well as a distribution system. Any library microfilming a book would add a permanent master copy and a service master to the central repository. Any library wishing to add a preservation copy to its own collections would be able to acquire, at cost, a copy of the service master.

Though NEH funding encouraged collaboration among libraries, centralization lost out because libraries aspiring to research status established their own individual preservation offices, and preservation became a recognized career track within individual institutions.Federal and philanthropic funding continues to support preservation within individual libraries and archives rather than to promote centralization of preservation in a single institution or handful of institutions. Thus, NEH has supported microfilming nineteenth century newspapers state by state and the National Agricultural Library has supported microfilming projects in state libraries to protect endangered materials documenting agricultural history.

Not surprisingly, this decentralized and local approach coincided with the local history movement in the 1980s and increased attention to conservation and preservation of local heritage resources of all sorts. NEH supports brittle-book microfilming at a number of university libraries that avoid redundant effort by sharing information about materials scheduled for filming.

Today preservation has become part of the management of a modern library, embracing not only the reformatting of texts but also the improvement of library buildings and their internal environments, the conservation and repair of items in library collections, the adoption of commercial standards for books and paper, the education of readers and staff about handling and caring for fragile materials, the training of librarians in preservation, and the adoption of disaster planning and recovery strategies. We have learned a lot from scientific study about library materials and how to manage them, and awareness of such research must become part of professional librarians' training and library management. Effective preservation programs require organizational coordination to ensure an appropriate and consistent standard, to reduce unnecessary redundancy, and to enable future users to find the materials. Preservation increasingly requires value judgments about whether to retain an original book, journal, or other artifact or just its intellectual content. That question is growing as libraries confront a huge additional set of preservation concerns and challenges associated with digital content.

Retriving Digital Archives

Digital information is inherently more fragile than traditional technologies such as paper or microfilm. It is more easily corrupted or altered, without recognition. Digital storage media have shorter life spans and require access technologies that are changing at an ever increasing pace. Because of these technological advances, the time frame in which we consider archiving becomes much shorter.

"Digital electronic archiving (DEA)" is defined as the long-term storage, preservation and access to information that was "born digital" (created and disseminated primarily in electronic form) or for which the digital version is considered to be the primary archive. Based on the analysis during this project, there is no common agreement on the definition of long-term preservation; the time frame is long enough to be concerned about changes in technology and changes in the user community.

Primary attention is given to operational and prototype projects involving scientific and technical information. The study is international in scope. It includes a variety of data types applicable to scientific and technical information, including data, text, images, audio, video and multimedia, and a variety of object types, such as electronic journals and monographs, satellite imagery, biological sequence data, and patents.

The issue of archiving digital objects brings together several normally diverse communities-archivists, records managers, librarians, data center managers, and data producers. There is so much activity among various groups that it is difficult to encapsulate the general state of DEA. However, there are a few general models that can be highlighted as emerging. The models have genesis in one of the diverse communities, but may have applicability to others.

It is noteworthy that many of the major projects in digital archiving are of a cultural or historic nature. Four major organizational models-Data Centers, Institutional Archives, Third Party Repositories, and Legal Depositories-were identified. An additional conceptual model for interoperable archives is also described. These models are based on differences in the information flow, the management of the life cycle functions of the archive (creation, management, preservation, and access), responsibility and ownership of the data, and the economic model.

The most mature archival model is that of the data center. Three subcategories of data centers were identified based on the degree of homogeneity and centralization. Centralized data centers, such as the National Digital Archive for Datasets (UK), have numerous contributors, but a central repository and administration. This model allows for easier integration of the data and more consistent adherence to standards.

However, there may be little backup for the central repository, particularly if funding is cut. It is also difficult to include new data producers with varying data models, standards and primary audiences. Federated data centers, like the NASA Distributed Active Archive Centers (DAACs) operate in a distributed, but closely guarded environment with common standards and practices, and a single user interface. There is redundancy in the federation's ability to respond to user needs.

With looser standards, more partners may be involved more easily. Cooperative data centers do not currently exist, but there is a prototype under development between the San Diego Supercomputer Center, the U.S. National Center for Environmental Analysis and Synthesis, and the Long Term Ecological Research Network.

The aim is minimal metadata and system standards, acknowledging the diversity of data types, models and structures in ecological science. On the whole, the data centers are also the simplest organizational model. The intellectual property rights are generally clear, because the owner is the funding agency. The economic model allows free access by the funding agency and, since many of these are government sponsored or internationally developed data banks, the public also has free access.

Additional charges may be levied for extraordinary services or for access for commercial purposes. However, it is unclear how well the practices of these data centers, which have large volumes of relatively simple data, would migrate to other communities and object types.

Institutional archives are generally a department or branch of an institution that collects and preserves the intellectual capital for that institution. These institutions can include publishers, data producers, societies, cultural organizations, government agencies, academic institutions and industries of various types. Institutional archives generally have some level of ownership of the information. Often access is limited to members of the organization, to subscribers, or to partners in a particular project or venture.

Many corporations and institutions archive only what is required by regulation, fearing legal ramifications if certain information is retained. However, there are organizations such as pharmaceutical, chemical and petroleum companies, where internal scientific and technical information is critical to the perpetuation of research and development.

Institutional archives may also increase as the knowledge management technologies connected to intranets reach a wider market. In addition to their primary role as vendors, electronic publishers, or jobbers, they may also provide digital archiving as a service to their clients, which are primarily learned societies and publishers. This is the most complex organizational model for archiving, because there are numerous roles being played by the participants.

Often the economic model for the archiving is not clear, because it is bundled with the other services that the publication service is providing. Examples of Publication Service Providers who also provide archiving services include ingenta, Ltd. and HighWire Press. Repository Management Agents are an emerging model in DEA. These organizations act as trusted third party repositories, but do not serve any other function in the value-added chain.

Public Use of Library Information

Today, school decision-makers for school library programs-school boards, superintendents, principals, teachers, even school librarians themselves-are unaware, or insufficiently aware, of the impact that good library information programs are having in many schools, and could be having in others. In

October 1998, Commonwealth Libraries made a Library Services and Technology Act (LSTA) grant to PCBL for this purpose.

The learning and teaching role supports the instructional goals of the school in both content (standards and subject curriculum) and process (information literacy skills). The information access and delivery role encompasses the more traditional responsibilities of the school librarian, those of developing the school library's collection and services and providing access to them.

Program administration, includes both management of the program and larger training and advocacy functions within the school community. The mission of the library program is to ensure that students and staff are effective users of ideas and information. Guidelines for School Library Media Programs dealt with the value of the mere presence of a library with a professional librarian, reflecting the lack of centralised library service, particularly at the elementary level. Willson showed that students demonstrated superior gains on the Iowa Test of Basic Skills (ITBS) in elementary schools with a centralised library and a professional librarian. Likewise, Becker compared ITBS scores between students in elementary schools with and without libraries and found that the presence of a library and the guidance and function of a librarian appeared to exert significant influence on pupil achievement in some information-gathering skills areas.

Student access to the school library was also significantly greater in schools with professional library personnel than in schools without them. Yarling found that the addition of a well-equipped and managed centralised library had a significant impact on the performance of elementary school students in library-related skills, particularly outlining and note taking. Students who used a new fully staffed and equipped elementary school library also showed significant improvement in library skills test scores in the study by Ainsworth.

Guidelines for School Library Media Programs in 1988 referred to various aspects of the school librarian's teaching role. Aaron studied a group of eighth grade students who participated in a program in which a full-time school librarian was added to the teaching team. In addition to showing significant improvement in language arts, spelling and math computation, the students in the experimental group experienced improvement in their self-concept. Gengler looked at differences in the ability to apply selected problem solving skills between sixth grade students who were instructed by a classroom teacher and those who received additional instruction from an elementary school librarian.

Findings showed that the mean score on a problem solving skills examination for the librarian-teacher instructed group was significantly higher than for the teacher instructed group. Hastings and Tanner looked at whether improved English language skills could be developed at the tenth grade level through systematic library experiences rather than the traditional emphasis on formal English grammar. In a study by Hutchinson, English teachers gave tenth grade students special library skills instruction and practice over a two-week period.

Library usage among the students increased regardless of their academic grade point averages. Hale found that an experimental group of twelfth grade students who were given a variety of library services and resources and the opportunity to work independently under the supervision of the librarian showed "remarkable enthusiasm" for learning. Barrilleaux focused on a comparison of the achievement of junior high school students in general science classes in which textbooks were used with students who used reference materials in the school library rather than a textbook.

Results showed that for all investigated educational outcomes, the use of library materials without a basic textbook was the superior method of instruction. Much of the research taking place after the introduction of Information Power: Guidelines for School Library Media Programs in 1988 focuses on the instructional role of the school librarian. Lance, Welborn and Hamilton-Pennell found that students whose school librarians played an instructional role, either by identifying materials to be used with teacher-planned instructional units or by collaborating with teachers in planning instructional units, tended to achieve higher test scores. A study by the Library Research Service in Colorado also found that students earned higher reading scores in schools where the librarian played a vital instructional role, including planning instruction with teachers, providing information literacy instruction, providing in-service training for teachers, and evaluating students' work.

Nevertheless, several researchers have identified a gap between theory and practice. Person found a discrepancy between the real and ideal role perceptions of school librarians. While they were aware of the roles identified in the Guidelines, they didn't perform them as often as they would have liked.

Pickard also studied the gap between theory and practice of school librarians performing the instructional role and found that less than 10 percent of her sample appeared to be practicing the role to a great extent. Angelo verified this finding in a study which showed that the majority of school librarians were performing duties of the traditional librarian, such as student orientation and assisting students and teachers in finding materials, while a low percentage were performing planning and consultation roles. Kuhne concluded that school libraries need to be more integrated into the curriculum and that the school librarian could play a much more distinctive teacher role than he or she does today. Van Deusen and Tallman found that more than half of her sample of school librarians did not assess student work at all during the study period.

Today, school librarians successfully involved in resource-based learning were energetic, healthy and enthusiastic; showed leadership abilities; had theoretical understanding of resource-based learning; had the ability to translate theory into effective instructional plans; and were knowledgeable about specific learning resources. These librarians saw teaching as their primary function. Farwell found that school librarians could play a pivotal role in the successful implementation of collaborative planning if they were knowledgeable about the curriculum, the library collection, information literacy instruction, and instructional design and delivery.

Another aspect of the school librarian's learning and teaching role identified in Information Power: Building Partnerships for Learning found that teachers and school librarians both strongly agreed that the librarian should work with teachers in helping students to develop the habit of reading. In the school library field, a few research studies to date have looked at the connection between integrating information literacy skills into the curriculum and improved student learning.

In Australia, Todd, Lamb and McNicholas studied Year-Seven and Year-Eleven students and found that integrating information skills into subject content, with collaboration by classroom teachers and school librarians, had a positive impact on student learning, including better understanding of subject content and improved test scores. Todd analysed the impact of integrated information skills instruction in a Year-Seven science class. The two treatment classes recorded significantly higher annual science scores than the control classes.

Access and Delivery of Quality Resources

The information access and delivery role includes providing quality resources and technology that support the curriculum, offering convenient and flexible access to the school library's resources and services, and providing a welcoming environment which is conducive to learning. Early studies focused on service level and collection size as predictors of academic achievement. Greve discovered that the most valuable predictor of student test scores was the number of volumes in the school library.

Thorne examined the reading comprehension and library skills of students using the augmented services of a Knapp Project library versus the nominal services of a second junior high school library in a two-year study. Findings revealed a significant difference in the mean gains of the experimental group over the control group in reading comprehension and library skills.More recent studies have focused on the connection between students' achievement in reading and access to print resources, particularly in libraries. The Colorado study by Lance, Welborn and Hamilton-Pennell concluded that the size of a school library's staff and collection is the best school predictor of academic achievement. Elley compared the scores of students from 32 countries on the 1992 International Association for the Evaluation of Educational Achievements (IEA) Reading Literacy Study with data on the home environment and school and public libraries.

A Library Research Service study reported that students are likely to earn higher reading scores if there is a relationship between the school library program and local public libraries. Such a relationship might include public library staff presenting booktalks at the school library, and the local public library providing a summer reading program.Several researchers point to the potential importance of the school library as a factor in equalising access to print resources for disadvantaged children. McQuillan found a strong negative correlation between poverty and print resources at home. He concluded that school and public libraries could help increase access to print for low-income communities and schools, thus improving their students' reading achievement.

Halle, Kurtz-Costes and Mahoney reported that the number of books in the homes of low-income, African American children was related to children's reading scores at the end of the following year. They concluded that providing access to children's books through libraries may be one of the most important things disadvantaged communities and schools can do. McQuillan studied the public library use of language minority students and found that Spanish-speaking households are much less likely to have access to books, and therefore fewer opportunities to further literacy development.

Unfortunately, school libraries often appear to reflect the economic conditions of their communities. Krashen and O'Brian reported that socio-economic status was the most powerful predictor of student reading achievement in the Los Angeles Unified School District. Both Krashen and McQuillan made the point that the low student reading scores in California could be traced to the deplorable state of its school and public libraries.

Size of the school library collection has been shown to be a positive predictor of student academic achievement. Similarly, McQuillan reported that SAT scores were positively correlated with the number of books per student in the school library. Koga and Harada investigated the attitudes of students in Australia, Japan, Korea and Thailand towards school libraries and found that students with a keen attitude toward learning tended to use the library more often and demonstrated better academic achievement.

A Library Research Service report showed that states with above average reading scores on the 1994 NAEP reading test have schools where students visit the school library more frequently and borrow more books and other materials. The role of the school librarian in developing and providing access to the library program has received a fair amount of attention in the research. Pembroke found that, when school librarians provide reading guidance or a bibliography, reluctant fifth grade readers can be motivated.

Martin found that as library services increased (including reference, information skills, curriculum integration, interlibrary loan, reading guidance, and technical assistance), third grade test scores also increased. She found a statistically-significant relationship between all the school library variables (collection size, expenditures for the collection, staffing, and services) and overall achievement in grades 3, 5, and 11, indicating that the whole is greater than the sum of its parts. A Library Research Service study reported that students are likely to earn higher reading scores if there is a collection development policy for the school library. K. G. Alexander's study of four exemplary school librarians found that they all provided continuous access to their libraries; assisted individual users; designed flexible circulation policies; used innovative methods to promote their libraries; and developed collections which supported all areas of the curriculum.

Gehlken reported that in all three blue ribbon high schools studied, the school librarian flexibly scheduled classes; organised and cataloged the collection; provided an inviting climate conducive to learning; assisted students in traditional and electronic methods of information access; and involved faculty in the selection of materials. The libraries in all three schools were organised, automated, easily accessible, and provided materials in a variety of formats across all levels and subject areas. The library facilities were inviting, aesthetically pleasing, safe, and user-friendly.

The role of technology in promoting student achievement has been the focus of some recent studies. In their review of educational technology research, Sivin-Kachala, Bialo, and Langford concluded that using technology has a positive effect on student achievement, attitudes toward learning, and student self-concept. Paul, VanderZee, Rue and Swanson reported that using the Accelerated Reader technology-based literacy program had a positive affect on student academic performance and attendance rates, especially for socio-economically disadvantaged children in urban areas. Wenglinsky found a positive correlation between computer use and academic achievement in mathematics, but only if computers were used to convey higher-order skills or engage in learning games. Use of computers for drill and practice, the lower-order skills, was negatively related to academic achievement for both fourth and eighth grade students.

Significantly, disadvantaged groups had less access to those aspects of technology that positively affected educational outcomes. There is perhaps no place where the school librarian's role has changed more in the last ten years than in the integration of technology. McCarthy found that less than 50 percent of the New England school libraries in her sample had automated circulation and cataloging systems, and these were mostly in middle and high school libraries.

High-achieving schools tend to have more technological resources. Baule found that schools with exemplary technology were also more likely to have high-quality school library programs. Yetter observed that the school libraries in successful resource-based learning schools had modern, spacious facilities designed for flexible use and access to technology.

Gehlken noted that all three blue ribbon schools studied had libraries which were committed to increasing student access to technology, and which had the flexibility and electronic capabilities to accommodate the changing needs created by new technologies. Students identified the electronic catalog, computer printer workstations and copying machines as some of the most important services provided by the school library program.

As Wenglinksy demonstrated, it is not the amount of technology or computer use that counts in promoting student achievement, but how it is used. Many researchers have found no correlation between reading achievement and amount of computer software available. Technology must be integrated into the school library program.

A Library Research Service report concluded that students earn higher reading scores if their school library programs incorporate the latest information technology. Such technology includes a district-wide catalog, access to online databases, resources available through a local-area network, and access to the World Wide Web and the statewide library network. The program administration role involves effective management of the human, financial and physical resources of the school library program.

This role also provides leadership within the larger learning community. Adequate staffing, budget, and administrative support are key to the success of this role. Yetter found that schools that had successfully implemented resource-based learning had a common understanding and support from the principal, teaching faculty and school librarian about the centrality of the library program in the school's instructional process. These schools provided planning time for teachers and school librarians to work collaboratively, clerical support for the school librarian, flexible scheduling in the school library, and principal support of the library program. Likewise, Farwell determined that in schools with successful collaborative planning, the principal served as an advocate for collaborative planning and information literacy instruction, and provided financial support for the library program, adequate clerical staff, and time during the school day for school librarians and classroom teachers to plan together.

There appears to be a two-way relationship between administrative support and school librarians performing the instructional role. In schools where there was fiscal and organisational support for the library program, including automated systems and paid support staff, van Deusen found that school librarians performed the instructional consultation role to a greater extent. Lumley concluded that instituting a curricularly integrated and flexibly scheduled library program required leadership on the part of the school librarian as well as principal support, resulting in strong leadership roles for the librarian in curriculum, instruction and staff development. Martin also found a significant positive relationship between school library staffing and student achievement, especially in high school reading. Schools employing more library staff had higher achievement test scores.

A Library Research Service study showed that student reading scores were higher in schools where there is a state-endorsed school librarian and where the school librarian is supported by an aide. School librarians in effective schools tend to have good planning, communication and management skills. The basic library procedures and processes in their school library programs functioned smoothly. A Library Research Service report indicated that students are likely to earn higher reading scores if there is a plan for the development of their school library program. The involvement of a school librarian in technology-based staff training can support student achievement. Wenglinsky found that teacher's professional development in technology and the use of computers to teach higher-order skills were both positively related to academic achievement in mathematics and the social environment of the school. A very important administrative role for the school librarian is to obtain an adequate budget for the library program.

Angelo's study of Massachusetts school library programs revealed that more than 90 percent were operating at the minimum level according to state standards in the areas of personnel, collection, and budget. Lance, Welborn and Hamilton-Pennell found that students at schools with better funded libraries tend to achieve higher average test scores, whether their schools and communities are rich or poor and whether adults in the community are well or poorly educated. Bruning also reported a positive relationship between student achievement measures and the proportion of a school district's budget spent on library materials, for both high- and low-income districts.

These findings are particularly significant since studies seeking a relationship between school spending as a whole and student performance have shown mixed results. Traditionally, conventional wisdom dictated that the larger the collection, the better. As electronic sources of information proliferate and the value of up-to-the-minute information increases, this assumption becomes more questionable. Another wildcard related to this issue is the age of library collections.

A larger collection is not necessarily a better one, if it consists increasingly of deteriorating volumes of obsolete information. Although few school libraries have budgets that include personnel costs, many have budgets for print and non-print materials, electronic access to information, and miscellaneous operating expenses. Additional items called for expenditures on computer equipment and other capital purchases. Partial correlation was used to weigh the effects of school library staffing on academic achievement while controlling for each of several school and community conditions.

This technique is especially useful in assessing complex relationships among several potential predictors, because it weighs the importance of each predictor variable while ruling out the effects of another. It is intuitively obvious that the status of library information programs may depend on more general school circumstances, just as those circumstances, in turn, may be driven by community conditions.

The community and school variables included represent major antecedent conditions that might explain away that impact. For instance, the possibility that a correlation between the level of school library staffing and test scores might be a spurious result of generally high levels of staffing in a school was addressed by including the teacher-pupil ratio. For all statistical techniques, separate analyses were conducted for elementary, middle, and high school levels. After the direct effects of all school library conditions on test scores were determined via bivariate and partial correlation, their indirect effects from one to another were calculated.

Several characteristics of school library programs beyond staffing help to explain the relationship between library staffing and academic achievement. These characteristics include: school library expenditures, information resources, information technology, and staff activities that help to integrate information literacy into the school's approaches to standards and curricula. The success of any school library information program in promoting high academic achievement depends fundamentally on the presence of adequate staffing-specifically each library should have at least one, full-time, certified school librarian with at least one full-time aide or other support staff member. When the relationship between school library staffing and test scores is controlled for socio-economic differences, the relationship reveals itself to be a dynamic one in several ways. When the relationship between school library staffing and achievement is controlled for differences in adult educational attainment, the relationship is weakened for all three tested grades.

The relationship is weaker still, however, at the high school level compared to the elementary and middle school levels. This finding suggests that school library programs can compensate better for a lack of parental education before rather than after students reach the mid to late teens. When the relationship between school library staffing and achievement is controlled for the race/ethnicity of students, it is weakened slightly at elementary level and remains little changed at middle school level, but increases dramatically at high school level.

This finding suggests that, while school library programs are challenged to compensate for the cultural disadvantages of many minority children in the early years of public education, those programs are more successful at compensating for such disadvantages as students mature. Predictably, economic differences (e.g., median family income, percent of families living in poverty) have the most consistently undermining effect on the relationship between school library staffing and reading scores. It is difficult for the best school library program to foster students' learning when their home life is defined by the privations of poverty. Children from poorer families are less likely to live in homes where books and other information sources are readily at hand, and where a home computer providing access to the World Wide Web can be taken for granted. Nonetheless, even when economic differences are ruled out, the relationship between school library staffing and test scores remains both positive and statistically significant.

While controlling for some school and community conditions (e.g., average teacher's salary, community socio-economic conditions) weakens the relationship between school library staffing and achievement, more often there is little change, and, in one case (e.g., race/ethnicity), the relationship is even strengthened over time. Because none of these other factors explains away the relationship between school library staffing and achievement, that relationship is likely to be one of cause-and-effect. At both elementary and secondary levels, increases in library staffing are also linked to increased access to computer resources.

Notably, computers counted in this study are those either in or under the jurisdiction of the school library program as well as any computer elsewhere in the school-in classrooms, computer labs, studios, or offices-that have networked access to library resources. An interesting distinction in these findings between elementary and secondary levels is that, for both levels, as library staffing increases, computers with access to licensed databases increase, while, for secondary level alone, staffing increases are linked with increases in computers with Internet/World Wide Web access. These findings probably reflect the increasing time and money commitments of most librarians to licensing and promoting use of well-organised, up-to-date, high-quality databases as well as the active concern of some public officials and interest groups about very young children having completely open access to the Web.

The mere presence of a large collection of books, magazines, and newspapers in the school library is not enough to generate high levels of academic achievement by students. Such collections only make a positive difference when they are part of school-wide initiatives to integrate information literacy into the school's approach to standards and curricula. Rich collections of information resources can only help to improve the learning environment if the school librarian is in a position to mobilise them to that end. The relationship between having access to such resources and having school librarians who are actively engaged in enriching the learning environment is important at all grade levels, but is especially important at the elementary level. The successful integration of information literacy into a school's approaches to standards and curricula depends on more than traditional library resources alone.

In today's global information-based economy, information technology plays as important a role in promoting students' academic achievement as it does their later financial success. At both elementary and secondary levels, activities involved in integrating information literacy happen more often where school library programs have carefully developed, well organised, widely deployed computer networks.

The successful integration of information literacy in a school depends, in part, on the school library program managing a computer network that provides access to the library's catalog, and the Internet/World Wide Web. Such networks are not limited to computers in or under the jurisdiction of the school library program, but can-and should-include networked computers throughout the school, so that students and teachers can access needed information in classrooms, labs, studios, and offices.

Students at the highest scoring schools averaged reading scores in the upper 80's, while their counterparts at the lowest scoring schools averaged scores in the mid-70's. Higher achieving schools often spend twice as much-or more-on their school library programs as lower achieving schools. At the elementary level, annual school library spending average over $14,000 and just over $7,000, respectively, for higher and lower achieving schools. At the high school level, higher scoring schools spend about $22,000, while lower scoring schools spend less than $10,000. Such differences in buying power have been demonstrated to have a direct effect on the size of the school library program's collection of information resources.

While school librarians are common among the schools participating in this study, the level of such staffing varies. The level of certified school librarian staffing varies as much as six hours per week in middle schools. Differences in the level of support staffing are even more dramatic. At elementary and middle schools, higher achieving schools have 25 to 35 hours per week, respectively, of support staff, while lower achieving schools average half as much help, if any at all.

When support staff is limited or non-existent, school librarians are not free to manage library expenditures, resources, and technology or to engage in key activities that ensure the integration of information literacy into a school's approaches to standards and curricula.

References

Lorie, R.A. *A Methodology and System for Preserving Digital Data.* Proceedings of the Second ACM/IEEE- CS joint conference on Digital Libraries, Portland, Oregon, USA. 2002.

Michelle Q. Wang Baldonado and Steve B. Cousins. Addressing heterogeneity in the networked information environment. *New Review of Information Networking*, 2:83-102. 1996.

Miller, Rush G., "Shaping Digital Library Content." The Journal of Academic Librarianship 28, no. 3 : 97-103. 2002 .

Moore, R., Baru, C., Rajasekar, A. et al. Collection-Based persistent Digital Archives. *D-Lib Magazine*, March and April 2000.

Trusted Digital Repositories: Attributes and Responsibilities. An RLG-OCLC Report, May 2002, http://www.rlg.org/longterm/repositiories.pdf

8

Web-based Library Services

Due to the tremendous growth and continuous development of technology, the role of library becomes more responsive in making the users techno-savvy. Technological developments have affected not only the formats and sources of the information, but also how and where to provide library services. Libraries and their resources have partially moved to the virtual world of the Internet. As a result, library users can access the resources from outside the physical library. In an effort to reach users accessing the library via their computers, many libraries and library consortia are extending their services to include virtual reference. Technology now allows users to submit their queries to the library at any time from any place in the world. Web Based Services, Digital Library Services, Internet Library Services and Electronic Library Services are terms with similar meanings.

As more libraries move towards providing services in a digital environment, the improved access to remote library collections is making the use of electronic information resources more realistic and more attractive. Traditional online services had transformed themselves into internet-based online services using web-based technologies. From traditional online services to today, four generations of information retrieval tools have passed that assist users in searching the World Wide Web.

The first generation of information retrieval tools was designed for use with bibliographic databases. The first generation provided access to references to the end documents rather than to the documents themselves, and indexing and searching were thus applied to document surrogates, such as titles or abstracts. These tools require considerable human efforts to collect, arrange, code, and annotate the various resources. A primary benefit of the first generation of tools is providing users with easy browsing capabilities.

The second generation of tools attempts to collect and index resources as an automated function. Automatic collection and indexing reduces the amount of human effort. The ability to search through massive amounts of information and locate the desired information for the user is the primary benefit of the second generation of tools. The third generation deals with World Wide W eb Meta search engines, such as Harvester and Meta crawler.

The fourth generation involves new ideas such as search agent technology currently being developed to search for information on the web.

Web-based search engines are as a means of finding relevant pages on the Internet. Different search engines, directory, meta-search engines, gateways, subject portals, electronic journals and on line databases each type could be used in a different way, from simple keyword searching up to peer-reviewed web sites.

A digital Library service manages and develops electronic services, the library websites and library staff. According to White, it can be defined broadly as 'an information access service in which users ask questions via electronic means e.g., email or web forms'.

Library service on the internet requires many of the same qualities as traditional references: accuracy, promptness, courtesy, an understanding of the information need. It provides users with the convenience of accessing information in their own time, saving them traveling cost and time and new options for answering reference questions. The provision of these services is not constrained by the traditional opening hours but can be offered on a 24-hour, seven-days-a-week basis known as 24/7. And while there may be a disadvantage in not having a face-to face encounter, there are many advantages to this new medium and the greatest advantage is that many more users can be helped by using electronic library services.

Today, users may have access a variety of textual information resources. There are different kinds of web-based reference resources and services for accessing information from libraries such as OPAC, Gateways, Portals, Subject Portals, Electronic Journals, Online Databases, Subject Directories and Search Engines. These resources overlap considerably in the type of information they cover, and sometimes it is difficult to distinguish between some of them. A library should have a good collection of these resources like selected Web links, subscription resources, and library materials in well-organized pages for serving better services to their users.

Many libraries and organizations are providing digital reference service through collaborative services. Existing library consortia are adding digital reference to current shared services, and networks of libraries. Some regional library consortia are offering member libraries the opportunity to share reference questions with each other using the Internet and other technologies.

Websites as Information Resource

Websites today come in many different forms. These range from simple collections of static pages that display the same information to all visitors, through to pages which are created and displayed dynamically in response to specific queries. In addition, many websites now do something - they enable visitor details to be captured, online orders to be taken and personalised information to be displayed based on user profiles. Thus, some websites can be considered to be more like a software applications than a set of publications. Each form of web-based activity poses a different set of challenges for those who seek to keep and preserve records of them over time.

In its most basic form, a website may be nothing more than a collection of static documents sitting in folders on a server and tied together with hyperlinks. These documents share a common address - the domain name in the universal resource locator (URL), such as 'naa.gov.au'.

A static website maps URLs directly to file system locations. The only interactivity provided by static sites is in the links which enable movement from one document to another or from one part of the site to another. Static sites are relatively simple to archive, for example by making and keeping:

— copies or snapshots of the site 'as a whole' (ie the functionality of the internal links is not destroyed); and

— logs of changes (eg when and how documents are removed, replaced or updated).

Many websites utilise forms to collect information such as comments and requests, from visitors. While these sites are still largely static publication mechanisms, agencies keeping records of such sites must also pay attention to:

— the information provided when the visitor fills in the form (usually stored in a 'back end' information system);

— the form itself; and

— the human readable source code of the script or program which enables the form's functionality.

Websites are sometimes used as front ends, or user interfaces, for accessing an organisation's database(s). Site users search prepared lists or put together their own searches which, in turn, query the content of a database. The information returned from these queries is displayed as an HTML (hypertext mark-up language) document to the user.

In many cases, documents exist as objects in a database. Each document will have its own unique identifier, usually reflected in the URL. This means that a user can bookmark the particular document and return to it later without reconstructing the original search query (provided the document has not been deleted from the database).

Even if the site's main or top-level pages are static, dynamic data access websites raise some additional issues for agency recordkeepers. Not all users 'see' the same website. At designated levels, the pages displayed on users' browsers are based on what they ask for, therefore user queries are an integral part of generating the website and may need to be captured. Information contained in databases behind the site may be continually changing.

An increasing number of websites are being built which generate all of the pages 'on the fly'. This means that the component parts of each individual page - its content, structure and presentation - are generated dynamically using a combination of databases and style sheets based on:

— a stored set of user preferences;

— a stored set of access profiles;

— a user query; and/or

— the capabilities of the user's browser.

In these situations, the website does not exist in any single or easily capturable form. Each user sees a different 'site' based on their stored preferences and access rights, current needs, and the capabilities or limitations of the technology they are using. Although the end result for the user might be a set of static pages, the processes which build the pages involve the use of a number of software tools. This is the point at which websites become more like software applications than electronic publications. Agencies need to consider how to archive dynamically generated web resources in a fully functional state.

The major issues these sites raise for agency recordkeepers is the need to choose whether to use an object-based or an event-based approach to keeping records of web resources and activities. That is, an agency needs to determine whether it wishes to focus on keeping records of:

— the individual transactions between clients (users) and servers (agencies); or
— the objects that comprise the content of the site at any given time.

Following are the fundamentals of good web-based recordkeeping:

— Take a systematic approach
— Assign and document responsibilities
— Determine requirements for records
— Apply metadata
— Capture records into a recordkeeping system

In keeping records of web-based activity, there are certain fundamental procedures that all agencies should observe. These rules are not unique to web-based recordkeeping. They are commonsense approaches which organisations, as a matter of course, should implement as part of their regimes for managing information resources - whether these are web resources, electronic or paper-based records, or data in legacy systems.

Application of Metadata

The application of metadata is central to the successful management of all records, including records of web-based activity. Metadata needs to be applied:

— at different levels of resource aggregation;
— at different times; and
— for different purposes.

While compatible with the AGLS metadata set, this standard specifies additional metadata that agencies should use to describe the context, management, use, preservation and disposal of information resources - including online resources - which are also records. For individual records on websites and for other records of web-based activity, this means using metadata to describe:

- date and time of creation and registration of the record into a recordkeeping system;
- organisational context;
- original data format;
- the use made of the record over time, including its placement on a website;
- mandates governing the creation, retention and disposal of the records; and
- management history of the record following creation - including sentencing, preservation and disposal.

For copies or snapshots of entire collections of web resources, metadata should include:

- data and time of capture;
- links to the universal resource indicator (URI) including information about version and date of link to specified URI;
- technical details about the website design;
- details about the software used to create the web resources;
- details of the applications (including search engines) that supplement the web resources; and
- details about the client software needed for viewing the web resources.

Record-keeping System

The capture of record of web-based activity, together with sufficient recordkeeping/data should occur at the time the resource is posted to the website and the record created. To achieve this, agencies will need to have clearly defined procedures, appropriately assigned responsibilities and adequate systems to support this requirement.

Assessing recordkeeping needs is also crucial. Organisations need to assess the complexity of the records and recordkeeping requirements to ensure 'full and accurate records' are captured and maintained. Agencies should assess the ability of existing recordkeeping systems to capture and maintain records of web-based activity and to satisfy online recordkeeping requirements. Some websites will offer significant functionality requiring additional web-based records to be created and captured (ie a multimedia document may require the capture of plug-ins to maintain its functionality). A number of technological options are available to ensure that additional functionality (and the generated website records) are captured into the agency's recordkeeping system(s).

Many agencies currently operate in a mixed environment, dealing with both paper-based and electronic records. The capacity to capture and manage web-based electronic records in their native formats during this transitional period may be limited if the appropriate infrastructure does not exist. Websites are used for a number of purposes, including:

- disseminating (publishing) and sharing information;
- providing advice;
- working collaboratively;
- advertising goods and services;
- providing online services;
- conducting business transactions;
- soliciting responses and feedback; and
- providing a public record of special political, social or cultural events.

As one of the purposes of websites is to provide current information to visitors and customers, the content presented on a website changes. Changes may take place on a regular basis, with all new or updated material uploaded to the website once a day, week or month. In other cases, changes may occur on an 'as required' basis or, in the case of database-driven sites, in real time. For the purposes of both accountability and site maintainability, it is important that records of website content changes are made and kept.

In determining the best way for an agency to deal with tracking and recording content change over time, it might be helpful to use the following terms to refer to site changes:

- frequent - three months or less between changes;
- infrequent - more than three months between changes;
- regular - changes are made on a planned basis;
- irregular - changes are not planned, but made on an 'as required' basis.

An agency website's rate of change could then be categorised using one of four labels:

— regular and frequent;
— regular and infrequent;
— irregular and frequent; or
— irregular and infrequent.

Websites that change irregularly but frequently are likely to pose the most degree of risk to the agency because such changes are the most difficult to track. Of course, the extent to which this factor impacts on the overall level of risk is dependent on the other risk factors.

HyperText Markup Language

HyperText Markup Language (or HTML as it is commonly known) is a non-proprietary format markup system used for publishing hypertext on the World Wide Web. To date, it has appeared in four main versions (1.0, 2.0, 3.2, 4.0), with the World Wide Web Consortium (W3C) recommending 4.0 as the markup language of choice. HTML is a derivative of SGML - the Standard Generalised Markup Language. SGML allows you to create your own markup language but provides the rules necessary to ensure its processing and preservation. HTML is a successful implementation of the SGML concepts, and, as a result, is accessible to most browsers and platforms. Along with this, it is a relatively simple markup language to learn, as it has a limited tagset. HTML is by far the most popular web-publishing language, allowing users to create online text documents that include multimedia elements (such as images, sounds, and video clips), and then put these documents in an environment that allows for instant publication and retrieval.

There are many advantages to a markup language like HTML. As mentioned above, the primary benefit is that a document encoded with HTML can be viewed in almost any browser - an extremely attractive option for a creator who wants documents which can be viewed by an audience with varied systems. However, it is important to note that while the encoding can cross platforms, there are consistently differences in page appearance between browsers. While W3C recommends the usage of HTML 4.0, many of its features are simply not available to users with early versions of browsers. Unlike PDF which is extremely concerned with keeping the document and its format intact, HTML has no true sense of page structure and files can neither be saved nor printed with any sense of precision.

Besides the benefit of a markup language that crosses platforms with ease, HTML attracts its many users for the simple manner with which it can be mastered. For users who do not want to take the time to learn the tagset, the good news is that conversion-to-HTML tools are becoming more accessible and easier to use. For those who cannot even spare the time to learn how to use HTML-creation software, of which there are a limited quantity, they can sit down with any text creation program (Notepad for example) and author an HTML document. Then by using the 'Open File'; tool in a browser, the document can immediately be viewed.

In contrast, the concise guidelines to HTML that are available on-line (and usually as a "help" option from the menu of a Web client) are a good introduction to some of the basic SGML concepts. This is of real value to the user. The notion of marking up a text is quite often an overwhelming concept. Most people do not realise that markup enters into their life every time they make a keystroke in a word processing program. So for the uninitiated, HTML provides a manageable stepping-stone into the world of more complex encoding. Once this limited tagset is mastered, many users find the jump into an extended markup language less intimidating - and more liberating.

However, one of the drawbacks to this easy authoring language is that many of the online documents are created without a DTD. A DTD is the abbreviation for a document type definition, which outlines the formal specifications for an SGML encoded document. Basically, a DTD is the method for spelling out the SGML rules that the document is following. It sets the standards for what markup can be used and how this markup interacts with others. So, for example, if you create an HTML document with a specific software program, say HoTMetaL PRO, the resulting text will begin with a document type declaration stating which DTD is being used. As it stands now, web browsers require neither a DTD nor a document type declaration. Browsers are notoriously lax in their HTML requirements, and unless something serious is missing from the encoded document it will be successfully viewed through a Web client.

The impact of this is that while HTML provides a convenient and universal markup language for a user, many of the documents floating out in cyberspace are permeated with invalid code. The focus then moves away from authoring documents that conform to a set of encoding guidelines and towards the creation of works that can be viewed in a browser. This problem will become more severe with the increased use of Extensible Markup Language, or XML as it is more commonly known. This markup language, which is being lauded as the new lingua franca, combines the visual benefits of HTML with the contextual benefits of SGML/TEI. However, while XML will have the universality of HTML, the web clients will require a more stringent adherence to markup rules. While documents that comply with the rules of an HTML DTD will find the transition relatively simple, the documents that were constructed strictly with viewing in mind will require a good deal of clean up prior to conversion.

This is not to say that HTML is not a useful tool for creating online documents. As in the case of PostScript and PDF, the choice to use HTML should be document dependent. It is the perfect choice for static documents that will have a short shelf-life. If you are creating course pages or supplementary materials regarding specific readings that will not be necessary or available after the end of term, then HTML is an appropriate choice. If, however, you are concerned about presentational and structural integrity, the markup of document content and/or the long-term preservation of the text, then a user-definable markup language is a much better choice.

The late 1970s and early 1980s saw a consensus emerging that descriptive markup languages had numerous advantages over other types of text encoding. A number of products and macro languages appeared which were built around their own descriptive markup languages - and whilst these represented a step forward, they were also constrained by the fact that users were required to learn a new markup language each time, and could only describe those textual features which the markup scheme allowed (sometimes extensions were possible, but implementing them was rarely a straightforward process).

The International Standards Organisation (ISO) also recognised the value of descriptive markup schemes, and in 1986 an ISO committee released a new standard called ISO 8879, the Standard Generalised Markup Language (SGML). This complex document represented several years' effort by an international committee of experts, working together under the Chairmanship of Dr Charles Goldfarb (one of the creators of IBM's descriptive markup language, GML).

Since SGML was a product of the International Standards process, the committee also had the benefit of input from experts from the numerous national standards bodies associated with the ISO, such as the UK's British Standards Institute (BSI).

A great deal of largely unjustified mystique surrounds SGML. You do not have to look very hard to find instances of SGML being described as 'difficult to learn', 'complex to implement', or 'expensive to use', when in fact it is none of these things. People all too frequently confuse the acronym, SGML, with SGML applications - many of which are indeed highly sophisticated and complex operations, designed to meet the rigorous demands of blue chip companies working in major international industries (automotive, pharmaceutical, or aerospace engineering).

It should not be particularly surprising that a documentation system designed to control and support every aspect of the tens of thousands of pages of documentation needed to build and maintain a battleship, fix the latest passenger aircraft, or supplement a legal application for international recognition for a new advanced drug treatment, should appear overwhelmingly complex to an outsider.

In fact, despite its name, SGML is not even a markup language. Instead, it would be more appropriate to call SGML a 'metalanguage'. In a conventional markup language, such as HTML, users are offered a pre-defined set of markup tags from which they must make appropriate selections; if they suddenly introduce new tags which are not part of the HTML specification, then it is clear that the resulting document will not be considered valid HTML, and it may be rejected or incorrectly processed by HTML software (e.g. an HTML-compatible browser).

SGML, on the other hand, does not offer a pre-defined set of markup tags. Rather, it offers a grammar and specific vocabulary which can be used to define other markup languages (hence 'metalanguage'). SGML is not constrained to any one particular type of application, and it is neither more nor less suited to producing technical documentation and specifications in the semiconductor industry, than it is for marking up linguistic features of ancient inscribed tablets of stone.

In fact, SGML can be used to create a markup language to do pretty well anything, and that is both its greatest strength and weakness. SGML cannot be used 'out-of-the-box', so to speak, and because of this it has earned an undeserved reputation in some quarters as being troublesome and slow to implement. On the other hand, there are many SGML applications, which can be used straightaway, as they offer a fully documented markup language which can be recognised by any one of a suite of tools and implemented with a minimum of fuss.

SGML provides a mechanism for like-minded people with a shared concern to get together and define a common markup language which satisfies their needs and desires, rather than being limited by the vision of the designers of a closed, possibly proprietary markup scheme which only does half the job.

SGML offers another advantage in that it not only allows (groups of) users to define their own markup languages, it also provides a mechanism for ensuring that the rules of any particular markup language can be rigorously enforced by SGML-aware software. For example, within HTML, although there are six different levels of heading defined there is no requirement that they should be applied in a strictly hierarchical fashion; in other words, it is perfectly possible for a series of headings in an HTML document to be marked up as <H1>, then <H3>, followed by <H5>, followed in turn by <H2>, <H4>, and <H6> - all to achieve a particular visual appearance in a particular HTML browser.

By contrast, should such a feature be deemed important, an SGML-based markup language could be written in such a way that suitable software can ensure that levels of heading nest in a strictly hierarchical fashion (and the strength of this approach can perhaps become even more evident when encoding other kinds of hierarchical structure, e.g. a <BOOK> must contain one or more <CHAPTER>s, each of which must in turn contain one or more <PARAGRAPH>s, and so on).

There is one final, crucial, difference between SGML-based markup languages and other descriptive markup languages: the process by which International Standards are created, maintained, and updated. ISO Standards are subject to periodic formal review, and each time this work is undertaken it happens in full consultation with the various national standards bodies. The Committee which produced SGML has guaranteed that if and when any changes are introduced to the SGML standard, this will be done in such a way as to ensure backwards compatibility.

This is not a decision which has been undertaken lightly, and the full implications can be inferred from the fact that commercial enterprises rarely make such an explicit commitment (and even when they do, users ought to reflect upon the likelihood that such a commitment will actually be fulfilled given the considerable pressures of a highly competitive marketplace).

The essential difference has been characterised thus: the creators of SGML believe that a user's data should belong to that user, and not be tied up inextricably in a proprietary markup system over which that user has no control; whereas, the creators of a proprietary markup scheme can reasonably be expected to have little motivation to ensure that data encoded using their scheme can be easily migrated to, or processed by, a competitor's software products.

The SGML standard gives a very rigid definition as to what constitutes an 'SGML document'. Whilst there is no need for us to consider this definition in detail at this stage, it is worthwhile reviewing the major concepts as they offer a valuable insight into some crucial aspects of an electronic text.

Perhaps first and foremost amongst these is the notion that an SGML document is a single logical entity, even though in practice that document may be composed of any number of physical data files, spread over a storage medium (e.g. a single computer's hard-disk) or even over different types of storage media connected together via a network.

As today's electronic publications become more and more complex, mixing (multilingual) text with images, audio, and image data, it reinforces the need to ensure that they are created in line with accepted standards. For example, an article from an electronic journal mounted on a website may be delivered to the end-user in the form of a single HTML document, but that article (and indeed the whole journal), may rely upon dozens or hundreds of data files, a database to manage the entire collection of files, several bespoke scripts to handle the interfacing between the web and the database, and so on.

SGML operates on the basis of there being three major parts which combine to form a single SGML document. Firstly, there is the SGML declaration, which specifies any system and software constraints. Secondly, there is the prolog, which defines the document structure. Lastly, there is the document instance, which contains what one would ordinarily think of as the document. Whilst this may perhaps appear unnecessarily complicated, in fact it provides an extremely valuable insight into the key components which are essential to the creation of an electronic document.

The SGML declaration tells any software that is going to process an SGML document all that it should need to know. For example, the SGML declaration specifies which character sets have been used in the document (normally ASCII or ISO 646, but more recently this could be Unicode, or ISO 10646). It also establishes any constraints on system variables (e.g. the length of markup tag names, or the depth to which tags can be nested), and states whether or not any of SGML's optional features have been used.

The SGML standard offers a default set-up, so that, for example, the characters < and > are used to delimit markup tag names - and with the widespread acceptance of HTML, this has become the accepted way to indicate markup tags - but if for any reason this presented a problem for a particular application (e.g. encoding a lot of data in which < and > were heavily used to indicate something else), it would be possible to redefine the delimiters as @ or #, or whatever characters were deemed to be more appropriate.

The SGML declaration is important for a number of reasons. Although it may seem an unduly complicated approach, it is often these fundamental system or application dependencies which make it so difficult to move data around between different software and hardware environments. If the developers of wordprocessing packages had started off by agreeing on a single set of internal markup codes they would all use to indicate a change in font, the centring of a line of text, the occurrence of a pagebreak etc., then users' lives would have been made a great deal easier; however, this did not happen, and hence we are left in a situation where data created in one application cannot easily be read by another.

Furthermore, by supplying a default environment, the average end-user of an SGML-based encoding system is unlikely to have to familiarise him- or herself with the intricacies of the SGML declaration. Indeed it should be enough simply to be aware of the existence of the SGML declaration, and how it might affect one's ability to create, access, or exploit a particular source of data.

The next major part of an SGML document is the prolog, which must conform to the specification set out in the formal SGML standard, and the syntax given in the SGML declaration. Although it is hard to discuss the prolog without getting bogged down in the details of SGML, suffice it to say that it contains (at least one) document type declaration, which in turn contains (or references) a Document Type Definition (or DTD).

The DTD is one of the single most important features of SGML, and what sets it apart from - not to say above - other descriptive markup schemes. Although we shall learn a little more about the process in the following section, the DTD contains a series of declarations which define the particular markup language which will be used in the document instance, and also specifies how the different parts of that language can interrelate (e.g. which markup tags are required and optional, the contexts in which they can be used, and so on).

Often, when people talk about 'using SGML', they are actually talking about using a particular DTD, which is why some of the negative comments that have been made about SGML are erroneous, because such complaints should properly be directed at the DTD rather than at SGML in general.

Other than some of the system constraints imposed by the SGML declaration, there are no strictures imposed by the SGML standard regarding how simple or complex the markup language defined in the DTD should be. Whilst the syntax used to write a DTD is fairly straightforward, and most people find that they can start to read and write DTDs with surprising ease, to create a good DTD requires experience and familiarity with the needs and concerns of both data creators and end-users.

A good DTD nearly always reflects a designer's understanding of all these aspects, an appreciation of the constraints imposed by the SGML standard, and a thorough process of document analysis and DTD-testing. In many ways this situation is indicative of the fact that the creators of the SGML standard did not envisage that individual users would be very likely to produce their own DTDs for highly specific purposes.

Rather, they thought (or perhaps hoped), that groups would form within industry sectors or large-scale enterprises to produce DTDs that were tailored to the needs of their particular application. Indeed, the areas in which the uptake of SGML has been most enthusiastic have been operating under exactly those sorts of conditions - for example, the international Air Transport Authority seeking to standardise aircraft maintenance documentation, or the pharmaceutical industry's attempts to streamline the documentary evidence needed to support applications to the US Food and Drug Administration.

However, as a general rule, if users wish to write their own DTDs, or tweak an SGML declaration, they are entirely free to do so (within the framework set out by the SGML standard) - but the vast majority of SGML users prefer to rely upon an SGML declaration and DTD created by others, for all the benefits of interoperability and reusability promised by this approach.

This brings us to the third main part of an SGML document: namely, the document instance itself. This is the part of the document which contains a combination of raw data and markup, and its contents are constrained by both the SGML declaration, and the contents of the prolog (especially the declarations in the DTD).

Clearly from the perspective of data creators and end-users, this is the most interesting part of an SGML document - and it is common practice for people to use the term 'SGML document' when they are actually referring to a document instance. Such confusion should be largely unproblematic, provided these users always remember that when they are interchanging data (i.e. a document instance) with colleagues, they should also pass on the relevant DTD and SGML declaration.

Having identified the features you wish to encode, you will need to find a DTD which meets your requirements. Rather than trying to write your own DTD from scratch, it is usually worthwhile investing some time to look around for existing public DTDs which you might be able to adopt, extend, or adapt to suit your particular purposes.

There are many DTDs available in the public domain, or made freely available for others to use, but even if none of these match your needs, some may be worth investigating to see how others have tackled common problems. Although there are some tools available which are designed to facilitate the process of DTD-authoring, they are probably only worth buying if you intend to be doing a great deal of work with DTDs, and they can never compensate for poor document analysis.

Once again, there are many useful tools available to help convert from one markup scheme to another, but if your target format is SGML this may have some bearing on the likelihood of success (or failure) of any conversion process. As we have seen, SGML lends itself most naturally to a structured, hierarchical view of a document's content (although it is perfectly possible to represent very loose organisational structures, and even non-hierarchical document webs, using SGML markup) and this means that it is much simpler to convert from a proprietary markup scheme to SGML if that scheme also has a strong sense of structure (i.e. adopts a descriptive markup approach) and has been used sensibly.

However, if a document has been encoded with a presentational markup scheme which has, for example, used codes to indicate that certain words should be rendered in an italic font - regardless of the fact that sometimes this has been for emphasis, at other times to indicate book and journal titles, and elsewhere to indicate non-English words - then this will dramatically reduce the chances of automatically converting the data from this presentation-oriented markup scheme into one which complies with an SGML DTD.

Digital Records

Records are a by-product of doing business and they have an important role to play in doing it electronically. A simple way of defining a record is as a document that has taken part in a business process, and thereafter provides evidence of the transaction of that business. Records document business activity of all kinds, and are critical to corporate, democratic and historical accountability. They constitute a vital part of organisational and collective identity and memory, and provide important sources of value-added information. As records provide evidence of social and organisational activity, they need to be managed in ways which take account of their evidential nature as well as those characteristics they share with other information resources.In networked environments, records, like other information resources, need to be adequately identified, described and authenticated. They need to be readily accessible via common user interfaces to authorised users, and retrievable for as long as they are required, then to be disposed of in a systematic way. Terms and conditions of access, including freedom of information law, privacy protection and confidentiality requirements, need to be managed and monitored. But records, as accountability traces and evidence of business activity, have additional metadata requirements. Authoritative well-structured metadata which specifies their content, structure, context and essential management needs must be embedded in, wrapped around or otherwise persistently linked to them from the moment they are created if they are to continue to function as evidence.

The explosive growth of interest in the Internet in recent years has created a digital extension of the academic research library for certain kinds of materials. Valuable collections of texts, images and sounds from many scholarly communities—collections that may even be the subject of state-of-the-art discussions in these communities—now exist only in electronic form and may be accessible from the Internet.A number of well-designed locator services, such as Lycos, are now available that automatically index many of the resources available on the Web and maintain up-to-date databases of locations. But indexes are most useful in small collections within a given domain. As the scope of their coverage expands, indexes succumb to problems of large retrieval sets and problems of cross disciplinary semantic drift. Richer records, created by content experts, are necessary to improve search and retrieval.

Formal standards such as the TEI Header and MARC cataloging will provide the necessary richness, but such records are time consuming to create and maintain, and hence may be created for only the most important resources. An alternative solution that promises to mediate these extremes involves the creation of a record that is more informative than an index entry but is less complete than a formal cataloging record. If only a small amount of human effort were required to create such records, more objects could be described, especially if the author of the resource could be encouraged to create the description. And if the description followed an established standard, only the creation of the record would require human intervention; automated tools could discover these descriptions and collect them.

In US, the Online Computer Library Center (OCLC) and the National Center for Supercomputing Applications (NCSA) convened the invitational Metadata Workshop on March 1-3, 1995, in Dublin, Ohio to address this issue. Fifty-two librarians, archivists, humanities scholars and geographers, as well as standards makers in the Internet, Z39.50 and Standard Generalized Markup Language (SGML) communities, met to identify the scope of the problem, to achieve consensus on a list of metadata elements that would yield simple descriptions of data in a wide range of subject areas, and to lay the groundwork for achieving further progress in the definition of metadata elements that describe electronic information. Goals of the workshop included fostering a common understanding of the problems and potential solutions among the stakeholders and promoting a consensus on a core set of metadata elements to describe networked resources. Since the Internet contains more information than professional abstractors, indexers and catalogers can manage using existing methods and systems, it was agreed that a reasonable alternative way to obtain usable metadata for electronic resources is to give authors and information providers a means to describe the resources themselves.

The major task of the Metadata Workshop was to identify and define a simple set of elements for describing networked electronic resources. To make this task manageable, it was limited in two ways. First, only those elements necessary for the discovery of the resource were considered. It was believed that resource discovery is the most pressing need that metadata can satisfy, and one that would have to be satisfied regardless of the subject matter or internal complexity of the object. Secondly, the discussion was further restricted to the metadata elements required for the discovery of what were called document-like objects, or DLOs by the workshop participants. It was believed that DLOs are still the most common type of resource sought in the Internet and that whatever solution could be proposed for DLOs could be extended to other kinds of resources. More importantly, the likelihood of making progress on this challenging problem would be increased if attention could initially be restricted to something familiar. DLOs were not rigorously defined, but were understood by example. For example, an electronic version of a newspaper article or a dictionary is a DLO, while an unannotated collection of slides is not. Of course, the crux of the problem is that in a networked environment, DLOs can be arbitrarily complex because they can consist of text with callouts to images, audio or video clips, or to other hypertext documents.

The Metadata Workshop participants made no attempt to limit the complexity of DLOs, except to say that the intellectual content of a DLO is primarily text, and that the metadata required for describing DLOs will bear a strong resemblance to the metadata that describes traditional printed texts. The goal was to define a core set of metadata elements that would allow authors and information providers to describe their work and to facilitate interoperability among resource discovery tools. But because the core elements do not yield a complete description of objects in a networked environment, careful consideration was also given to mechanisms for extending the element set.

Dublin Core Metadata

The primary deliverable from the workshop was a set of thirteen metadata elements, named the Dublin Core Metadata Element Set (or Dublin Core, for short). The Dublin Core was proposed as the minimum number of metadata elements required to facilitate the discovery of document-like objects in a networked environment such as the Internet. The syntax was deliberately left unspecified as an implementation detail. The semantics of these elements was intended to be clear enough to be understood by a wide range of users.

The discussions at the Metadata Workshop revealed several principles that should guide the further development of the element set. Adherence to these principles increases the likelihood that the core element set will be kept as small as possible, that the meanings of the elements will be understood by most users, and that the element set will be flexible enough for the description of resources in a wide range of subject areas. These principles are intrinsicality, extensibility, syntax independence, optionality, repeatability, and modifiability.

— *Intrinsicality*: The Dublin Core concentrates on describing intrinsic properties of the object. Intrinsic data refer to the properties of the work that could be discovered by having the work in hand, such as its intellectual content and physical form. This is distinguished from extrinsic data, which describe the context in which the work is used. For example, the "Subject" element is intrinsic data, while transaction information such as cost and access considerations are extrinsic data. The focus on intrinsic data in no way demeans the importance of other varieties of data, but simply reflects the need to keep the scope of deliberations narrowly focussed.

— *Extensibility:* In addition to its use in dealing with extrinsic data, extension mechanisms will allow the inclusion of intrinsic data for objects that cannot be adequately described by a small set of elements. Extensibility is important because users may wish to add extra descriptive material for site-specific purposes or specialized fields. In addition, the specification of the Dublin Core itself will change over time, and the extension mechanism will allow revisions while maintaining some backward compatibility with the originally defined element set.

— *Syntax Independence*: Syntactic bindings are avoided because it is too early to propose formal definitions and because the Dublin Core is intended to be eventually used in a range of disciplines and application programs.

— *Optionality:* All the elements are optional. The Dublin Core may eventually be applied to objects for which some elements have no meaning. It also seems counterproductive to mandate complex descriptions if the creators of the content are expected to provide the descriptive material. A simple description is better than no description at all.

— *Repeatability*: All elements in the Dublin Core are repeatable. For example, multiple author elements would be used when a resource has multiple authors.

— *Modifiability:* Each element in the Dublin Core has a definition that is intended to be self-explanatory. However, it is also necessary that the definitions of the elements satisfy the needs of different communities. This goal is accomplished by allowing each element to be modified by an optional qualifier. If no qualifier is present, the element has its common-sense meaning; otherwise, the definition of the element is modified by the value of the qualifier. Qualifiers will be typically derived from well-known conventions in the library community or from the field of knowledge appropriate to the resource. Qualifiers are important because they give the Dublin Core a mechanism for bridging the gap between casual and sophisticated users.

The Dublin Core Metadata Initiative describes the Dublin Core metadata set as facilitating discovery; this term is often applied to the process of looking for resources in a broad cross-domain universe.

Functions of Metadata

In a digital library, metadata may be needed to help the user not only select an item appropriate for the current purpose but also to use it. Such metadata may include structural metadata that permits navigation among components of a single intellectual "object" or information about terms and conditions in a machine-parsable form that can be used to limit access to authorized users. Metadata is also required to manage content and to record information that will support future preservation activities. Metadata that leads users to resources in digital libraries (discovery, finding, collocation, navigation) and lets them choose resources for the task at hand (identification, selection).

The networked world has changed the expectations of information users by removing physical constraints. In the physical world, few question the practice of storing maps or manuscripts separately from books or locating the specialists who help users access and use the resources in different areas of a library or in different libraries.In the networked world, the digital libraries hold the potential to brings resources of many types together to the user's laboratory or desktop (or even palmtop). Some users will want first to cast a wide net as they trawl for information and then to draw it tight and precisely around the most relevant and usable resources for a particular purpose. The wide net calls for interoperability and commonality across domains and custodial communities, while assessment of fitness for a particular purpose often calls for rich and domain-specific metadata. One characteristic of a digital library is the accessibility of the content to the user.

In the traditional library, subject to the physical constraints of weight and distance, the user who selects lots of items that turn out not to be fit for the purpose at hand will incur a high cost. If users can delve straight into the content to aid the act of selection, some metadata conventionally recorded to support selection may be less essential. Users and builders of digital libraries also recognize the potential for navigation among related items. This feature was the fundamental function underlying the initial success of the World Wide Web.

Online, citations can lead directly to cited works and works can link directly to datasets or models they describe. Reference links and thumbnail images change the architecture for research and information seeking. Users can navigate using relationships between metadata records and relationships between resources from their desktop. The functions that metadata must support may not change in a digital library, but, in the new architecture and with new tools, it seems likely that metadata practices must evolve to provide the functionality cost-effectively in the new market. Content is also accessible for building services in a digital library. Metadata or surrogates can be derived or extracted from content files.

Today, a thumbnail is essentially part of the descriptive record for an image. In the collection of negative strips from the Farm Security Administration, many of the images were never captioned; access to the uncaptioned images within American Memory is primarily through navigation. Contact sheet displays of thumbnails are ordered using the processing number sequence on the negatives.

Automatic summarization and analysis of other forms of content is an active research area. The value of including basic metadata in the header of text marked up in SGML or XML is also well recognized. Text conversion projects following the Text Encoding Initiative (TEI) guidelines often use a mapping between elements in the header section of the marked up file to fields in a MARC catalog record. In some cases, the TEI header is derived from the catalog record; in other cases, a catalog record is derived from the header. For material published in digital form, the publishing community will maintain basic bibliographic metadata for its own purposes, including promotion and business-to-business dealings with booksellers. It will be inexpensive to include it in file headers. For example, the Open eBook Publication Structure specification includes tags for "publication metadata."

In a digital library, searchable text can minimize the need for metadata (particularly when items do not merit the expense of individual cataloging). American Memory has a popular collection, American Life Histories, for which the only item-specific metadata is a title (a display string needed for result lists) and an identifier; the text itself is searched to provide intellectual access. Creators of non-text materials also recognize the value in embedding such metadata within the files. Today, cameras can record the date and time of an exposure. If there is not already a camera with built-in GPS to record location, there will be very soon. Proposals for new digital file formats, such as JPEG2000 (for images) and MPEG-7 (primarily for sound and video) include the ability to embed descriptive metadata within the file.

Metadata Schema

The educational community has been active in exploring the functional needs of educators for finding and using instructional materials. Resources are available because of economic incentives to establish and manage online learning environments and government efforts to improve education. Some information tasks call for rich metadata. For example, a teacher may be looking for material to help him explain a very specific topic in a particular class. The teacher wants to be confident that the material makes appropriate assumptions about what the students already know, has already been used successfully in the classroom, will occupy an appropriate amount of class time, and will work on the equipment available. This level of specificity may be available in a service built by and for educators.

A metadata schema for instructional resources has been developed by the IMS Global Learning Consortium, Inc., a global consortium with members from educational, commercial, and government organizations.

Another area with specialized metadata needs is that of geospatial resources. The ability to build maps dynamically or relate geospatial facts from distributed sources of information is enhanced by commonality of metadata. Such capabilities can support government tasks such as emergency management, city planning, and tracking air quality or global climate change. The Federal Geographic Data Committee has developed a Content Standard for Digital Geospatial Metadata. There is worldwide standardization activity in this area in relation to metadata schemas and to the content standards for elements. The activity involves government, commercial and educational sectors.

As with the instructional metadata schemas, the functionality required by the creator and user communities, rather than traditional libraries, is driving these activities. The Visual Resources Association has developed a two-level hierarchical model for describing objects or visual works (such as paintings, sculptures, or buildings) and images of those works. A single set of metadata elements, the VRA Core Categories 3.0, can be applied to the works and to the images. This approach follows the so-called "1-1" principle, distinguishing characteristics of the image surrogate clearly from characteristics of the work. This principle emerged from the Dublin Core community but has provoked considerable controversy. It can not be applied in existing "flat" bibliographic systems without creating awkwardness and confusion for users through multiplicity of records and a burden on cataloging processes by requiring replication of work-level information in records for each surrogate image. A system that takes advantage of the two-level structure must allow searching across all records but present results that pull in work records automatically when a "hit" is at the image level.

The metadata schema used by the Art Museum Image Consortium (AMICO) has a similar hierarchical structure. The Visual Information Access (VIA) system at Harvard University uses a three-level hierarchy. Although the Encoded Archival Description (EAD) standard has been used primarily for describing collections of papers and records that have not been digitized, it too provides a hierarchical structure for description at different levels. The EAD metadata structure has been used effectively as the basis for digital library services, for example at the University of California, Berkeley (and now at the California Digital Library) and Duke University.

A more complex conceptual model has been proposed by the Documentation Standards Group International Committee for

Documentation of the International Council of Museums (ICOM-CIDOC). The CIDOC model is an object-oriented reference model that expresses a much more complex knowledge universe than the simple relationship of a descriptive record to a resource or even of a hierarchical structure of related descriptions and resources. It allows for descriptions not only of works, images, document, (conceptual objects) and objects (physical entities), but also of people (actors), places, and periods (time-spans). This model will form the basis for the Cultural Materials Initiative digital library project at the Research Libraries Group.

Full use of such a model will integrate gazetteers, biographical dictionaries, and encyclopedias, going well beyond the traditional use of authority records and thesauri. One example of a digital library enriched by integrating the use of reference resources such as biographical dictionaries and the Thesaurus of Geographic Names is Perseus, housed at Tufts University. In this digital library for the study of the ancient world, the books "talk" to each other. Names of places and people been identified automatically in the text and can be used as links to related information elsewhere in the corpus. This includes automated disambiguation of different places with the same name and of references to people who share names with places). Some of these rich metadata schemas or models have great potential for enriching the interaction with knowledge for users through collocation and navigation using the relationships expressed in the models and supporting knowledge organization systems, such as gazetteers, name authority files, and thesauri. The models are, however, unfamiliar and will require new tools to implement and deploy. The web sites that present them usually have FAQ (Frequently Asked Question) pages that emphasize that most features are optional. There is plenty of evidence that, unless there is strong economic motivation, introductory guidelines and basic tools are needed before complex standards gain broad acceptance.

Part of the genius shown by Tim Berners-Lee in his original standards for the World Wide Web was the simplicity of the specifications. The conceptual model could be explained on one slide and fleshed out in three more. Implementing a server was a few lines of code; a young programmer built a graphical interface (Mosaic) as a side project and the rest is history. The other aspect of Berners-Lee's genius was the instant integration of legacy content by supporting earlier Internet protocols now seldom mentioned (gopher, wais, news). Real-world experience with the simple (e.g. HTML) has led iteratively to better understanding of which extensions to its functionality are most essential.

Complex metadata schemas present a challenge for those with valuable legacy metadata to migrate or metadata maintained in rich, but different schemas. It is relatively easy to "dumb down" metadata records from a rich schema into a simpler one, for purposes of interoperable retrieval, while still maintaining the full richness in a master system. Transforming from one rich schema to another is usually more expensive and the benefits may not be obvious to the institutions or individuals most likely to bear the cost. At the other end of the spectrum, some digital library activities are focusing on allowing users to find resources across an information universe that spans communities, nations, types of information, and types of institution. The Dublin Core Metadata Initiative has been building consensus through a series of workshops and working group activities since March 1995. From the start this has been an international effort to develop a common core of semantics for resource description. The path has not been easy.

The Dublin Core Element Set (Simple Dublin Core) was submitted to NISO as a draft standard this year. The set has 15 elements; all elements are optional and all repeatable. The elements themselves are unlikely to be sufficient as an internal metadata schema for any particular project or application. Some proponents see the elements as the basis for a schema that can be extended by adding or refining elements; others prefer to see the set as a view of a richer, more complex description. This view can be used as a framework for mapping different element sets into a common set for indexing and searching. The DCMI has also developed a model for extending the simple element set while maintaining the objective of interoperability. Elements can be refined.

Tom Baker describes Dublin Core as a pidgin language in a discussion of simple and qualified Dublin Core. The existence of the 15-element set has provided an important focus for other interoperability initiatives. Simple Dublin Core was recently adopted as the core metadata record format for the experimental Open Archives initiative. This initiative is testing whether a simple mechanism that allows service providers to harvest metadata records from content repositories will facilitate and stimulate the development of valuable services that draw on content from many repositories. An initial impetus was the belief that access services could benefit from harvesting records for e-prints and other "grey" literature.

Records will usually have links back to the host repository through persistent identifiers for the full content. The concept also allows the development of comprehensive search services that include significant web-accessible resources currently hidden from the "spiders" that crawl the web on behalf of search engines. The so-called "deep web" includes the content of most digital libraries, such as American Memory, whose web presence is largely ephemeral, with records retrieved from a database in response to each search and displays generated dynamically. The Open Archives harvesting framework includes the ability to harvest records in other metadata formats.

The Open Archives initiative is based on the premise that simple records provide the first step to cross-domain discovery. Service-builders can choose to harvest records in a richer schema when available. Specifications for records marked up in the Extensible Markup Language (XML) must be made accessible for any schema used. Cross-domain discovery is the development of a very basic profile for the Z39.50 information retrieval protocol for cross-domain discovery. This specification also supports Simple Dublin Core marked up in XML as a transfer format for records. In many ways, the stimulus for this activity is the success of the World Wide Web. People clearly find value in web search engines, whatever their shortcomings. An enormous mass of information accessible from a single search box has clear appeal; many people prefer to try several queries and skim through pages of hits than to use Boolean queries to increase precision. The computational and linguistic tools built into commercial search engines are enhanced frequently. The architecture of cyberspace has changed the relationship between bibliographic control and access. Today, ironically, resources under good bibliographic control are likely to be less widely accessible than those simply mounted on the web. The motivation behind these simple-minded interoperability efforts is to encourage broad access to resources of value.

Digital Content

The fund of knowledge is represented by a much richer set of resources than static pages on paper, and resources beyond those traditionally found in libraries, even multi-faceted libraries like the Library of Congress. Knowledge has always been conveyed through buildings (and the archaeological sites they become), works of art, physical specimens of flora and fauna, artifacts of different cultures and lifestyles, and human memories.

Photography, sound recordings, and motion pictures have added to the fund of knowledge both in their own right as means of expression and as richer surrogates than words on paper. The digital era has added not only reproductions and analogs of older forms of information, but also new digital resources of enormous variety. Some fall into obvious categories. The broad category of datasets includes census and other survey results, gene sequences, images and other sensor data from space, geospatial information that allows maps to be generated dynamically, decades of financial statements for publicly traded corporations, directories of people and places, and structured lexical resources, such as dictionaries and thesauri. More complex digital resources include mathematical and chemical knowledge expressed in structural forms that permit dynamic manipulation, interactive software for education and entertainment, and collections of re-usable "open source" software code.

Digital libraries are being built to manage, serve, and support discovery of all these categories of resource. Some of these digital libraries are extensions of traditional libraries; many have developed from other well-established activities in organizing information. Dynamic information resources, such as the web site that delivers up-to-the minute details of event and results at the Olympic Games challenge all traditional practices for organizing and recording for posterity. However, this too could be represented as a series of snapshots of bit-patterns, a digital resource, a set of computer files.

The metadata required to support discovery and use of digital resources must clearly represent the intellectual nature and genre of the content; in a digital library, the fact that a resource can be represented by 0s and 1s is an assumption, not a useful categorization. Attempts to develop general hierarchical categorizations for genres or types of information have usually failed. The Type working group of the Dublin Core Metadata Initiative developed, with much debate and without unanimity even in a small group, a high-level list of types (the DCMI Type Vocabulary: DCT1): Collection, Dataset, Event, Image, Interactive Resource, Service, Software, Sound, Text. MARC records can hold information about the type of a resource in several ways. Svenonius notes that there are seven different places where a "document type" can be indicated. Each element or indicator has a different set of possible values. Given the different guidelines for use and the different functions these seven elements serve, type information in MARC records has proved impossible to use uniformly within American Memory.

Type indicators in the header are excellent as triggers for systems based on MARC records. They indicate what guidelines have been applied to content fields and therefore can be used to configure appropriate displays or procedures. However, the coded values can not be incorporated into a general keyword index, and are therefore unavailable to a user as a search term as they expect. The current feeling of the Dublin Core Type working group is that some communities will develop controlled lists of terms, but agreement across communities on the important categories or even common definitions for the same terms is unlikely. Lacking initial agreement on an acceptable "standard" typology, American Memory does not have explicit type values in all metadata records. This shortcoming means that searches limited to images may retrieve other categories of content, since the limit is actually by collection and some collections included will have text or sound as well as images. Colleagues agree that adding high-level type information consistently across the metadata records would provide more benefit for American Memory users than any other change.

Interoperability will certainly be well served if descriptive records shared or exchanged always include type information, even if all content within the repository or collection providing the data is of the same type. Based on experience with American Memory, users might be best served by the inclusion of any applicable terms from the DCT1 list and additional terms at finer levels of specificity. The user's objectives are supported not by raw metadata, but through the tools and systems that can take advantage of the metadata. In both library catalogs and digital library services, the functionality for discovery, finding, and collocating is determined not by the metadata but also by the indexes constructed for that metadata. Different systems provide different options for configuring indexes. Public interfaces to library catalogs usually combine different metadata elements into a relatively small set of indexes. For example, a keyword search by subject may find the term in any of the MARC subject fields. Once a record has been retrieved, elements can be labeled more specifically. Some digital libraries, including American Memory, take the same approach.

Individual elements that may be usefully distinguished (and labeled) to support the act of selection are lumped together to support discovery, finding or collocation. The University of Washington Libraries have used collection-specific element sets for their collections of digital reproductions; each set is mapped to the fifteen elements of the Dublin Core Metadata

Element Set for cross-collection retrieval. Retrieved records show the specific labels. For example, a collection of pictures of plants has a variety of fields relating to preferred soil quality and climate, whether the plant is native to the state, and other botanical details. For search purposes, these fields are all included in the Description index; on the display they are individually labeled. American Memory uses a similar approach. All descriptive notes are lumped into an overall text index; on display, a summary or abstract is usefully presented first and labeled as such. Many collections in American Memory call for unusual metadata elements, such as musical features for folk songs and descriptions of the key mechanisms in a collection of flutes. For searching, these are all treated as notes and included in the general keyword index. For display, however, the metadata format includes tags that are ignored by the indexer, but provide labels for use in the record display. The indexing approach currently used in American Memory was developed empirically and iteratively, based on data elements usually available across heterogeneous sources and expectations of content custodians and users; it has seven primary indexes that support searching of metadata.

The developers of the Alexandria Digital Earth Prototype at the University of California, Santa Barbara have described the framework they use for querying metadata from distributed sources. Based on experience over several years of working with geo-referenced information, they chose eight search buckets. For the most basic cross-domain discovery, the developers of the Bath Profile for Z39.50 identified Author, Title, Subject, Any. The Bath Profile effort is not strictly a digital library project, but has as an aim, interoperability between library catalog systems and "other electronic resource discovery services." The common text bucket proves invaluable when dealing with heterogeneous data and it is useful to include subject terms in this bucket. Indexing engines designed for full text will find word variants automatically, relieving users from knowing when formal subject terms use the plural form. The distinction between assigned subject terms and textual description is, nevertheless, valuable. In American Memory, it allows us to generate browse lists, which are actually static HTML pages with "canned" searches. The subject index also permits navigation from subject terms on record displays to other records assigned the same terms.

Although American Memory indexes the primary Creator separately from the other Contributors, searching and browsing for creators and contributors is usually done together. Combining the indexes has been considered. In American Memory, the addition of roles to Creators and Contributors proves valuable, particularly for non-text materials. Authorized forms for names are extremely valuable in American Memory. However, names within text are also an important access point. The Alexandria Digital Library is designed for powerful searching by geographic location and date range. Strict machine-parsable content standards are used for those metadata elements. American Memory users would love to be able to search more effectively by date and place. For much content in American Memory, unfortunately, dates of creation for the original item are uncertain and date-ranges recorded are often so broad as to be useless for discovery. For certain collections where chronology is important, normalized dates have been generated and can be used to sort search results.

The Alexandria Digital Library has chosen to index date of creation/ publication in the same bucket as date of coverage. In American Memory, there are many instances in which the dates are essentially equivalent. For published books and maps, the distinction is often important, but users may be interested in either or both. The Alexandria Digital Library uses special overlap and containment queries for date ranges and location. Such queries would not be efficient with a full-text engine, but American Memory users would like the capability.

Geographical location is an area in which traditional descriptive practices aimed at human-readable displays do not transfer well to digital libraries. In American Memory's metadata from heterogeneous sources, location may be expressed in many ways: as an informal place-name, as a subdivision in a topical subject heading, as a traditional subject heading or a hierarchical place name. Of these, by far the most useful for manipulating automatically with simple text-based tools has been the hierarchical place name. Users often know that they are looking for an image or for a map and would like to exclude other types of information from the start. Searching by more specific genre terms is also useful, for example for posters or cartoons. As pointed out earlier, type categories expressed in terms that users recognize should be available for limiting or searching. Controlled vocabularies are useful, but are likely to be domain-specific.

The emergence of XML (Extended Markup Language) and its widespread support as a syntax for exchanging metadata and content, particularly for e-commerce transactions and services, is stimulating the development of better tools for transforming and sharing metadata. This, in turn is leading to support for XML from vendors of database software and text-indexing engines. It appears clear that XML will provide the syntax for metadata exchange among digital libraries in the coming years. A few examples of its adoption to support interoperability include: the Bath Profile; MPEG-7; the Open Archives Initiative; and the Federal Geographic Data Committee. XML is also being used as a syntax to represent content objects, such as the proposed Open eBook standard.

American Memory has relied heavily on common indexing of heterogeneous metadata, with different element sets and in two different digital formats (MARC communications format and an XML-like syntax for simple (Dublin Core-like) records. Migration to an XML syntax with a formal DTD or schema is anticipated. Transformations from one XML metadata schema to another (especially from a rich one to a simpler one) can be facilitated using Extensible Stylesheet Language Transformations (XSL/T). This is just one example of the powerful XML-based tools emerging. XSL/T is already in common use for transforming finding aids marked up to the EAD standard (in XML) to HTML for display on the web. XML also includes the ability to mix and match metadata element definitions (semantics and syntax) from other schemas (using the "namespace" feature). As the flurry of XML-related activity on the World Wide Web Consortium web site in late 2000 shows, the general acceptance of XML signals the beginning of a further period of experimentation and development. Among the unanswered questions relating to the use of XML as a syntax for metadata is how soon (or whether) there will be widespread adoption of the Resource Description Framework, an elegant modeling framework for descriptive schemas.

RDF is layered on top of XML, using a particular XML-based syntax for metadata. RDF-specific tools will be needed to take full advantage of its potential for scalable interoperability. Whether the mix-and-match potential of XML namespaces will be widely exploited also remains to be seen. In the past, text-indexing engines, relational database management systems, and SGML-based storage and retrieval systems all offered different functionality to support the finding, collocation, and discovery objectives for digital libraries.

A text-indexing engine can handle heterogeneous metadata and full text in a single system; the capabilities for matching word variants (stemming) have been invaluable for American Memory. Features standard in relational database systems, however, such as sorting by date, have been implemented by additional programming. SGML-aware systems have advantages for substantial bodies of highly structured textual content, such as books and periodicals. Recently, products in one category have found ways to integrate the capabilities of another. ORACLE now has a full text search module, CONTEXT. Some text-indexing engines can now index text stored within relational databases. All such products are announcing "support" for XML. The other area where tools are emerging is in automated integration of thesauri and other knowledge bases to support more intelligent retrieval.

OAI-Protocol for Metadata Harvesting

OAI-Protocol for Metadata Harvesting (OAI-PMH) holds much promise for similar exchanges of metadata describing the collections of museums and other cultural heritage institutions. Materials in these types of collections often are not well indexed by commercial Web search engines. Metadata describing such holdings is hidden in databases, finding aids, and XML documents, or otherwise is not readily available to Web search systems, which typically understand little more than simple HTML. As a result, these materials remain hard to find and out of reach for many researchers. The utility of such a metadata repository will depend on many factors, including the development of more uniform metadata authoring practices across various communities of metadata providers.

Metadata is currently used primarily for a variety of local purposes, and the schemas to which collections conform have been adapted and tailored to meet local needs. Less attention has been paid to using metadata to support universal interoperability. With the advent of OAI and similar protocols, mapping local schemas to more universally standard schemas for the support of interoperability is gaining ground. Even assuming broader and more consistent application of metadata schemas designed to support interoperability, there remains considerable work to be done in learning how best to utilize aggregations of metadata describing heterogeneous information resources.

There is a need to normalize metadata so as to enable more consistent retrieval of results from cross-collection searches. Challenges also exist for presenting search results in ways that provide appropriate contextual information for the records retrieved. As of February, 2002, the Illinois OAI-PMH project has harvested metadata from twenty-five different institutions or consortiums. The resources described range from museum artifacts such as pottery and clothing, to archival manuscript and personal paper collections, to digitized photographs and monographs. The sets of harvested metadata range in size from the largest at 900,000 records to the smallest at 23 records. Some sites include metadata not relevant to cultural heritage mixed with more appropriate metadata. The institutions providing metadata are diverse, including academic libraries, museums, historical societies, public libraries, the Library of Congress, and special consortia such as the Colorado Digitization Project and the Alliance and Lincoln Trail Library systems in Illinois. Fourteen institutions have provided the Illinois OAI-PMH project team with snapshots of relevant metadata, in a few cases providing an entire database, which has then been made available from Illinois servers in a manner compliant with OAI-PMH.

While all of the metadata harvested from the registered OAI metadata provider sites was in the required Simple Dublin Core format (DC), metadata from the fourteen unregistered sites were given to the project in a variety of formats. These included finding aids formatted in encoded archival description (EAD), MARC format metadata describing bibliographic information, and local metadata schemas stored in HTML files, XML files, or proprietary database structures.To enhance cross-collection searching, local metadata schemas need to be mapped to standard schemas. Even with greater adoption of standard metadata schemas like DC, there remain wide variations in the use of authoring conventions and the depth of descriptive information included when creating metadata to describe cultural heritage collections.

The Open Archives Initiative Protocol for Metadata Harvesting (OAI-PMH) is a new and still evolving protocol designed to allow institutions to share metadata easily. It is hoped that the standard can help increase the discoverability of resources by scholarly researchers. The Protocol underwent one minor revision during its first full year of experimental implementation. Version 2.0 is scheduled for release in May 2002. The fundamental pieces of the protocol are its adherence to well-formed XML, its use of the HTTP standards for data transmission, and its requirement that metadata records shared via the OAI-PMH be made available in the DC metadata schema.

One of the common challenges in setting up an OAI-PMH metadata provider service is ensuring that the metadata to be exported is mapped properly into DC.

There are fifteen DC elements: Title, Creator, Subject, Description, Publisher, Contributor, Date, Type, Format, Identifier, Source, Language, Relation, Coverage, and Rights. Any or all of these elements may be used, and all are repeatable. Because much of the existing metadata about museum and special collections was developed with limited resources, using local schemas and with local needs in mind, the process of mapping to DC can be time and resource consuming and potentially frustrating. There is, however, a growing community of DC users and freely available tools to assist with this process. Harvesting done so far shows that metadata authoring practices differ both in the selection of DC elements used and the depth of information provided even within specific communities. As previously noted, DC elements are both optional and repeatable. These allow a significant degree of variation in the interpretation of which elements to use and how to use them when metadata are created in DC and when mapped to DC.

The Library of Congress American Memory Project, the American Museum of Natural History, the CIMI Demonstration Repository, and the Spurlock Museum to compare the use of DC elements. Within each set of sample records, calculated the percent of records that contain each of the DC elements and the average number of times an element is used in records that contain it. The usage variations are due in part to the intrinsic differences in the collections described by the metadata. However, some variations are clearly due to different decisions made by each institution when determining how to map their metadata into DC. These variations pose a challenge when attempting to build cross-collection search services and determining what depth of detail should be shown in record display. The variations can also influence how a search engine's ranking algorithm orders the result set.

Museums began to use personal computers for tracking information about their collections using a variety of proprietary databases. The use of proprietary software not specifically designed with the museum community in mind can lead to inconsistencies in the way collections are catalogued and tracked. The descriptive elements within a locally created metadata format and the degree of completeness when classifying and cataloging the items can vary widely from one organization to another. This may have the effect of diluting the potential for discoverability as searching aggregated repositories requires some degree of predictable structure and normalization of metadata terms or concepts. At the same time, one should not overlook the value of descriptive, locally created metadata applied to artifacts by professionals familiar with the collection and the museum. This is particularly valuable for collections used primarily by a local community of users. At the University of Illinois Spurlock Museum, FileMakerPro software is used to track the procurement, storage, stage of processing, and display of artifacts. It is also used to maintain descriptive information about the materials. The FileMakerPro database interacts with a Web server to provide public access to a portion of the collection. The decisions made about mapping the metadata were more time consuming than the time spent writing the scripts and manipulating the data. Here is an example of some of the decisions that were made for the cultural materials provided by Spurlock:

— *Subject:* One instance of the DC Subject element was included in each record. The decision was made to concatenate three fields from the original metadata records that could be considered equivalent to DC Subject. Colons were used to distinguish each of the three original strings that were concatenated to create the single DC Subject element. If there were not three values to concatenate, then the DC Subject filed would have two colons next to each other or a lone colon at the beginning or end of the element.

— *Date:* The Date element was qualified as DCQ date.created.

— *Coverage:* The Coverage element was qualified by appending Spurlock metadata field names to the DC element as DCQ coverage.spatial, coverage.temporal, or coverage.cultural.

— *Description:* Key words were added to the Description field values in the original metadata to clarify what was meant by the content of the Description element.

In addition to the mapping given below, 3 fixed DC Type values ("cultural," "physical object," and "original") were included in each Spurlock metadata record exported via OAI. One of the more challenging aspects of implementing the OAI protocol is mapping from metadata schemas designed to describe collections of materials to the DC metadata schema. Finding aids may describe as many as several thousand items or folders in an archive while DC has typically been used to describe individual items. Each EAD record includes metadata describing the entire collection and a "description of subordinate components" which lists the separate series, sub-series, folders and items found in the collection. Some EAD files reach hundreds of kilobytes, or even several megabytes, in size. The challenge is to allow the richness of such a large file to be exposed and made searchable alongside other records that describe a single item or a much smaller collection. Another challenge is due to the very flexible nature of the EAD standard designed to encourage participation by a large number of institutions. It is not surprising that the EAD records analyzed for the Illinois OAI-PMH project reveal many differences in tag structures and encoding patterns between institutions. Despite these differences, the records seem to have enough consistency to make a general cross mapping between EAD and OAI-DC possible. Although the EAD Application Guidelines include two recommended mappings to DC, one for the finding aid itself and another for the resources described in the finding aid, neither mapping will generate records adequate for use in an OAI repository.

While researchers are interested in discovering the existence of actual archives or manuscripts, metadata about the finding aid itself is also necessary in order to point effectively to the source records. For this reason, a flexible approach in mapping an EAD finding aid into an OAI record is needed. This top-level record becomes a base record for the finding aid and must be as complete, accurate, and concise as possible. The base record includes a link to the source EAD file as well as references to related parts of the collection. These related parts are described in other individual records and produce for each component level found within the EAD file's description of subordinate components. Although it is not possible to link these records to each other adequately using simple DC, a sophisticated use of qualified DC fields can produce linked records. This method will provide functional and easily searchable records. Metadata authoring practices as discussed above play important roles in determining the value of a cross-collection repository focusing on cultural heritage materials. Providing context for the metadata, normalization techniques, and developing the search engine and interface also need to be examined and explored for ways to enhance the discoverability of the collected metadata.

One real concern related to the development of cross-collection repository search tools is the context of the original artifact or digital resource. The value of information about the materials that may be found in museum collections and archives is often related to the context and the provenance of the object(s). For example, a photographic slide depicting part of a remaining wall of a basilica dating to the 4th Century would have less value if it were viewed out of the context of the architectural structure it represents. It is not good enough simply to make the slide available for viewing; it needs to be put into a proper context. Ideally, the holding institution of the artifact or digital resource will determine the appropriate context. When the repository encounters URLs embedded within any of the metadata fields, they are mapped to the DC Identifier element. The links sometimes lead to the holding institution or organization's Web site, to the digital display of the resource's record from the holding institution or organization's database, or to an actual display of the resource itself. Given the non-persistent nature of many URLs, it is possible that providing access to them may lead to a large number of dead links over time. With regularly scheduled re-harvesting of the metadata, changes to the URLs should be reflected in the records and therefore allow to avoid excessive dead links. For an example of a repository that has made thoughtful consideration of these efforts, consider the metadata collection contributed to the Illinois OAI-PMH project by TDC, the Teaching with Digital Content project. This project provides a searchable database of images that can be used by K-12 teachers to develop teaching modules that meet specific curriculum requirements. Partners providing metadata for the project include museums, the Illinois State Library, the Chicago Public Library and others. All the metadata has been entered into a database in a format that meets the specific needs of the TDC project and does not conform to DC. However, the display of the records is very clean and consistent and maps well into DC for the purposes of the Illinois OAI-PMH project. With a link directly to the Teaching with Digital Content resource provided from a URL that has been mapped into the DC Identifier field, the context is easily maintained by providing more background information about the record when the user clicks on this link.

Normalization of Metadata

In order to provide context internally and to enhance discoverability of metadata records in a cross-collection repository, some normalization of the metadata is desirable. That normalization can be done on several of the DC elements, including Type, Format, Coverage, and Date. Effective normalization requires to:

— Understand how the element was interpreted by metadata providers and which elements in other metadata formats were mapped to the DC element;

— Identify which - if any - vocabularies were used by data providers;

— Determine whether there is any controlled vocabulary that the project team could successfully apply to all of the data providers;

— Apply vocabulary to the metadata to augment the 'native' vocabulary;

— Build mechanisms into the search interface that would take advantage of the normalization; and

— Gauge the success of the normalization for resource discovery.

The metadata providers used elements in a variety of ways. For example, the DC Date element was used for the date the digital item was created, the date the physical item was created or published, and the date an item was added to a collection. Because OAI-PMH requires use of simple DC, the qualifiers that may have explained these values further were not present. Similarly the variety and specificity or generality of controlled vocabularies also influenced the next steps in the normalization process. Each DC element was examined to determine the focus for normalization for that particular element. While the Date element suggests a need to choose between options like 'date created' or 'date contributed' and the particular format the value is displayed in, the Type element required to focus on the range and specificity of vocabulary used.

Once the vocabulary is developed, the values in the metadata are mapped to the vocabulary terms. The actual normalization of the data is an automated process. Following the mapping, values from the vocabulary are added to each record as additional. After new records are harvested, the system compares the values of specific elements with the mapping already done and adds appropriate terms from the vocabulary where applicable. If a term that has not already been mapped appears, it is flagged and looked at by human eyes. The last step is to provide services so that users can take advantage of the normalization process. The ability to limit searches or sort results by type of resource or to search for specific date ranges or geographic areas is each made possible by the normalization process.

The Process of Metadata Harvesting

Metadata harvesting will be an important part of the interoperability toolkit for libraries. But it is just a first step. Communities that have close affinities with libraries, such as museums and other archival institutions, have good reason to use different descriptive practices. Those practices, and the terminology used: "necessarily depend on conscious or sub-conscious assumptions about who will use it and how". A resource that is of potential use in many contexts may need to be described in several ways and using several vocabularies. In US, the Library of Congress (LC) was an early adopter of the OAI Protocol for Metadata Harvesting to make records for some of its digitized historical collections available for integration into other services. The American Memory team was attracted by a protocol for sharing its resources that promised to be straightforward to implement with no deleterious effect on the primary users. The promise was borne out in practice; the mechanics of harvesting are working well and records for additional collections are being made available every few months.

To non-librarians, the MARC communications format, used by the Library of Congress for its catalog records, was unfamiliar and often seen as a significant hurdle. The American Memory interface was designed for users to locate individual items, not to download batches. On several occasions, LC made an entire collection (records and images) available on an "as-is" basis. Assembling batches for download and explaining what was being delivered was time-consuming, but for an entire collection and a partner with the ability to handle the metadata as it came, it was feasible. Often, what was requested was a substantial subset of a very large collection. LC did not have the resources to do the selection or build a custom batch for download and the requesting institution did not have the capacity to receive the full collection and sift through it. Neither party had the tools or resources at hand to transform the metadata from one form to another. Many worthwhile requests for material to repurpose led to nothing because the effort involved in responding to such requests on an ad hoc basis was simply too great.

During 1996, two task forces of the newly-formed Digital Library Federation (DLF), a group of 15 research libraries engaged in projects involving digital content, met several times to consider recommendations for descriptive metadata and for an architecture to provide common access to the growing pool of resources digitized by member libraries. Both task forces found a variety of practices and local imperatives that would have to be accommodated in any shared approach. For example, three institutions were taking different "standard" approaches to the description of photographs. At LC, the Prints and Photographs Division uses MARC records and follows Anglo-American Cataloging Rules (AACR2) supported by additional rules for describing older and unpublished visual materials. At Harvard, there was strong support, for example from the Graduate School of Art and Design, for the tiered approach represented by the Visual Resources Association's proposal for a core descriptive framework that distinguishes between records for underlying works and records for images of those works.

At the University of California, Berkeley, a commitment had been made to archival practice rather than item-level cataloging for reasons of economy; collections of photographs would be described in archival finding aids, to be marked up in SGML (now XML) using the Encoded Archival Description Document Type Definition (DTD). Practices and technical capabilities also varied widely across university campuses; libraries could not dictate practice to academic departments doing their own digitization or creating their own digital content unless they could provide resources or services to offset the costs of compliance. Rather than attempt to establish a single architectural design, DLF chose to start by promoting exploratory discussions, prototyping, and standards development for components that would be required in any architecture, such as authentication of users, and linking from references to cited articles. Several DLF organizations joined in a proposal to the Mellon Foundation for a project based on a pooled collection of finding aids and a common structure for complex hierarchical objects representing digitized manuscripts, photographs, and other archival objects.

Out of the experience with this XML-based metadata structure has come the more general METS standard, which is now being explored by many institutions as a mechanism for encoding the structure of complex digital objects. However, by 1999, the goal of shared access to the high-quality digital resources in the collections managed by DLF member institutions seemed no closer. Ironically, the convenience and effectiveness of the Internet search engines, such as Lycos and Google, meant that random Web pages were more conveniently available to the students and researchers these libraries served than the resources they carefully selected and cataloged. Rather than being in static HTML pages that could be indexed by the search engines, the managed resources were hidden behind a database query interface, part of the "hidden" Web.

Open Archives Initiative (OAI)

Open Archives Initiative (OAI) and its early history is well documented elsewhere. Services could be specialized, for example, by discipline or by intended audience, or comprehensive and cross-domain. The content described could be digitized historical materials as easily as e-prints. The protocol to support collaboration among organizations building collections of papers and reports deposited by authors could be applied by libraries and museums wishing to build virtual collections of cultural heritage materials. Technology for collaboration can be independent of any particular incentive to collaborate.The enthusiasm from that first meeting led the Library of Congress to play an active role in the Open Archives Initiative. The metadata harvesting approach proposed had a great deal in common with the initially ad hoc approach LC had taken in integrating into American Memory materials digitized by institutions with awards through the LC/Ameritech competition. Based on LC's experience with the competition, many characteristics of the initiative and the harvesting protocol were immediately appealing. These included:

- the emphasis on keeping technical barriers to entry low for those with valuable resources to share through metadata;
- the recognition that requirements for interoperability should not place unacceptable loads on the primary services of institutions choosing to provide access to their content;
- a planned period of practical experimentation followed by review;
- the combination of a very generic common denominator metadata schema that would be mandatory with the ability to exchange records in more specific schemas;
- the potential to integrate, for purposes of discovery, resources from libraries, museums, historical societies, and other cultural heritage institutions with a variety of descriptive traditions;
- suitability for use in any future program similar to the LC/Ameritech competition or for any organization wishing to repurpose records or content from American Memory;

— and an opportunity to make the resources digitized for American Memory more broadly available and useful, by allowing others to harvest the records conveniently and integrate them into services aimed at different audiences and taking advantage of new technological developments in information retrieval.

From a longer-term perspective, it seemed likely that a simple mechanism for metadata harvesting could provide a substantial body of metadata to support deeper collaborative exploration of interoperability. Interoperability involves agreements at several levels. In the context of the NSDL, the NSDL core integration team identified three levels of agreement needed: technical, content-related, and organizational. Costs of complying with agreements at any level inhibit adoption but without agreements the functionality that can be achieved is limited. A simple protocol for harvesting metadata seemed to offer low-cost participation at the technical level. If a large pool of metadata records were available for harvesting, pragmatic exploration of costs and benefits of fuller agreements at the other levels could follow. Content-level agreements would cover metadata schemas and guidelines for the content and encoding of values for metadata elements. The experience with integrating the heterogeneous records for collections digitized through the LC/Ameritech competition led to some sense of what minimal normalization was necessary for metadata records to be useful in American Memory. However, a larger "marketplace" of metadata and services established with the use of metadata harvesting might lead to broader consensus as to what is most important. Organizational agreements would cover matters such as governance of a consortium building and running a service based on metadata harvested from members.

By November 2000, with strong encouragement from Winston Tabb, the Associate Librarian for Library Services, the Library of Congress had committed itself to early implementation of the Open Archives Initiative Protocol for Metadata Harvesting (OAI-PMH) as a data provider using selected collections from American Memory as a test. The Library of Congress has been distributing catalog records since 1901, first on cards and since around 1968 in machine-readable form; making records for digitized content available for harvesting continues the tradition of adapting to new opportunities provided by new technology. Tabb also saw participation in the initiative, and other activities supported by DLF, as important for the Library of Congress, particularly in the light of criticisms of isolation in the recent report, LC21 A Digital Strategy for the Library of Congress.

The commitment was possible because the barrier to entry appeared low enough not to draw significant resources away from American Memory itself. This assessment proved true in practice. The first implementation took about 40 hours of programmer time, including analysis and testing. Mappings and conversion tools that were already used for American Memory or managed in LC's Network Development and MARC Standards Office (NDMSO) were reviewed, updated, and used to advantage. These included Perl language routines for parsing MARC records, a one-way mapping from MARC to simple Dublin Core, and a table to translate characters from the ALA character set used in LC's MARC records to UNICODE.

The first records to be made available would be those already upgraded to serve both in LC's main catalog and for indexing in American Memory. These already supported links to the content based on persistent identifiers resolved using a Handle Server, developed by the Corporation for National Research Initiatives (CNRI) and deployed at LC. Procedures for updates to American Memory could be easily extended to update the OAI data-provider service. The computer processing required to support harvesting requests was not expected to have a perceptible effect on response time for American Memory users. Also in late 2000, the DLF put out a call to members asking for lists of digital content for which they were willing to share metadata through the harvesting protocol.

At LC, this call was passed on to the custodial divisions responsible for content in American Memory described by records in the MARC format. Another mechanism to broaden access to their content was greeted enthusiastically, particularly because the links from the metadata records would bring users to the LC site, where more context for the collections would be available and users could follow leads to other related materials. At the January 2001 public release of version 1.0 of the protocol, David Woodward was able to announce that LC's data-provider service, for which he was the programmer, was up and running with records for two American Memory collections of digitized historical materials available: roughly 3,000 records for maps, and 200 records for ballroom dance instruction manuals. The records were harvestable in two formats, the full MARC records in a simple XML schema established for OAI-PMH and in unqualified Dublin Core in the XML schema.

Version 1.0 of the protocol was released in January 2001 with the expectation that there would be a period of experimentation for at least a year. Starting in September 2001, a technical committee was established with membership drawn from institutions actively using OAI-PMH to make metadata available or to harvest metadata and build a service.

LC was invited to participate, not only because of its experience as an OAI data provider, but also because of the importance in the library community of MARC records as a carrier for metadata. The outcome of this process was version 2.0 of the harvesting protocol; the differences are outlined elsewhere. There are many differences in detail, but the underlying philosophy of a low barrier to entry remained. Proposals were accommodated if there was sufficient support, several through optional extension features. LC is taking advantage of the option to provide descriptive records for "sets" of records that can be harvested as a group. Among the additions proposed but not adopted was support for distributed querying. Proponents were encouraged to participate in the activity now known as ZING (Z39.50-International Next Generation). This activity includes a number of initiatives by Z39.50 implementers to make the accumulated wisdom and functionality embodied in 20 years of experience more broadly available and lower the barriers to implementation. Simple Dublin Core was retained as a mandatory metadata format, because no other obvious candidate exists.

Version 2.0 of the OAI-PMH protocol proved as straightforward to implement at LC as the initial version. Based on experience over the first year, a revised architecture was developed to support more convenient and robust updates and additions. LC's OAI service divides records into OAI sets on the basis of American Memory collections or groups of collections. As of late 2002, there were ten sets, with one set being the aggregation of four photograph collections also available as separate sets. The implementation of OAI-PMH is programmed in Perl, taking advantage of the popular CGI.pm library to process and respond to HTTP requests. SGML processing routines from James Clark were used to handle the character conversion. For the first version, responses to the Identify and ListSets verbs were both in static files. ListIdentifiers requests were answered from an index, stored as a file, which mapped record identifiers to sets. The OAI verbs that return records access the source files of MARC records in the standard (ISO 2709) communication format, with dynamic conversion (using Perl) to XML.

The principal change when implementing version 2.0 was to use three tables in a relational database (using MySQL) in place of the simple set-identifier index. The tables represent OAI sets, OAI items, and the set-item links that indicate set membership. Sets can be added and related information edited through a Web form. Perl is still used for the HTTP processing, querying the MySQL database, and dynamic conversion from the source MARC records. Implementation of the new version at LC took roughly 60 hours of programmer effort, including analysis and testing. It was completed during the beta-test period and in operation before the official release of the protocol in June 2002.At NDMSO, the year leading up to the release of version 2.0 of OAI-PMH saw related developments in response to industry trends and requests from the library community. The trends included the growing adoption of XML following the stabilization of the XML schema definition language in May 2001 and the emergence of compliant software tools, the desire in libraries for a "lite" version of MARC encoded in XML, and the interest in metadata harvesting as part of the interoperability toolkit for libraries. NDMSO has developed two MARC-related XML schemata.One of these schemata is recommended in the new OAI release as a replacement for the original oai_marc schema. This MARCXML schema can be used to encode any MARC21 record. Like oai_marc, the tagging of this "slim" schema indicates the structure of a MARC record in fields and sub-fields, allows round-trip conversion without data loss, and will not need modification with the minor changes to the MARC standard that happen routinely. In February 2003, LC's cataloging distribution service made test files available in MARCXML for evaluation and prototype development.The second schema, known as MODS (Metadata Object Description Schema), is still at an early stage of development. Introduced in June 2002 and revised in early 2003, it is intended as a multi-purpose bibliographic element set for library applications. Unlike MARCXML, MODS includes only a subset of MARC elements and sometimes regroups them. MODS uses familiar words as element names rather than relying on MARC's numeric tags to convey semantics. In Fall 2002, LC made its OAI-harvestable records available in the MODS format in addition to MARC21 and simple Dublin Core.

These records provide richer semantics than Dublin Core and will support experimentation with the new format. The implementation uses an XSLT stylesheet to convert MARCXML records to MODS. NDMSO intends to maintain a suite of such tools for manipulating and transforming records between MARC and MODS. Implementing OAI-PMH as a data provider has had several beneficial side-effects for LC. Program code for converting records in the MARC Communications Format to an XML format can be used in many circumstances. Experience gained with special characters has been applied in other contexts through the development of mappings among MARC 21 characters, UNICODE, and character entities for HTML and SGML. Unusual characters in LC's records have also helped harvesters test their handling of UNICODE. Having records formally validated and tested by automated transformations by harvesters picks up errors that may be hidden by local interfaces or simply not noticed. This finding is consistent with experience with the LC/Ameritech competition. When records were brought into American Memory and subjected to different indexing and display routines, errors exposed were often found to cause undetected anomalous behavior in the original system too.

The Library of Congress has registered its OAI server for American Memory collections in the central OAI registry, which means that others can harvest and re-purpose records without LC being aware of it. This is nothing new for LC. Its records are available for copying from bibliographic utilities, such as OCLC and RLG; users of Z39.50 have been able to download records directly from LC's main catalog for well over a decade. Indeed, one of the key benefits to LC from the harvesting protocol is that no special arrangements have to be made when others want to get the records and use them in another service. LC has a particular interest in the use of its records in services with a focus on cultural heritage or humanities scholarship, and services that integrate materials from libraries, museums, historical societies and other archival institutions. The Research Libraries Group (RLG) has harvested records (in the MARC format) for several collections for integration into its cultural materials service. Dublin Core records for all collections are harvested by two services described elsewhere in this issue: OAIster at the University of Michigan and the University of Illinois-Urbana Champaign (UIUC) Cultural Heritage Repository. Records have also been harvested by the Perseus Digital Library. The mechanics of harvesting appear to be working well.

Now that records for a substantial body of cultural heritage content are easily harvestable, organizations and communities can begin to build on this base to support learning and scholarship through richer interactions with the resources accumulated in archival institutions. To achieve this will likely require communities to adopt more detailed agreements about metadata or make commitments to federated organization. Costs associated with metadata content can be daunting. Identifying and characterizing a resource and placing it in an intellectual context is expensive. Local needs take priority and upgrading existing records on an individual basis is seldom an option. Few doubt that "better" metadata lets people find what they want more easily, but a compromise between quantity and quality is often necessary. For pictures, music, and other cultural resources that do not include full text or spoken words that can be searched, human expertise is essential to provide summaries, assign topical and genre terms, indicate where and when a work was created, or relate it to other works.

Because of the expense and investment, change in practices is inevitably slow. Most standards and formal consortial agreements allow a great deal of flexibility so that legacy records can be handled. Motivation to modify records or practices, or to develop and test more complex conversion tools, will exist only if there is obvious benefit to the unit bearing the brunt of the workload. The Library of Congress is aware that it could improve the records it makes available for harvesting in a number of ways, with more or less effort, but needs evidence or guidance from service builders to indicate which modifications would be most valuable and which irrelevant. Indications are beginning to surface. Some inferences can be drawn from an analysis from the team building the UIUC Cultural Heritage Repository and the approach to metadata normalization for that service. The section on data content in RLG's description guidelines for participants in the Cultural Materials Alliance indicates the aspects that are most significant in building their service.

The least expensive way to improve LC's records in the short term would be through modifications to the transformation from the source record into formats for harvesting. LC's current transformation from MARC to simple Dublin Core is extremely basic. Element values are copied directly without conversion to another vocabulary or encoding scheme. Where codes are converted to terms, MARC terminology is usually used, because it matches the semantics of the coding scheme. In some cases, this results in terms that do not correspond to common usage or map cleanly to categories in other metadata schemes. Issues and questions that have come up in relation to simple (unqualified) Dublin Core records include:

— *Title:* The mapping to simple Dublin Core omits all title information except from the MARC 245 field. This is on the assumption that multiple titles will be confusing for service builders if the main title cannot be distinguished. However, significant information will be missing. For example, songs are often known by words from their first lines or choruses rather than the title on the published score.

— *Date:* The value for Date is taken from the statement of publication, distribution, etc. This field is intended for human reading, and the cataloging rules provide methods to indicate uncertainty and approximation, or date ranges when the resource being described is not a single item, and even to concatenate several dates for different events. For cultural heritage materials, uncertainty about the date of creation or distribution is common. The result is that the Date element is neither easily machine-processable nor useful for sorting.

— *Description:* For American Memory materials, note fields can be very significant for discovery: they can include summary descriptions, information about provenance, or biographical details. LC has chosen to include almost all categories of notes as Description elements. Some notes may be of little value for discovery, but because the range of information included in general notes is very broad, it is not easy to distinguish notes that are logistical or administrative from those that provide intellectual context for the resource.

— *Creator/Contributor:* The current mapping uses only Creator and includes all values for MARC fields 100-111 (Main Entry Name fields) and 700-720 (Added Entry Name fields). The semantics of the distinction between main entries and added entries in MARC is not the same as the distinction between Creator and Contributor. In particular, since only one main entry name is permitted, authors beyond the first are added entries. The American Memory experience leads us to believe that a distinction based on role with relationship to the resource being described is more significant for cultural heritage materials than either the MARC distinction or the Dublin Core distinction. Unfortunately, neither the unqualified version of Dublin Core nor the approved qualifiers can represent this distinction. Questions to service builders at UIUC and OAIster about their preferences received somewhat uncertain responses.

— *Type:* This element, which corresponds to the genre or nature of the resource, what it is rather than what it is about, is perhaps the most complex of all. Those thinking about the issue for the first time often assume that a hierarchy of genres can be established for general use. All attempts in the library community have failed, and those with experience, including the DC Type Working Group, believe that genre vocabularies will continue to be developed by communities and for specific contexts.

Some of these issues will not be a problem when transforming MARC records to the MODS schema, since MODS inherits the relevant semantics from MARC. This is not a coincidence, since experience with American Memory and mappings to metadata schemes used in other communities were among the inputs to the development of MODS. Others, in particular those related to dates and genres, will continue to be a concern when transforming records from sources based on MARC records and AACR2/ISBD practices.

References

Janes, Joseph. "The Internet Public Library: an intellectual history." *Library Hi Tech*, 16(2), 55-68. 1998.

Keller, M.A., Reich, V.A. and Herkovic, A.C. 'What is a library anymore, anyway?', *First Monday*, 8.5, May 2003, http://firstmonday.org/issues/issue8_5/keller/index.html

Ladner, Sharyn J., and Hope N. Tillman. Using the Internet for reference. *Online*, 17(1), 45-51. January. 1993.

Levy, David M., "Digital Libraries and the Problem of Purpose." *D-Lib Magazine* 6, January. 2000.

Liu, Ying, and Anita S. Coleman. Communicating Digital Library Services to Scientific Communities. *LIBRES* 14, no. 1. 2004.

Logoze, Carl, and David Fielding, "Defining Collections in Distributed Digital Libraries." *D-Lib Magazine,* November.1998.

Bibliography

Beagrie, N. and Jones, M. *Preservation Management of Digital Materials: A Handbook*, London. 2001.

Bertot, John C., "Libraries and Networked Information Services: Issues and Considerations in Measurement." *Performance Measurement and Metrics*, 2004.

Bishop, Ann Peterson. "Document Structure and Digital Libraries: How Researchers Mobilize Information in Journal Articles." *Information Processing and Management* 35 May 1999.

Blandford, Ann, and George Buchanan. "Usability of Digital Libraries: A Source of Creative Tensions with Technical Developments." *TCDL Bulletin*, Summer 2003.

Borgman, Christine L. *From Gutenberg to the Global Information Infrastructure: Access to Information in the Networked World.* Cambridge, MA: The MIT Press, 2000.

Doty, Philip, "Policy Analysis and Networked Information: 'There Are Eight Million Stories'..." in *Evaluating Networked Information Services : Techniques, Policy, and Issues.* Medford, N.J.:Information Today, 2001.

Fenton, E. & R. Schonfeld.. "Digital Preservation Library Periodicals Expenses: Variance between Non-Subscription Costs for Print and electronic Formats on a Life-Cycle Basis." Presented at the Fall 2003 CNI Task Force Meeting, Portland, OR, 8-9 December 2003.

Friedlander, A., 'The National Digital Information In frastructure Preservation Program,' *D-Lib Magazine*, 8.4, April 2002, http://www.dlib.org/dlib/april02/friedlander/04friedlander.html

Janes, Joseph. "The Internet Public Library: an intellectual history." *Library Hi Tech*, 16(2), 55-68. 1998.

Keller, M.A., Reich, V.A. and Herkovic, A.C. 'What is a library anymore, anyway?', *First Monday*, 8.5, May 2003, http://firstmonday.org/issues/issue8_5/keller/index.html

Kessler, Jack, *Internet digital libraries: the international dimension*, Boston and London: Artech House.

Ladner, Sharyn J., and Hope N. Tillman. Using the Internet for reference. *Online*, 17(1), 45-51. January. 1993.

Levy, David M., "Digital Libraries and the Problem of Purpose." *D-Lib Magazine* 6, January. 2000.

Liu, Ying, and Anita S. Coleman. "Communicating Digital Library Services to Scientific Communities." *LIBRES* 14, no. 1, 2004.

Logoze, Carl, and David Fielding, "Defining Collections in Distributed Digital Libraries." *D-Lib Magazine,* November.1998.

Lorie, R.A. *A Methodology and System for Preserving Digital Data.* Proceedings of the Second ACM/IEEE- CS joint conference on Digital Libraries, Portland, Oregon, USA. 2002.

Michelle Q. Wang Baldonado and Steve B. Cousins. Addressing heterogeneity in the networked information environment. *New Review of Information Networking,* 2:83-102. 1996.

Miller, Rush G., "Shaping Digital Library Content." The Journal of Academic Librarianship 28, no. 3 : 97-103. 2002 .

Moore, R., Baru, C., Rajasekar, A. et al. Collection-Based persistent Digital Archives. *D-Lib Magazine*, March and April 2000.

OCLC/RLG Working Group on Preservation Metadata. "Preservation Metadata and the OAIS Information Model: A Metadata Framework to Support the Preservation of digital Objects." 2002.

Rothenberg, J. Ensuring the Longevity of Digital Information. *Scientific American,* 272(1):24-9. 1995.

Rowlands, Ian, and David Bawden. "Building the Digital Library on Solid Research Foundations." *Aslib Proceedings* 51, September. 1999.

Rowlands, Ian, and David Bawden. "Building the Digital Library on Solid Research Foundations." *Aslib Proceedings* 51, September 1999.

Saracevic, Tefko. "Digital Library Evaluation: Toward an Evolution of Concepts." *Library Trends* 49, Fall 2000.

Schatz, Bruce R. "Information Retrieval in Digital Libraries: Bringing Search to the Net." *Science*, 17 January. 1997.

Schwartz, Candy. "Digital Libraries: An Overview." *The Journal of Academic Librarianship* 26, November. 2000.

Shiri, Ali. "Digital Library Research: Current Developments and Trends." *Library Review* 52, no. 5, 2003.

Smith, Abby. *Strategies for Building Digitized Collections*. Washington, DC: Digital Library Federation, Council on Library and Information Resources, 2001.

Suleman, Hussein,et.al., "Networked Digital Library of Theses and Dissertations: Bridging the Gaps for Global Access—Part 1: Mission and Progress." *D-Lib Magazine* 7, September 2001.

Trusted Digital Repositories: Attributes and Responsibilities. An RLG-OCLC Report, May 2002, http://www.rlg.org/longterm/repositiories.pdf